AF519091

# International Communications

# INTERNATIONAL COMMUNICATIONS

Naval Prabhakar
Narendra Basu

Commonwealth

**International Communications**

© Authors

Edition : 2019

ISBN 81-311-0024-3

*Published by* :
**COMMONWEALTH PUBLISHERS PVT. LTD.**
e-mail : commonwealthbooks@gmail.com

*Distributed by* :
**CAMPUS BOOKS INTERNATIONAL**
**ARPAN PUBLICATIONS**
4831/24, Prahlad Street,
Ansari Road, Darya Ganj,
New Delhi - 110002
Ph. : 23275511, 23257835
e-mail : arpanpublications@gmail.com
campusbooks@hotmail.com

*Typesetting by* :
**Rishu Computers**
Delhi

*Printed at* :
**Divine Digital Press**
Delhi

# Preface

International communication is vital, and particularly during periods of crisis. It provides us with the opportunity, a necessary opportunity, to gain an understanding of others in this world and furthermore to gain deeper insights into ourselves. In recent past, significant changes have occurred in the communication field. These changes have implications for both national and international communication flows. These flows have advantages as well as disadvantages. They have also raised a number of issues concerning politics, economy and culture in different countries and prompted them to evolve a framework of communication of their own in keeping with their own needs. It is, therefore, necessary to understand the nature and content of communication flows between and among nations and the organisations that are involved in these tasks.

This book deals mainly with the concept, problems and prospects of international communication. It introduces the international communication agencies and organisations having global networks. The value of information mightiness, media trends in the age of globalisation, imbalance in the international flow of information, issues in universal access to communication and information services etc., are also described in detail. It also analyses the rise and fall of the political move to bring about a new world information and communication order.

**Naval Prabhakar**
**Narendra Basu**

# Contents

# 1

# Information Mightiness

## Power of Information

Information is a term with many meanings depending on context, but is as a rule closely related to such concepts as meaning, knowledge, instruction, communication, representation, and mental stimulus. Although many people speak of the advent of the "information age," the "information society," and information technologies, and even though information science and computer science are often in the spotlight, the word "information" is often used without careful consideration of the various meanings it has come to acquire. Advances in information technology (IT) are affecting most segments of business, society, and government in many if not most regions of the world. The changes that IT is bringing about in various aspects of life are often collectively called the "information revolution."Many of these changes could over time prove to be profound; some may have already done so.

A wide range of national and international political, economic, and societal issues arise from these changes, both now and in the future.Understanding the various impacts that advances in IT will have and the likely nature of future changes that IT will bring about, in different societies all around the world, and the issues (i.e., problems and opportunities) that will arise from these impacts and changes is very important-and also quite difficult. It is important because IT is likely to change the 21st-century world just as much as the steam engine, railroad, and telegraph changed the 19th-century world, and just as much as electricity, the internal combustion engine, automobile and airplane, and the telephone, radio, and television changed the 20th-century world.

It is difficult because, while the technology developments that enable and drive the information revolution are more or less the same throughout the world, a large number of factors -social and cultural, political and governmental, business and financial-shape each society's approach to those technology developments. These factors interact in a variety of ways, both straightforward and subtle, and are subject to numerous variations in nations throughout the world, leading to many different national or regional manifestations of the information revolution.

### *Information Shaping the Economy*

Revolutionary advances in information technology reinforce economic and social changes that are transforming business and society. From this revolution emerges a new kind of economy - the information economy - in which information is the critical resource and the basis for competition. Old ways of doing business will be challenged and sometimes defeated.

At the social level, a corresponding new society is also emerging. This society's information capabilities are pervasive, making it substantially different from an industrial society. It is: much more competitive, more democratic, less centralized, less stable, more able to address individual needs, and friendlier to the environment. These changes dictate, for all countries, a major agenda of structural adjustment. Advanced countries are rapidly pursuing their version of the agenda, and developing countries must do so as well or risk exclusion from a global economy and severe disadvantage in the competitiveness of their goods and services.

## INFORMATION REVOLUTION

Information technology is changing how we work, play, learn, travel, and govern. "Throughout the world, information and communication technologies are generating a new industrial revolution already as significant and far-reaching as those of the past. It is a revolution based on information, itself the expression of human knowledge. Technological progress now enables us to process, store, retrieve and communicate information in whatever form it may take, unconstrained by distance, time and volume.

This revolution adds huge new capacities to human intelligence and constitutes a resource which changes the way we work together and the way we live together." The diffusion of information technologies to all areas of human activity causes accelerating change in economies and societies. Knowledge, inputs, and work products of industries, governments, and professions can be captured as digitized information, which can then be processed, duplicated, stored, and transmitted at ever lower costs. Markets, industries, and society must adjust to vastly different economic rules. Yet information technology often outruns society's capacity to apply it effectively and wisely. Widely known is the diffusion of products with information at their core. Less widely recognized but even more significant, key organizations, markets, products, and services from all sectors depend increasingly on information technology. Companies can raise the efficiency of production and management with networks of facilities and markets. Sophisticated information processing capabilities are increasingly within reach of small and medium enterprises, communities, and private homes. "Entire enterprises and industries could not exist at their present scale and complexity" without information technology, including financial market transaction volume, credit card charge volume, mutual funds, video games, travel reservations, international telephony, and discount retailing.

Information processing capabilities and reliable, inexpensive telecommunications combine to spawn an unprecedented kind of information infrastructure. Established networks attract a broadening base of participants, and they interconnect nationally and globally. The endpoint is a global information infrastructure, widely anticipated if not yet here. In developing countries, access to this infrastructure is inadequate, and progress depends on telecommunications policy reforms not yet implemented. Yet there is an opportunity for leapfrog - new technology can provide better, cheaper links to subscribers, while competing global operators can provide low-cost long distance connections. Developing countries can deploy telecommunications for lower costs per capita than was spent by the industrial world. For basic telephone service, the gap between industrial and developing countries is still large but narrowing.

The information revolution will not soon be slowed by technological limits. Advances in information technology are startling and continuing apace. Fundamental limits are still remote, and many constraints believed to be fundamental in the past have been breached. The knowledge to successfully apply information technology is another matter. The limits of this knowledge are readily apparent in the many failures and deficiencies of information systems at all levels. Improvement is occurring, but slowly. This problem is, if anything, worse in developing countries.

In software, better knowledge and techniques are increasing programmer productivity and enabling routine reuse of software modules in the manner of integrated circuits. Trends include: object-oriented programming, an emerging market for software components, and software agents. Most striking, and most revolutionary, is the emergence of a global information infrastructure. At a very fast pace, electronic superhighways of broadband fiber optic lines and satellite channel capacity are being deployed worldwide, creating a strong infrastructure for the global information economy. Data networks are being built on the basis of this infrastructure to allow large, uncontrolled information flows within global organizations and to the public. Computing, telecommunications, publishing, broadcasting, and entertainment industries are converging into a new industry to create products and services made possible by this infrastructure. At the same time, issues of accessibility, intellectual property protection, fair competition, content regulation, and cultural preservation arise, and they are far from being resolved. Access to the global information infrastructure by developing countries is inadequate and dependent on major telecommunications policy reforms yet to be implemented.

International telephone traffic has been expanding about 16% per year for the last 10 years, about 4 times the pace of the global economy. The Internet has about 20 million electronic mail users worldwide, growing 20-30% per quarter. "Internet is so big, and growing so fast, that it cannot be ignored. Nevertheless, it has flaws, notably serious security problems." The World Wide Web provides multimedia browsing for the Internet. The World Wide Web allows Internet users to browse efficiently through huge amounts of information in myriad formats from computers worldwide. The enthusiasm of volunteers has made the Web very popular, accounting for about 3% of Internet traffic and growing twice as fast as the Internet itself. So far, it is only increasing the information gap between rich and poor countries."

New economic rules distinguish an information economy from an industrial one and blur the lines between industries. Work products of many industries and professions can be captured as digitized information. Information can be replicated at negligible cost. Information can overcome time and distance constraints. Information can substitute for other factors of production: land, labor, capital, and energy.

Effects on employment patterns are complex and shifting. Because of lower wages, developing countries gain skilled jobs by export from industrial countries through telecommunications. But this advantage is only temporary for any particular country, because wages for skilled service jobs in developing countries will rise with demand, the knowledge content of these jobs will increase, and the advantage might shift to other countries that are more effective in building knowledge and skills. "Developing countries can no longer expect to base their development on their comparative labor advantage - that is, on cheap industrial labor. The comparative advantage that now counts is in the application of knowledge. The segments that comprise the world economy-the flows of money and information on the one hand, and trade and investment on the other-are rapidly merging into one transaction. They increasingly represent different dimensions of cross-border alliances, the strongest integrating force of the world economy. Both of these segments are growing fast.

Those countries which have market economies have prospered so much more than those that have not that today nobody dares propose a solution to underdevelopment that disregards the market. Although severe transitional problems hamper income growth in these countries, they will undoubtedly become major consumers and competitors in the next decade. International trade in goods has increased to the point where global production and sourcing prevail. International trade in services is increasing as a share of total trade, and developing countries are catching up by exporting high-skill and low-skill services.

Investments and money flow globally through an increasingly integrated and volatile financial market. Information systems built on telecommunications are essential for this expanded global market. An unambiguous lesson of the last 40 years is that increased participation in the world economy has become the key to domestic economic growth and prosperity. Integration is the only basis for an international trade policy that can work, the only way to rapidly revive a domestic economy in turbulence and chronic recession.

### Commercial services

International trade in commercial services has been growing. Trade in services has also increased as a fraction of total trade. This occurred as the country experienced a trade deficit fueled by open trade policies. Unable to shore up the falling peso through open market operations, the government had no choice but to devalue precipitously. The two major countries with fastest growth in participation in the world economy also have fastest growth in their domestic economies.

Competition increases through the globalization of trade and investments and the entry of developing countries into markets formerly dominated by industrial nations. Markets for industrial countries expand as incomes rise in developing countries. Competition on low-value-added goods and services intensifies with new entrants, technological progress, and skill-based efficiencies. As profits erode, developing countries with low labor costs can exploit this advantage only temporarily. Without flexible labor markets, countries cannot base development strategies on these products. Investment in training to develop a skilled labor force pursued together with the elimination of barriers to entry and exit can foster the whole economy into a dynamic growth pattern.

Fast growth is common in developing countries. Nine out of 10 countries achieving export growth rates over 10% from 1980-92 were developing countries. In the information economy, firms compete with knowledge, networking, and agility. Those that lag behind risk shrinking market share or extinction. To remain competitive in a global market, firms depend more on knowledge than on natural endowments or low labor costs. Knowledge and networking are the enablers of flexible manufacturing, just-in-time production, total quality control, and other industrial innovations.

Effective communications and alliances are essential for rapid response to competition. Firms must reinvent themselves, sometimes repeatedly, to cope with agile competitors from the same industry, from related industries, and from around the world. Knowledge, the new resource for economic performance, is not in itself economic. It cannot be bought or sold. The acquisition of knowledge has a cost, as has the acquisition of anything. But the acquisition of knowledge has no price. Economic interests can therefore no longer integrate all other concerns and interests.

Entire industries transform and emerge through adjustment to the new economic, social, and technological environment. Products and processes are redesigned around information technology. Outsourcing of support functions focuses industries on their core business and creates new service industries. The supply chain is compressed through information exchanges, and industrial networks become virtual corporations in continuous contact with consumers. New technologies generate entirely new industries, and traditional industries rediscover their competitive advantage in knowledge utilization and information handling. AT&T went from being a telecommunications company to being a networking company, putting together people, information, and services.

China Railways became not just an efficient passenger and cargo railway carrier but also a telecommunications carrier in competition with the monopoly state carrier through fiber optic and switching capacity developed for its own use. Closer links between non-bank lenders and borrowers, and electronic auctions of well-defined monetary products, are eliminating the need for traditional banks. Relationship banking in narrow niches has given ground to securitization and other sorts of price-based finance, creating a greater role for global credit-rating agencies. A new category of goods that adds up to a new industry is emerging from the merger of skills and information of the education, entertainment, and personal computer industries. Point-of-sale technology changed the balance of power between retailer and manufacturers. Merchants such as Wal-Mart tell consumer goods manufacturers what they want and where they want it. The nature of work has been transformed to tasks which are easily exportable electronically and where the local economy has cost advantages - white collar services as opposed to raw materials extraction. New business is acquired through electronic markets - bulletin boards and contacts in electronic communities. New work patterns have emerged within the company - less need for central offices, less presence in the capitol city, employees located anywhere, mixed nationality teams, more emphasis on teams and projects.

The company enjoys close cooperation with customers and suppliers, and the borders of the company have become indistinct. Requirements for operations have shifted from the physical office to electronic networks of workstations. Contractual relationships with employees allow flexible contracting for projects as needed. The company requires unrestricted international flows of investments and payments. Flat corporate structure, with international ownership and teams of workers assembled as needed, requires strong global governance based on transparency of electronic transactions.

### *Information Revolution and Social Transformations*

These changes go far beyond economics and technology to affect society in broader ways. As a great social leveler, information technology ranks second only to death. It can raze cultural barriers, overwhelm economic inequalities, even compensate for intellectual disparities. High technology can put unequal human beings on an equal footing, and that makes it the most potent democratizing tool ever devised. Social and organizational control based on closely-held information is no longer possible when information is ubiquitous and inexpensive. Democracy and decentralization rise, and hierarchical organizations flatten. Travel, work, and consumption patterns change as electronic networks replace stores, factories, and workplaces that exist largely to facilitate information exchanges. Products and services of all kinds become information-intensive. Uncontrolled flows of information increase, creating opportunities for social reorganization. Who takes care of the social challenges of the knowledge society. Neither the government nor the employing organization.

Demand for institutional accountability increases. Spurred by increasing availability of international information, the public is increasingly unwilling to allow public and private organizations to operate in secrecy. At the same time, the spread of democracy creates new opportunities for people to participate in public decisions. Institutions of all kinds, but chiefly government, must promptly change their roles and must operate under permanent scrutiny by stakeholders. A new kind of institution - the nongovernmental organization (NGO) - rises to prominence as it slowly replaces government in the social agenda. The increased accountability of private enterprises through financial market disclosure requirements is worth noting: Capital flows worldwide on portfolio investments generate a demand for credible financial reports, corporate audits, and credit ratings.

An environmental agenda rises. The preservation of the environment has become the concern of a well-informed public worldwide. This increased awareness of environmental changes is due in large part to global communications. Accountability for resource use and pollution increases. Economic growth cannot be pursued at the expense of the environment, lest such growth become unsustainable and threaten the health of the entire world. Yet concern for the environment has significantly different connotations in developed and developing countries. The striking image of the Earth rising over the moon's horizon, taken by Apollo astronauts and copied worldwide, has changed forever the way that we view the planet. The information in the image, and the fact that it could be copied freely, created its social impact. Broad-based membership organizations such as Greenpeace have developed powerful global communications systems.

A remarkable international agreement on the curtailment of chloroflourocarbons has demonstrated almost unanimous support, substantial changes in chemical production, and progress in consumption patterns. This despite the fact that the benefits are somewhat ambiguous and cannot be captured by specific countries. Human development and poverty alleviation, long-established goals of economic and social development, are increasingly a prerequisite for international competitiveness.

Communities everywhere, informed through television of how others live, aspire to higher standards of living and place increasing demands on their leaders. Disease and malnutrition are recognized by their victims as mainly economic and political problems, creating pressures for change that reverberate internationally. Education is recognized as a basic human right and the path to higher incomes. This rising social agenda is spearheaded by increasingly influential nongovernmental organizations. Intellectual and artistic products of national cultures can be preserved and disseminated with information technology. But creative cultures and societies can also be overwhelmed by the influx of outside information, and sinister uses of information technology, notably computerized weaponry, certainly exist.

The information adjustment - to achieve macroeconomic and political balance in an environment of uncontrolled information flows and global competition, trade, and investment. Societies all over the world correctly see major challenges and opportunities from advances in information technology. The higher the level of development, the higher the level of computing expenditure in a country.

Developing countries must also adjust or suffer exclusion from the global economy and severe disadvantage in the competitiveness of their goods and services. They are threatened with a new and dangerous form of information poverty that could further widen the gap in economic status and competitiveness. The necessary adjustment is sweeping and complex. It is also risky, for wholesale diffusion of information technology can result in waste and social deterioration. It can be no accident that there is today no wealthy developed country that is information-poor, and no information-rich country that is poor and undeveloped. This advantage will accrue not only to the telecommunications industry, but also to such industries as manufacturing, banking and entertainment and to such activities as education and healthcare.

*The information revolution is very real*

— Diffusion of information technology increases.

— No technological limits are in sight.

— Global information infrastructure emerges.

— Market economies prevail worldwide.

— Global trade and investment are increasing.

— Global competition increases.

— Firms compete with knowledge, networking, and agility.

— Industries transform and emerge.

*Information revolution and social transformations*

— Society is being reorganized.

— Demand for institutional accountability increases.

— An environmental agenda rises.

— The social agenda gains importance.

— Culture can be preserved and destroyed.

Fortunately, the information revolution creates both the challenge and the means necessary for successful adjustment. It also creates new possibilities to attack vexing problems of poverty, inequality, and environmental degradation with the potential to achieve unprecedented gains in economic and human development.

The first countries to enter the information society will reap the greatest rewards. They will set the agenda for all who must follow. By contrast, countries which temporize, or favor half-hearted solutions, could, in less than a decade, face disastrous declines in investment and a squeeze on jobs. Information is critical to the social and economic activities that comprise the development process. Telecommunications, as a means of sharing information, is not simply a connection between people, but a link in the chain of the development process itself.

## Opportunities and Challenges

Information technology and telecommunications in developing countries can transform old challenges and create unprecedented possibilities for sustainable economic development, just as it has for business in the industrial world. Too narrow a definition of appropriate technology ignores the profound social implications of technology and risks consigning the world's poor to a life of third-rate capacity and opportunity. Information technology, when designed for the right job, can be deployed even in regions that lack adequate water, food, and power. This technology can be effective for many tasks, not least human and economic development. In fact, this technology is often indispensable in meeting basic needs.

Educate more people and support lifelong learning. Education pays. Rewards to an individual for an educational investment include more employment options, higher income, and better future prospects. Education is the best route to improved status for women worldwide. The need for continued education and training persists throughout a person's career. Export of low-skill jobs requires primary education of good quality, including language skills. Export of high-skill jobs requires advanced and lifelong training. Information systems have supporting roles in education - efficient administration, low-cost delivery, and production of appropriate educational materials. Computer-based training is an effective tool for lifelong learning.

Make governments more efficient, accountable, and transparent. Large productivity increases in government services are possible with information systems that simultaneously increase speed, volume, quality, transparency, and accountability of transactions.

Well-designed information systems can become major instruments of public policy - powerful tools to implement, enforce, and evaluate policy reforms. Public administration is, by its very nature, highly information intensive. Government business can be considered as a series of systems, such as education, health, defense, public revenue and expenditures, natural resources management, social security, etc. Public administration relies heavily on the use of information and communication technologies to gather, process, and diffuse information within both public and private domains.

Increase effectiveness of economic reforms. Economic reforms often fail in implementation due to weak compliance. Good monitoring mechanisms can help. Information systems designed in conjunction with reforms are more likely to be effective, however. Through information systems, it is possible to embed policy reforms into institutional processes and transactions, which can then be readily monitored and audited. Strategic decisions and policy reforms related to trade were fundamental, and the information systems were the vehicle for their implementation and enforcement. The combination of trade policy change and computer support was rapidly and widely accepted by the trade industry.

Monitor and protect the environment. Environmental monitoring, inherently data-intensive, is more effective using information technology, primarily geographic information systems. These systems are already practical and increasingly inexpensive. The data captured are of lasting value beyond their initial use. International cooperation for monitoring and advice is fostered by environmental networks.

Information technology also provides effective tools for regional planning based on dynamic modeling. Protection of the environment begins inside the factory with integration of pollution control and energy conservation into manufacturing processes. Process control depends on information systems for both design and operational functions. Many information-intensive services are inherently clean. Telecommuting can reduce environmental impact even further.

Satellites are increasingly being used to provide early warning of infestations of insects such as desert locusts and tsetse flies by combining satellite data about vegetation patterns, moisture levels, and weather with ground-based data. The images are expensive, and interpretation requires deep technical expertise. Dependable, timely predictions of pest infestations can help to prevent serious damage to health and agriculture.

The database and simulation models revealed important observations that were helpful during project design and execution. Existing map and photographic information were utilized beyond their initial intent, supplemented with field work where necessary. Existing data would have been difficult or impossible to use manually.

Reduce information and income inequalities. The relationship between access to information and level of income is strong and becoming stronger at both the national and the international level. The information revolution threatens to increase inequity, but it also provides tools to reduce poverty.

A pro-poor agenda of technology-improved access to education, health care, and information is increasingly possible for developing countries. Rural and poor urban communities can be integrated into economic life, and thereby raise income levels, through information services. Appropriate regulatory incentives can be designed to encourage provision of rural telecommunications on a commercial basis. Satellite networks, wireless communications, public telephones, and community information centers are effective arrangements. One fisherman simply holds up a newspaper to establish the date while another records the company-owned bulldozers plowing under mangroves in the background. Community information centers can extend the reach of information services to under-served rural and urban areas.

Community information center vignette: In a large room in a small town, a community information center provides diverse information services in response to community needs: public telephone and fax, government service directories, regional employment listings, agricultural prices from brokers in several cities, posting crop and pest observations for the agricultural extension agent, electronic mail for distance education radio courses, and self-paced training. In many parts of the developing world, women do much of the agricultural work. They may take crops to market or negotiate prices for their crops or livestock. In such cases, the benefits of telecommunications in getting information about prices and markets and in getting expert advice from extension agents should apply to women. Natural disadvantages, especially geographic remoteness, are inconsequential for some information-intensive industries. In some cases, time zone differences can be turned to advantage. Advanced telecommunications is allowing small towns to hold on to new jobs and attract new ones and to experiment with telemedicine, distance learning, and other services.

Markets for information goods and services are young, growing, and exceptionally mobile. In this dynamic situation, there are many opportunities and some successful models for creating new industries in developing countries. These industries can provide information products, such as components and equipment, custom software, or exported provision of services. They can also help to improve the information components of traditional products, a fast growing aspect of many industries.

The software industry in India has been able to take advantage of its low-cost, highly skilled work force and with the benefit of international communications links has become a major producer of software (India ranks second among competing countries in software/services exports).

Announcing plans to invest in the Indian subcontinent, the Singapore government recently revealed its intention to fund and develop a 58 acre high-tech industrial park in Bangalore (in southern India). Scheduled to open in late 1995, the Bangalore Information Technology Park will comprise factory, office, and residential areas to meet the needs of manufacturing companies engaged in electronics, computers, and telecommunications. AT&T and IBM are expected to be the anchor tenants, but other global technology companies have also expressed interest, including Texas Instruments, Motorola, and Siemens. The park is intended particularly to attract foreign computer companies that want to form partnerships with Indian firms.

The ability to widely and cheaply disseminate very detailed design information is changing the traditional manufacturing process. Making an original design for a product can account for half of its life-cycle cost. Computer-aided design can dramatically cut cost and time requirements and improve accuracy. Developing countries may be able to skip entire stages of industrialization if they are able to incorporate computer-aided design, information systems, and flexible manufacturing into their nascent industries. However, these capabilities require large investments and extensive training.

### Promote Small and Medium Enterprises

Small and medium enterprises (SMEs) are vital engines of job creation. They have played a key role in production and diffusion of information technology. They are quick in bringing new products to market, getting into and out of fast changing niche markets, and setting up spin-off companies. The needs of SMEs can be addressed through self-sustaining service systems and networks for training, technical cooperation, accounting, purchasing, marketing, banking, government licensing, and taxation.

The role of the state is therefore partly to fill the supply-side gaps related to serving mainly SMEs - especially those without experience in buying consulting services. This can be done directly by state consultancies like the Irish MCS and AMT Ireland services and the US Manufacturing Technology Centers, or through programs that manage and refer users to accredited private firms. Low level white collar procedural tasks are being exported, with major changes in this direction expected in the next 10 to 15 years. In India, about 100 jobs were created to rekey information from original reports by the UK police force on nonstandard forms onto official forms.

Participation in global trade requires at least cheap and efficient customs procedures, but the need goes much further, extending eventually to the exchange of detailed market information around the world that allows local companies to tap export markets in both rich and poor countries. Local goods and services must therefore be globally competitive; if not, the national and international markets for the inferior goods and services will evaporate under attack from better suppliers anywhere in the world. Increasingly, goods and services with information components are more competitive, and the implicit knowledge component dramatically affects quality and price.

It is easy to get excited about the opportunities, but the information revolution dictates new needs for developing countries that must be addressed, whether exciting or not. Fortunately the information revolution also provides the means to address this urgent agenda of adjustments. Developing countries will pay a high cost if they lag behind. Without fast and successful adjustment, a developing economy can be hampered in many ways: Local production may be less competitive in international markets against better-quality, lower-priced, and more flexible products. Productive firms might lose market share due simply to inability to connect to international trading networks and to participate on equal terms in markets. Research and development might stagnate without convenient access to international science networks. There is a real and present danger of deepening inequity of access to information both within and among countries.

The information revolution confronts countries with a major new equity issue, not of wealth but of information. If the adjustment agenda does not lead a country toward widespread access to information services, those without access will face a double hardship, lacking both information and economic opportunity. Governments, the private sector, local communities, nongovernmental organizations, and international organizations such as the World Bank Group all have a role to play in creating information economies in developing countries. The broader and more effective the partnerships among these agents, the faster the adjustment will occur. The most important role of partnerships is to create consensus on strategic priorities and commitment by the various stakeholders to a national strategy to create or enhance information infrastructure in developing countries. A national strategy must include identification of the sectoral reform policies and strategic investments needed to deploy the infrastructure as well as priorities for implementation. Reaching strategic consensus is a difficult but very important initial step toward an information economy. Government action and reform can build competition. Private sector competition fueling growth of telecommunications and information industries could not have taken place in advanced countries without complementary government action and reform. Nor could have development of national infrastructures, without public investment in certain critical areas or changes in laws and regulations. Asian informatics strategies have public and private support.

Create an information-friendly environment, characterized by coherent telecommunications reform and information policies; laws protecting investment, intellectual property, and individual privacy; open and well-regulated information and communication markets; education policies that favor a skilled labor force; and effective regulatory and standard-setting institutions. Such an environment supports availability, diversity, and low cost of information services and products. Clearly, the task of creating such environment falls to not one but all of the partners for development. A national information infrastructure consists of both the telecommunications networks and the strategic information systems necessary for widespread access to communications and information services. Deployment of this infrastructure is a task of ten years or more and billions of dollars in most developing countries. It is possible only through the efficient functioning of national and international markets for financing, engineering, and management services. An information-friendly environment is a precondition for investments. While the role of the private sector is paramount, the government and often international organizations such as the World Bank Group also play key roles as legislators, regulators, advisors, and guarantors. There is a correlation between telecommunications investment and economic growth.

Rural telephone switches are being produced by and for India. In 1980, India had fewer than 2,500,000 telephones, almost all of them in a handful of urban centers. The country had only 12,000 public telephones for 700,000,000 people, and 97% of India's 600,000 villages had no telephones at all. India was using its priceless foreign exchange to buy the West's abandoned technology and install obsolete equipment. The technological disparity was getting bigger, not smaller. By 1987, a three-year effort by many of India's great young engineers had produced a series of telephone switches, manufactured in India to international standards, and adapted to village use.

The costs of telecommunications are falling, according to desk research and case studies from 26 developing countries that explores options for commercial supply of rural telecommunications. The emergence of the global information infrastructure presents an extraordinary opportunity for developing countries, sometimes called telecom lite. The new infrastructure is characterized by a variety of low-cost options for local connections, competing global operators for long-distance services, digital transmission, and low-cost, reliable, simple network access with increasingly sophisticated terminals. This model for the telecommunications infrastructure allows developing countries to leapfrog the industrial world's enormous investment in wired local loops, the most expensive part. Developing countries can provide better service at a much lower cost per subscriber. With radio and satellite options for the local loop, widespread deployment of telecommunications becomes affordable, and developing countries can have the technical support to coexist with commerce in the information age.

Strategic information systems for developing countriesinclude sector-wide information systems for education, health, public sector management, and transportation. Electronic payments, education and science networks, trade facilitation, disaster prevention and management, and national statistics might also be defined as strategic systems.

An information system provides a societal capability based on the use of information that encompasses its full context of people, institutions, policies, processes, incentives, data, information technology, and infrastructure. A strategic information system provides a fundamental capability of such importance that it can enhance the scope and efficiency of an entire sector and economy.

The Global Positioning System, originated by the US Department of Defense, gets increasingly wide civilian use by pilots, shippers, hikers, rescue workers, surveyors, and others for work and recreation. The capability increases efficiency in many industries and transforms the market for geographic products and services. Current aviation units cost about $500 and pinpoint their position to within 100 meters anywhere on the globe. Demand for specialized informatics professionals, computer literacy throughout the workforce, and lifelong training are challenges for most countries in the face of rapidly changing technology and shifts in job mixes. Meeting the demand will require the efforts of universities, private companies, training institutions, computer societies, and accreditation councils.

Effectiveness of telecommunications technologies for secondary and post-secondary education has been fairly well documented. Research on the costs and benefits is much more limited. Hewlett Packard provides interactive voice and data communications in more than 100 classrooms worldwide, and estimates that its system delivers training at one-half the cost of traditional classes.

Social networks based on electronic communications are needed to enable alliances that connect institutions in agriculture, education, health, banking, industry, and other sectors. Once operational, these networks multiply opportunities for technical cooperation, research, coordination, information sharing, and private transactions. Electronic customs clearance, transportation arrangements, and other electronic commerce capabilities have reduced import and export transaction costs substantially for many countries.

Toolnet is a network for small scale development projects that fosters exchange of information, experiences, expertise, and solutions to technical problems. It provides multifunctional electronic mail to link field workers, local organizations, technological institutions, international development organizations, and individuals to each other and to national and international networks.

Printed scientific information has been doubling every 12 years. Journal subscription prices doubled in 8 years. A 1994 directory lists 440 electronic journals and research newsletters, up from 110 in 1991. Proponents and some agreements are emerging on electronic low-cost dissemination of scholarly work, but not yet agreement on refereeing, scholarly priority, journal of record, and other issues traditionally resolved by print journals. Scholarly journals could become an anachronism. In this change is an opportunity for developing countries: Participation in international research will depend on ideas, results, and evaluations by peers, not on location.

### *Constraints and Hazards*

The information revolution fuels change of remarkable pace and scope, but also of remarkable unevenness. Failures and horror stories litter the history of the information industry. Even the success stories, when scrutinized, reveal formidable social and technical complexities. The power of information technology, which has so much potential for social good, can also be harnessed for selfish, dangerous, or even destructive ends.

Developing and deploying information systems and telecommunications capabilities is socially and technically complex, even in the face of technological advances and obvious potential benefits. Countries need to marshal substantial resources, often from abroad, to accomplish this task. They need to establish effective incentives and management schemes to facilitate adoption and effective use of new systems. The transferring of investment and operation responsibility for the telecommunications infrastructure from the public to the private sector is an urgent and particularly complex task. It involves sacrificing local short-term revenues and control to gain the investment volume and service improvements that a competitive private sector can supply. A training program was developed to train computer programmers, develop their organizational skills, and instill in them the importance of accountability.

In the absence of appropriate policy incentives, adequate quality standards, and competitive discipline, a society could allocate scarce development resources to information infrastructure investments that create waste or perversely increase social inequality. Such is the case when telecommunications services are available only to the urban rich, when incentives favor use of technology more for recreational than productive purposes, and when an excessive share of investments are directed toward military purposes. Wasteful information infrastructure investments also can occur because of inadequate definition of the expected benefits and inadequate measurement of the actual results. Benefits in terms of societal capabilities and institutional objectives can be and should be defined for projects, but it is very complex to measure the results objectively, and it is tempting to hide behind alleged intangible benefits.

### *Cultural preservation versus social disruption*

An information society should both benefit from and contribute to worldwide cultural assets. A balance should be maintained between import of artistic, recreational, and educational products and local generation and consumption of culture-enhancing products. Without that balance, the information revolution could weaken the cultural ties that bind communities and nations. The information revolution greatly facilitates production, publishing, and international dissemination of cultural products by individuals, citizen groups, and communities.

Enhanced access to telecommunications and broadcasting creates opportunities for those who would enhance culture, society, and human life, as well as for those who would diminish or destroy them. Social control through information censorship is unworkable, yet information technology creates threats to individual privacy. Advocates of a benevolent and fair society must accept new responsibilities for influencing access to communications.

Information technology has an increasing capacity to capture the knowledge and expertise required for many human tasks and to repeat those tasks with an unprecedented degree of speed and precision. This capacity constitutes a singularly powerful force for transformation of the employment landscape for both high-skilled and low-skilled jobs.

Many low-skilled jobs will be lost. Others will migrate to the lowest bidder. Countries can compete for the migrating jobs, but they must mainly count on massive retraining to raise the skill level of the workforce as a whole. High-skilled jobs will increase their wage differential, but the information revolution will reduce the number of jobs in this category as human skills are increasingly automated. Furthermore, many of the remaining jobs will be performed by a shrinking pool of highly effective suppliers who best master technology and knowledge for competitive advantage. An extreme problem of managing change affects individuals, firms, professions, and countries. Even in the best of circumstances, the transition will put some industries and countries at a severe disadvantage. This transformation of employment reinforces the urgency and strategic importance of education and the need for lifelong learning at all levels. Both theory and evidence suggest that in the long run new technology should create more jobs than it destroys. But the long run can take a long time. Unfortunately there may be prolonged lags between job losses and the creation of new jobs. And the new jobs may anyway be inappropriate for the displaced workers. Governments can help by making workers more adaptable through improvements in education and training and by removing obstacles to free markets in labour and in goods and services.

# 2

# Patterns of International Communications

## Media in the Internet Age

Nationalism, nation-building, and prominence of national over other identities have been prominent and global forces in the past century. They ensue from globalization in the nineteenth century connected with industrialization and the mass communications revolution that industrialization included. The twentieth century's one truly new organizational form was the inter-national organization in which the members were national states, culminating in the United Nations Organization but including others from labor to finance to culture to food and agriculture, each predicated on nations as members.

The breakup of empires — from the Ottoman at the beginning of the century to the British and French in mid-century to the Soviet at century's end — ratified national states as the only legitimate kind. If this is the 20th century story, many now believe its undoing is the story of the future and that communications technology is central to the process. For some, new communications technology is making the nation is more problematic that it has been for 2 centuries. Many political scientists are skeptical of more extreme claims for this revolution. Nations and states are still major facts of life throughout the world, as people compete to define them and to control them. Arguably, there are fewer political forms now than a century ago; even religious communities have come to assert themselves in national forms, most recently as the ruling Hindu party in India, and through the apparatus of states as never before.

On the other hand, defining identity and the state that moved to the air waves a generation ago now are being reshaped by newer information technologies. The key social features of new information technologies - from cassette recorders and VCRs to satellite television and the Internet - are lower barriers to entry and the possibilities of wider participation as producers, not just consumers, of mediated communication. From television and the spread of mass media a generation ago, today's signature information technology is the Internet, a world-wide "web" of information and medium of communicating that has captivated journalists and academics whose working communities it expands.

Socially, the Internet arrives in developing countries along with other technologies that together open channels of communication, choice, and, with the Internet, participation in an expanding public sphere fostered by popular access to new media. Some comparisons help to put this development into perspective. Where print fostered the ethnolinguistic nationalism that now seems so natural, and mass media fostered the mass audiences that were the twentieth century's distinctive realization of "citizenship," post-mass media foster audience fragmentation, viewer choice, participation, and a generally more symmetrical relation between senders and receivers of messages. One is the expanded access for more people to participate in mediated communication, from the commercial to the cultural. The monopolies of broadcasting, and particularly of state broadcasting that served nation-building projects in the Third World, are opened to a wider range of participants and interests. The other effect is to extend participation beyond previous confines of time and space. The first impact of new communications technologies is a migration of practices that were previously restricted to more private realms into a more public one. The increasingly ubiquitous mobile telephone in Arab countries is not just a business tool but equally, even more so, a way of keeping continuously in touch with family and friends while outside the home. Mediated communication becomes more dyadic, more interactive, more vernacular. One consequence is seen in satellite broadcasting opening possibilities of a more diverse Arab cultural space in television that reflects diversities, which were previously excluded by monopoly broadcasting, not least in the flourescence of unscripted television dealing with everything from religious and political to personal and lifestyle issues. The consequence here is a breakdown of social distance, particularly between forms of discourse and rights to participate.

In this transformation of mediated communication into a more vernacular, more interactive, more nearly "natural" channel, the Internet stands out for expanding participation in whatever it touches. For several years, an energetic and ever-changing group of Palestinian students and professionals overseas have taken discussion of the challenge of Palestinian nation-building to Internet. While the migration on-line of opposition politics first attracts attention, coming behind it are more widespread attempts to use the medium to imagine and reimagine alternative Arabias of regions, generations, and particularly of growing middle classes. Some are literary, others cultural; some nostalgic, others imagine the future. The multiplicity and specificity of responses mirror capabilities of the technology to first to open the public sphere to more actors and then to widen that public sphere itself.

More senders and more messages, and more space for them, does not mean an effortless transition to new communities of communication. Communication is a social process and embedded in social networks, which are its real authors. Instead of a global village, there are globalized villages, as such networks break the limits of time and space previously inscribed by earlier means of communication. The social dynamic of extension in space and compression of time make possible, for instance, the participation of Palestinians of the diaspora in the project of nation-building, or the abilities of NGOs to internationalize their issues and leap over the heads of local authorities to mobilize a "virtual" community of supporters, or at least of listeners. User-driven information technologies, such as exemplified in the Internet but not limited to it, facilitate including those overseas, or for those overseas to assert inclusion, in previously more local issues. But it is prudent to keep in mind that these may be different forms of recruitment. Interestingly, the very communications technologies that many fear will bring cultural dilution first make just the opposite possible; and what looks like diversification in one setting may really be enhancement, such as of homeland and diaspora populations.

Globalization in the information realm only selectively reverses some trends associated with the period of high nationalism, while augmenting others. Globalization's features of multiple, cross-cutting transnational ties, and the extensions of cultures into "cyberspace" first extend professional and national cultures, and then inscribe their diversities. Those include cultures and projects of nation-building and imagination. Potentially, they take on new lifas actually they take on new people, or at least the circle of public discussion. It is not only the dramatic case of dissident politics moving to on-line in search of global forums; there are other voices as well, which do not address international audiences in addressing audiences internationally.

So the effect of the Internet is not to undermine boundaries, except of participation, but to affirm and to provide a new outlet for it, new opportunities to pursue it, and above all for new people or additional people to join the discussion of it. The common anxiety that new information technologies like the Internet portend fragmentation generalizes from a mass media model that equates audience fragmentation with cultural-ethnic parochialism. To some, it seems as if the projects of nationalism are becoming undone by more people participating in them. Some, contemplating this widening participation, anticipate a post-national age in which special interest groups replace more integrative identifications, such as with nations. Perhaps, but special interests are just that — special — and apart from a tiny avant garde of enthusiasts, cyberspace does not replace the real thing. What its technologies do, however, is provide for re-presentations of real diversities that are subordinated in the mono-channel regimes of mass media. If the Internet were a place, it would be — like any other — one where people bring values and interests, some of which are subordinated in pursuit of others that are advanced to define a community. Among the first values and interests so far are altogether conventional ones of religion and nation, which already organize networks of actors and communication.

The emergence of new forms is a slower process than the migration of old ones: it took nearly a century for newspapers to emerge from the revolution of printing books, for instance. With this caveat in mind, part of the history of new information technologies during the past century in the Middle East has been to provide new arenas for new people and in which to address issues of identity that their advent brings to the public sphere — with the press early in the century, again through mass media in mid-century. Now, there is a new opportunity, and one might anticipate part of the response to it will be a similar pattern.In the short run, new technologies from cassette recorders to the Internet facilitate networks that are already international. Those of religion are quite old and already "transnational." Some of the more vibrant uses of the Internet today ensue from such quarters. Others, such as of NGOs, are products of more recent political economy, although not without precedents. Others are "cultural" in the narrower sense applied to entertainment, and still others are incipient as voices of similar but otherwise weakly linked class interests. Down-market information technologies create an arena in which they converge, and converge with other alternatives to more strictly national models; but while these are similar as alternatives, they are different alternatives. The similarities have disadvantages as well as advantages, as for instance NGOs are often locally assimilated to the models of opposition politics, even as oppositional movements can take on some NGO features by recruiting international constituencies.

In the longer run, this blurring of boundaries aligns the use and impacts of more participatory information technologies with the processes of contemporary globalization. These include taking local discussions "off-shore," reintegration with diasporas and with their interests, identities, and networks, and a coming to the fore of creolized discourses. Here is where the blurring of boundaries starts. And here it becomes possible to imagine contradictory processes - the extension of networks that is a conservative force and the expansion of discourse that fragments authority - that meet in new media technologies.

## Journalism in an Age Globalization

Perhaps the most significant development of the last two decades in international communication is the increasing concentration of mass media ownership within and across national borders. This process has been facilitated by a world-wide trend toward deregulation and privatization of the mass media. Concentration of mass media ownership has had two significant implications for the ways news is assembled and disseminated world-wide: First, concentration of ownership and privatization of mass media has been accompanied by commercialization of news and other cultural products, a trend that is characterized by aesthetic, technical, and professional standardization at the global level. And second, alliances between the international "media moguls" such as Rupert Murdoch and forces of political conservatism has led to increasingly "soft" media content. These phenomena are part of the process of globalization.

These trends in the political economy of international mass communication have left little space for information that questions the status quo, and even less space for material that forcefully advocates even limited structural change. A prevailing model of journalistic practice that emphasizes neutrality, "facts," authority, official expertise, and so on, has helped ensure that alternative views and oppositional voices remain largely unheard. The widespread use of the prevailing model, the origins of which can be traced to the rise of a "professional" journalism in Europe and the United States, has aided the owners of mass media corporations in their world-wide expansion by ignoring or, at best, not fully analyzing important global developments such as the social, political, and cultural implications of the international corporate concentration of mass media firms.

What consumers of mainstream mass media often are left with is generic news content that emphasizes titillation, sensational events, and politically "safe" topics. Contextualized and critical discussions of social and economic trends, deep analysis of the human condition, and material that provides genuinely useful information for mass media consumers is often consigned to the back burner, if not the dust bin. Consequently, the potential for journalism to nurture and expand any semblance of civil society, a space relatively independent of the state and the market, where open discussion and debate about the terms of social organization, the direction of public policy, the bases of cultural identity can take place among individuals, organizations, and other interest groups, is undermined. For example, because commercialized mass media need large audiences to survive financially, they may respond by eliminating political news or avant garde entertainment deemed by the owners to have the potential to displease certain segments of their audience. The result is that the range of issues discussed in the news is reduced. And when an issue or problem deemed acceptable is discussed, the range of acceptable perspectives on the issue also is relatively small. Consumers of this kind of artificially narrow and perhaps irrelevant information may begin to feel increasingly alienated and disconnected from the civic life of their communities. They may develop a sense that they are without relevant, actionable information and, therefore, powerless to control the course of their own lives.

This chapter is to consider how the journalism profession, on the one hand, and journalism educators, on the other, can respond to the detrimental impact international concentration of mass media ownership has had on journalism and news consumers.

### *International Concentration of Mass Media*

Currently there are five major corporate players in international mass communication. These giants are News Corp., Disney/Cap Cities, Time Warner, Viacom, and TCI. In addition, two other "mini-giants," General Electric and Westinghouse have global ambitions. Of these seven firms, all but Viacom and TCI have major news components. News Corp. is the owner of or significant partner in newspapers, television stations, and satellite broadcasting systems (including STAR TV and Sky TV) around the world. Disney/Cap Cities owns ABC. Time Warner's recent acquisition of Turner Broadcasting, which created and owns CNN, gives it a major international presence in news gathering and dissemination. General Electric owns NBC and Westinghouse owns CBS. All of these mega-corporations but one are based in the United States; News Corp. is based in Australia. There are several other significant players in the international mass media. Among them are Japan's Sony Corporation, France's Havas and Hachette, Germany's Bertelsman AG, Holland's Philips Corporation, and the emerging Globo of Brazil and Televisa of Mexico. Nevertheless, News Corp., Disney/Cap Cities, Time Warner, General Electric, and Westinghouse epitomize the trend toward the international concentration of ownership among mass media firms.

The growth of global mass media firms has been fueled by a parallel move toward deregulation and privatization of mass media organizations. This is most clearly evident in the broadcasting sector, which in many countries of the world had been maintained as nonprofit, public service, state supported entities. As the forces of capitalism and entrepeneurship have emerged as the dominant model of economic organization, the state has receded as a regulator of the market place . This development has allowed the global media giants to enter into partnerships with dozens of national mass media firms around the world to produce, provide and/or disseminate news and entertainment to domestic markets.

Advances in satellite broadcasting has secured the presence of the giant mass media firms in the cultural and information market place of every region of the world. If the current trend continues, as McChesney and others have noted, the day when most of the world's entertinment and journalism is provided by, or at least is somehow connected to, one of global mass media firms is not far o. Of course, this does not mean that every person in the world will consume identical news and entertainment products. The content will be linguistically tailored and otherwise culturally adjusted to serve specific regions by institutional and individual users at the local level. But the invariably pro-profit and market orientation of the firms along with staunchly conservative political orientation of their owners, will mean that some views, perspectives, ges, etc., will be off limits.

### Prevailing Model of Journalism

Journalism is an industrial art. The inverted pyramid, the 5 W's lead, and associated techniques are as much a product of industrialization as tin cans." Essentially, prevailing model emphasizes "objectivity" and neutral observation;

letting the "facts" speak for themselves; and heavy use of officials and experts as sources and attributions. It is a model that results in journalism that describes events with little analysis, relies upon polls and statistics to show social trends but without providing historical context, and provides no vehicle of expression for ordinary people at the grass roots level.

It is precisely the type of journalism that serves the interests of the owners of the global mass media firms because it avoids asking deeper questions about the exercise of power, the dispensation of social justice, and the prospects for cultural survival. Raising these types of issues under the prevailing model of journalism is difficult because it would force the journalism profession to jettison the notion of neutral, detached, "industrial" reporting. As a result, the news consumer is confronted each day with a numbing array of stories about political scandals, celebrity divorces, natural disasters, "horse race" reporting of politics, official pronouncements, and so on. Journalism of this type does not fulfill the role of journalism in modern participatory democracies in which people participate in jointly deciding the direction and nature of civic life. The type of news now produced by the application of the prevailing model of journalism does little to facilitate deliberation and discussion of pressing social concerns of the day among news consumers. In fact, the prevailing model of journalism results in news that may distance news consumers from one another in that the news stories do not provide information relevant for decision making; a sense of how the information (assuming it was relevant to begin with) is related to deliberations about public affairs; or a recognition of shared values upon which to make decisions related to the civic life of the community.

### *Principles for an Alternative Journalism*

For journalism to assume a more meaningful social and civic role, it must do what the prevailing model does not allow. It must raise fundamental questions about power, social justice, and culture. This effort requires that whenever appropriate, journalists take a stand, actively interpret "facts," let ordinary people speak about their experiences, and make moral and ethical judgments about the nature of capitalism

Such an approach requires specific reporting strategies that move away from the short-sighted, myopic definitions of news and how to cover it. Also, the idea of journalistic objectivity must be recognized as a myth and must be replaced by a view of journalistic work in which the reporter is an integral part of and involved in the community which he or she reports. Such an approach would emphasize processes rather than discrete events, dynamic explanations rather than static descriptions, bottom-up rather then top-down flow of information, a wide range of sources rather than officials and experts, and an explicit commitment to social change rather than professed neutrality.

Journalists would replace the dry, mechanical recitation of "facts" with evaluation and interpretation. Clearly these tasks represent the rudiments of a very different model of journalism than the one prevailing world-wide.

The following chart compares the prevailing model of journalism with an alternative model journalism, which is labeled "emancipatory journalism" to highlight the liberating and democracy-enhancing potential of mass communication.

***Prevailing model Emancipatory Model***

In the prevailing model the emphasis is on providing factual accounts of seemingly disconnected events drawing upon the words of officials and the legitimacy of science (experts, polls, statistics) as evidence to support the account. The primary purpose is to describe the event by recounting the "who, what, when, and where," and less frequently the "why" and "how" of the story. In the emancipatory model, the emphasis is on understanding how apparently discrete events fit into ongoing processes.

Journalists interpret the meaning and significance of the "facts of the case" rather than letting the facts speak for themselves. To understand the subject upon which they are reporting, the journalists rely not only on officials and experts but also on ordinary local people and their grounded knowledge about the situation. The purpose of their work is to provide an explanation of why the news is relevant and a cognitive "map" that attempts to illuminate the significance of the current historical moment.

While the prevailing model of journalism reports facts perceived to be the truth and makes a conscious effort to remain detached from the subject of the story, emancipatory journalism makes explicit efforts to promote reform and encourage social action. Emancipatory journalism can encourage action simply by providing information that makes people aware of services, opportunities, and problems that need attention. Readers can then act immediately and personally on information salient to their needs. Emancipatory journalism also can encourage reform by, for example, keeping the problems related to development on the agendas of policy makers so that they may be forced to take action leading to emancipatory social change.

Emancipatory journalism reports news in a fashion that uses a holistic approach, is people-oriented, and emphasizes advocacy. The holistic approach implies a recognition that globalization is a process and not an event. The enormously complex interconnections and trajectories of globalization may contribute to feelings of alienation and anxiety for those living through the process. Emancipatory journalism may counteract these forces by providing the cognitive mapping necessary to establish a sense of physical and cultural orientation to news consumers.

Emancipatory journalism can, for example, compare the current conditions with similar processes in other regions or countries and point out the unique needs and accomplishments of the local community. Emancipatory journalism can discuss current conditions in the context of their cultural relevance and historical significance; point out the cultural implications and consequences of change; assess how people's needs are being met; and propose culturally relevant models for future plans.

The people orientation of emancipatory journalism can help facilitate reconstruction of cultural identities. Through the broadly democratic dialogic and "bottom-up" nature of emancipatory journalism, local communities can develop a set of concepts and theories that provide the basis not only for understanding the contradictions of international capitalism, but also for critiquing them and proposing alternatives. The advocacy emphasis of emancipatory journalism helps to create, maintain, and strengthen a space for resistance with news that helps propose visions of the future that make significant the current battles for autonomy, integrity, and security.

### Public Journalism

The basic idea behind public journalism is to have news organizations purposefully use their resources and activities to educate and interest people in becoming more active citizens. To carry out this task, news organizations must capture and then report accurately what citizens think are the most pressing issues of the day and then provide a forum for anyone who wished to express views. In this regard, the news organizations may sponsor public meetings at which the community voices its views, bring policy makers together to discuss public concerns, or merely open up an opinion section in which members of the community can express their views.

The entire model is not easily applied in the classroom, but the information gathering and reporting part of the model fruitfully can be used to teach students information-gathering techniques other than the standard journalistic interview, and to convey a sense that reporters can be connected to the Communities they report without sacrificing their professionalism. The concept is based on getting the editorial personnel to think of the whole community as its constituent; not just those people who the advertising department is after but the poor, youth, minorities, those on fixed income, the elderly, etc. The entire community becomes the subject, sources, and market for the newspaper.

One of the most useful lessons students learn with this model is the blurring of lines between news beats, between "hard" news and analysis, and between reporter and community. Beats are no longer relevant because the whole community is the unit being reported in each story. The journalists learn that they can be a positive influence on the life of the community as they view their specific story from the perspective of the total community.

Among the most satisfying results of teaching these alternative models in the classroom was that students and instructors were forced to think about the world in different ways and to reconceive their idea about what the social role of a journalist might be. Connecting students to the community as active participants seemed to revitalize students' interest in the profession. Instructors were challenged to show the usefulness of the alternative models in an era when the prevailing model is not only pervasive but is widely accepted among most of the journalism industry as the only legitimate model of reporting and writing news. The most difficult lesson was that some students will resist learning models of journalism that are different from the prevailing model.

Most American students have accepted the basic principles and myths of the prevailing model. They have done this probably as a result of widespread and more general acceptance of capitalism as a model of social and economic organization. Most students do not find the concentration of mass media ownership troubling so they do not see the negative consequences of this trend for diversity of information and democracy. If they cannot see these problems, they cannot see they need to alter existing methods and models of journalistic practice. Thus, teaching alternative models of journalism must be accompanied by a broader critique of the political economy of the mass media.

Another lesson learned is that students found it difficult to sustain a systemic or holistic perspective of the community, in which each element of the community is interconnected. Part of the problem here is that if the holistic approach to reporting is used only in one course or sequence, students only think in terms of the total community for part of the time they attend classes. The entire journalism curriculum must think in terms of "total community coverage" for emancipatory journalism education to work effectively.

The Internet was a mixed blessing. It proved an excellent resource for background information and also for material that prompted ideas for localized stories about national or international trends. However, some students did not go beyond what they found on the Internet. Some students viewed use of the Internet as a shortcut to the field research they needed to complete assignments. Teaching alternative models of journalism is an important task given that the prevailing model often does not enhance diversity of voices and democratic deliberation. But challenging the prevailing model, which is supported by the economic, political, and cultural power of the international mass media firms that are growing more powerful through international concentration of ownership, is a difficult task. It requires more than piecemeal efforts in which the alternative models are taught only in some classes or some sequences. It requires a concerted effort on the part of journalism educators to deliberate about the role journalism should play in society.

## Consequences of Globalisation

The electronic media and communication sector, which ranges from telecommunication networks and the Internet, through to radio, television and film, is itself among the most active in the current drive for the globalization of production, markets and trade. Although varying among the subsectors, its rate of expansion has been phenomenal, the centralization of ownership has been among the most marked, the transition from national public ownership to global private ownership is almost total and international trade has expanded apace. This has been accompanied by the reorganization of hardware, software and content production, and the global redistribution of activities.

The social consequences of the globalization of the sector itself are comparable to those of many other sectors, and include the restructuring of employment relations and conditions, and international competition for footloose capital based on cheaper labour. While these issues are very important in themselves, rather than being given special consideration on their own, they should be seen as part of the overall issues surrounding globalization. Yet the sector, in its current trajectory, occupies a special place in processes of globalization that sets it apart from others. It has a unique impact in two directions. The first is as an enabler of globalization.

The media and communication industries are a leading sector in facilitating overall globalization. In the first place, the role of telecommunication is critical to globalized production strategies. It is inconceivable that the pace and depth of globalization could have been sustained over the past decades in the absence of sophisticated telecommunications networking. Furthermore, content industries, such as television, music, video, film and the Internet, directly through advertising and indirectly through the promotion of consumerist and individualistic lifestyles, are at the forefront of cultural preparation for consumerism, an essential precondition and accompaniment to the opening up of new markets for a huge variety of products, and to the breaking down of cultural and other barriers.

Directly in their role as enablers of globalization, the social consequences of the media and communication sector are primarily mediated through the sectors that they facilitate. For instance, the social consequences of facilitating the emergence of globalized financial transactions and manufacturing industries are ultimately a function of the globalization of these sectors, while the social consequences of the opening of markets for "lifestyle" products, such as fast food and cosmetics, are a result of the growth of these sectors. But these impacts bring us beyond the main focus of this presentation. The second special characteristic of the globalization of the media and communication sector is as a powerful agent in the transformation of social, cultural and political structures.

This is, of course, partly the flip side of media and communications as a means of opening new markets and softening up cultures for consumerism, although there is more to it than that. It is this set of side effects of the globalization of media that have the most impact of all, namely the evolving cumulative impact of the gradual commercialization of media and communications on critical social functions, such as the formation of individual and community identity, cultural and language diversity, the capacity to participate in the political process and the integrity of the public sphere, the availability of information and knowledge in the public domain, and the use of media for development, educational and human rights purposes.

These areas, the vital functions that media and communications must play in a society that respects democracy, human rights and economic, social and cultural needs. This chapter also highlights the major risks that are involved in the current process of the global commodification of media outputs and productions, and the commercialization of the dynamic that drives them. Priorities are also suggested for avoiding these risks in the context of international institutions and civil society.

At stake is the type of communication and media environment that are from the local to the global levels for future generations. Major forces are strongly propelling down one route, the commercialization of media sectors and outputs, subsuming media and communication 'products' under general market rules. An alternative route, currently much weaker, would lead us down the road of media and communications focused on fulfilling human needs and reinforcing human rights under a revised and invigorated structure of global governance.

The crossroads metaphor is apt. If we travel down the former route, it becomes increasingly difficult to make our way back, as changes are locked into place, ratchet-like, by powerful institutions with an armoury of enforcement mechanisms and sanctions at their disposal. But building an impetus to move in the human rights direction will demand a conscious and coordinated effort from advocates in international institutions and in civil society.

Media products are different, not least because they are more than mere consumer goods: in important respects they also "produce" us. Mass media and electronic media in today's highly differentiated and compartmentalized world are becoming the primary means through which people interact with each other, beyond their immediate everyday contacts.

Beyond even an individual's relationship to society, the very mode in which society as a whole realizes its aspirations and fulfils its claims to offer freedom and democracy to its members, to support rational and fair legal, political and social institutions, indeed its legitimacy in claiming to act in the best interests of people in general, are all ideas and realities that are represented and brought to us primarily by the media. The notion of "media products" seems somehow too feeble to encompass the role that they play in our lives.

In listening to, watching and reading media, we do not just consume, we interact. We interact with other people, and through them with society in general. We interact with ourselves, sometimes unconsciously, with our sense of sharing a common culture and of being a part of something beyond ourselves. Virtually every society has therefore developed two distinct ways of governing media: firstly as a sector of economic activity, and secondly for their role in politics, society and culture. Each follows a separate rationale and is deployed in different configurations by different societies. The two approaches consist of:

— regulating the media as a sector of the economy, or industry regulation, similar to that of other economic sectors. In a market economy, this usually involves regulating in the interests of people as consumers by preventing market dominance, sustaining competition, ensuring a legally secure foundation, for instance for intellectual property rights (IPRs), and ensuring that public resources, such as radio spectrum, are allocated fairly; and

— regulating to sustain and strengthen the social, cultural and political role of media and communications or societal regulation. This is regulating in the interests of people as social, cultural and political actors, and includes the regulation of content and the policing of acceptable "outer limits" of specific content, based on social norms.

This may involve everything from support for public service media to limits on advertising, expanding public domain information, universal service obligations and the censorship of content.

Forms of regulation often come into conflict. Too strong an emphasis on regulation as an industry in a market economy may be at the expense of the media's social or cultural roles. For instance, intellectual property rights by their nature involve a trade-off between the monopoly economic rights of content owners and public domain information available freely to all. From a human rights perspective, societal regulation should have clear preference over industry regulation in areas of conflict, but also in terms of determining overall priorities.

Within industry regulation, where they conflict, but also in general, the rights of consumers should be preferred over the interests of industry. Powerful countries, with a view to global dominance, promote corporate needs over those of people as consumers of media; and societal regulation, along with people's social, cultural and political needs in relation to media and communications, are shoved to the bottom or ignored altogether.

As the media globalize, questions of regulation are posed at the international level. As the national boundaries of media are gradually relaxed, the international level emerges. Media and communications issues have therefore developed their own international institutions, or have become integrated into the activities of existing general purpose institutions.

## Communication Governance

### *Media governance institutions*

The International Telecommunication Union (ITU), founded in 1865 and the oldest of the four institutions, is responsible for the allocation of radio spectrum across borders, terrestrially and via satellite, for the purposes, among others, of telephony (mobile and fixed), data, television and radio. The use of spectrum is coordinated to prevent interference and border "spillover", and slices of it are allocated to different uses and users. Since it is a scarce public resource, its allocation among users is an important and contentious issue at the international level.

The ITU also divides out the satellite orbital slots, including the valuable and scarce geo-stationary orbit. A second major function of the ITU is in standardization for telecommunication networks. The standardization of equipment and protocols can also be highly contentious, as it is tied up with issues such as market control. A further activity has been to facilitate the so-called "accounting rate" system, whereby telecommunication operators reimburse each other for the use of their networks for the completion of calls in another country. In net terms, many poorer countries have, for a number of reasons, benefited from these cross payments, which sometimes yield significant amounts of foreign exchange.

The ITU is also concerned with extending telecommunication to less industrialized countries, but has only very limited means by which to do so.The ITU therefore has responsibility for several narrow but critical areas of strong interest to governments, corporations and civil society alike. The United Nations Educational, Scientific and Cultural Organization (UNESCO), on the other hand, has much "softer" responsibilities. But these extend to many areas of social concern.

UNESCO is important less for its formal powers and its capacity to enforce multilateral agreements, than as a forum for voluntary cooperation on issues of mutual concern across a wide area, and for raising and debating issues of global import. UNESCO in its early decades was instrumental in many conventions, declarations and congresses, overseeing agreements on issues such as the exchange of audio-visual content for educational use, cross-border direct satellite broadcasting and copyright exemptions for development purposes.In the late 1970s to the mid-1980s, it came to the fore as a debating arena for global communication issues in the context of the New World Information and Communication Order (NWICO).

However, its fingers were badly burned, as Cold War politics and the entrenched positions of some of the major powers eventually led to the defeat of voices calling for more open and democratic global media flows and structures. UNESCO has never fully recovered in terms of facilitating vibrant debate, and indeed the United States has still not rejoined it after leaving in the mid-1980s believing, probably correctly, that it can wield more influence by remaining outside. In 1995, the UNESCO-sponsored World Commission on Culture and Development put forward some significant proposals regarding media, raising the idea of a tax on the use of spectrum, with the proceeds to be utilized for non-commercial programming for international distribution, and questioning the growing concentration of media ownership.

However, it is probably indicative of UNESCO's broader constraints that these failed to be ratified, or even discussed, at the follow-up intergovernmental meeting in 1998. Established in 1998, its main function is to manage the process of assigning names and 23 numbers for the Internet, an issue that has gradually taken on huge commercial and legal significance. ICANN initially saw itself as primarily technical, but its management of IP addresses and of the Domain Name System (DNS), which ultimately controls the routing of Internet traffic, quickly moved into economic, political, social and even cultural domains.

ICANN is interesting not just for what it does, but for how it does it. It is constituted as a non-profit private-sector corporation under Californian law, with a view to allowing the United States Department of Commerce to maintain ultimate control over the DNS (which it still does). This places it in the non-governmental sector. Its governance is still in transition, and has not as yet attained stability, although the at-large membership (Internet users who registered for the process) did have the opportunity to elect five of the 19 directors, the rest coming from the initial board and nominated by associated organizations. Its fragility has been underlined recently, with a decision by the ICANN board to back-pedal on civil society participation, and the robustness of the basic structures has been called into doubt. Nevertheless, it does point to the feasibility of different approaches.

Although WIPO is a United Nations agency set up to oversee intellectual property rights (IPRs), the WTO (which is not a United Nations organization) gained decisive pre-eminence with the signing of the TRIPS agreement in 1995. The WTO now has at its disposal some of the strongest policing and enforcement powers ever ceded by governments to an intergovernmental body, and it uses them extensively in the field of copyright. The copyright industries, such as film, music, books, television and magazines, include the world's largest media corporations, and the WTO underwrites and enforces their rights in all the TRIPS signatory countries.

The WTO is also the forum in which these rights have become, on the one hand, narrower, retaining only the model used by wealthy countries, and on the other, deeper in terms of duration and breadth. In telecommunications, since the shift from monopoly national providers to competitive international supplies, the trade paradigm of the WTO has also come to the fore. An area of interest here is universal services policies, under which governments can require cross-subsidization from large business users and urban areas to domestic and small users and rural areas.

The WTO Agreement permits this only where they do not interfere unduly with competition - a vague formulation that is yet to be tested. The move to privatized trade in telecommunications is also leading to the redundancy of the ITU's accounting rate system and to the net loss of foreign earnings for some of the poorest countries. Finally, the WTO is active in the field of media products. In the area of magazines, newspapers and other non audio-visual media, countries are not allowed, on pain of strong financial or trading sanctions, to introduce barriers to market entry on the basis of the protection of cultural integrity.

An attempt was made in the Uruguay Round to lay down the same rules for film, video, television and audio-visual products, which failed due to European and other opposition.

Intergovernmental organizations (ICANN being an odd one out) are ultimately subject to control by governments. In formal terms, they exercise no more power than is (more or less voluntarily) ceded to them by governments. Not that all governments are equal - a range of pressures can be brought to bear by powerful governments to force others to cede their authority to a treaty or agency.

The WTO, for instance, is regularly accused of being the arena for such strong-arm tactics. But governments in general remain the most powerful single set of actors.Nevertheless, when intergovernmental agreements are reached and ratified, they exhibit a tendency to take on a life of their own, and the central role of the administering agency in interpretation and implementation lands it in the driving seat. Accordingly, the agencies are gradually carving out a sphere of influence and must thus be considered as actors in their own right.

The global private sector, through multinational corporations and their well-funded associations and lobbying bodies, is also a major force on the international scene. Its avenues of influence extend everywhere, through some major governments, which virtually identify the national interest with that of their corporations, by sitting on the arbitration boards of the WTO, recruiting their former senior officials and the concerted long-term lobbying of international agencies. However, in media and communications, as in other areas, the private sector does not always speak with one voice. For example, the issue of copyright over pages downloaded from the Web pitted the "copyright" industries against the Internet and telecommunications industry, with the former seeking to extend copyright to even temporarily downloaded pages. The latter won out at the end of the day, and the Web for the moment retains that aspect of public access.

Nor does the private sector always get its own way. Non-commercial non-governmental organizations (NGOs) have enjoyed special access to the United Nations system since its foundation (oddly, the ITU is an exception, and the WTO, which is not a part of the United Nations system, also closes out NGOs from any formal role). The role of NGOs has gradually expanded and taken on concrete forms in terms, for instance, of access to information and influencing agendas. However, it is outside institutions, for example through mobilization at major events, that civil society organizations are currently flexing their muscles and staking a claim to be heard. In relation to media and communications, civil society has so far as a whole been largely, and surprisingly, silent, viewing the media primarily as tools to promote their agendas, rather than as active and hugely influential agents in their own right. But this may be changing.

## Influences and Trends

Media trends, and how to influence them, must be set in the wider context. Dominating this context is the new phase of globalization which is characterized, on the one hand, by a diminishing role in certain respects for the nation State, coupled with the limited and declining capacity of most United Nations multilateral agencies to cope with expanded global governance tasks. Into the vacuum, deliberately engineered by powerful nations, are stepping liberalized industries across commodity, service, information and communication technology sectors, with their own integral and exclusive forms of "governance" and control, overseen by their favoured international institutions, including the WTO, G8 and OECD.

The risk for United Nations agencies is that they will flounder in the wake of these unelected elites.A simplified global institutional dynamic can be identified. United Nations multilateral agencies, with at least some claim to upholding balanced global development, are struggling against a trade and commercial paradigm based on private property and contractual rights driven largely by non-United Nations organizations, especially the WTO, and supported by the more powerful governments and the interests of private capital.

Although they are unable to act in concert, the majority of world governments are probably on the side of more balanced development, as are most United Nations agencies themselves, in accordance with their remit and secretariats, and civil society. But the media industry is not only a lead sector in the rise of the trade paradigm. It provides many of the tools and instruments that drive it along. The media, and especially cultural content industries, help prise open new international markets through advertising and the promotion of the consumerist lifestyles in which entertainment is usually packaged.

The pace of globalization would be almost inconceivable without telecommunications and information and communication technologies (ICTs) in general. It is because the media occupy this key double role that attempts to influence their course of development will always confront the larger forces of globalization. As micro-expressions of these macro-trends, a number of distinct intertwining strands are likely to influence the future media landscape.The first of these strands is the declining role of most governments and United Nations organizations in the governance of media and communications, and the ascendance of the trade paradigm. In this respect, five points have stood out over the past decade or two:

— the transfer to the WTO of sovereign government power in the area of telecommunication and intellectual property rights (IPRs), and possibly in the future regarding audio-visual products and the capacity to protect cultural diversity and identity;

— the loss of IPRs by WIPO to the WTO and the consequent strengthening of trade and competition rules over human rights, cultural and social considerations;

— the general decline of the ITU as the global governing body in telecommunication, with much of its previous domain moving over to trade and market mechanisms;

— the inability of the multilateral organizations to agree on the regulation of foreign direct satellite broadcasting, and the consequent absence of regulation in the sector;

— the careful distancing of UNESCO from political issues and any debates casting doubt on the supremacy of the trade and market paradigm; and

— the failure of the United Nations system to gain governance over the Internet, underlined by the creation of ICANN as a non-governmental and non-representative body receiving its power directly from the United States Government.

Many of the above are actively pursued by governments, belying any simple argument concerning the eclipse of the nation State by some competing power. The loss of sovereignty to global market forces is seen by many at the individual level as being to their commercial benefit. Both the European Union and the United States, for instance, anticipated and achieved huge benefits from the opening of telecommunication markets in less developed countries (for which the long-term benefits are a lot less clear). However, the net effect is the loss of the sovereign power of governments and its transfer to selected multilateral organizations, and most significantly the WTO. The second strand is the related emergence of closed quasi-governance organizations controlled by the private sector, pushing market mechanisms to the fore in media and communications.

The private sector is already a major player, perhaps the most powerful, in the global arena. Yet it falls short of what it needs to achieve its ultimate ambition: freedom to operate when, where and how it wishes in an unrestricted global marketplace for all media and communications products. The constraints faced by the private sector in this respect include: the exclusion of the audio-visual sector from the WTO Uruguay Round agreement; market barriers based on cultural preservation; the inability to buy and sell satellite slots and radio spectrum at will; continuing government ownership of some telecommunications networks and media, as well as universal service obligations; time-consuming negotiations in United Nations agencies; and public interest regulation at the national level. These and other nuisances cramp the style of private sector operators and cost them profits.

The concepts of the Global Information Infrastructure and the European Union's Global Information Society were refined here, in close consultation with business and landing them firmly in the driving seat. Civil society and development issues travel in baggage class, offered amid much publicity some pilot projects and fine-sounding but ultimately self-serving plans for bridging the "digital divide". Latterly, entirely new entities have been coming into being to represent business and patron governments, such as the Global Business Dialogue on Electronic Commerce and the Global Information Infrastructure Commission, the core objectives of which are to plot a future for governance in which business interests are permanently to the fore. Nevertheless, the trend towards private sector governance faces an ongoing legitimacy deficit. Credible and durable governance structures are not yet in sight. A third strand affecting the future of media and communications is the tentative emergence of the influence of civil society and the rise of "people's media".

Although civil society, in the form of NGOs, has long been recognized within the United Nations system, it was only at the Earth Summit in 1991 that it began to take on a more organized and collective role, moving on from individual consultations with ECOSOC and the specialized agencies. But it was because of NGO activity outside the United Nations system, at least formally, that the other players began to sit up and take notice. The success achieved in opposing the Multilateral Agreement on Investment (MAI) initiative and the street demonstrations against the WTO, G8 and others, converted civil society into a new category of actor on the global scene, the implications of which are still being played out. In media and communications, however, there has been little direct action, and only slightly more in formal intergovernmental structures. The organization of civil society around media and communications can be seen in terms of three trends:

— One of these is the emergence of international advocacy and activist groups in media and communications concerned with global trends and pushing for enhanced democracy and the right to communicate. These include the People's Communication Charter, the Platform for Communication Rights, the World Association of Community Radio Broadcasters (AMARC), the World Association for Christian Communication (WACC), the Communication Rights in the Information Society (CRIS) campaign, the Association for Progressive Communications (APC) and many others.

— Another trend is the more frequent inclusion of a right to communicate and similar calls in the statements and goals of (non-media) umbrella NGO and civil society entities and events, such as the World Civil Society Conference and the World Social Forum in Porto

Alegre in January 2001 and 2002. This suggests that the issue is slowly but steadily gaining a profile across civil society as a whole.

— A third trend is the growth of community or "people's media" in many countries across the world, motivated in large part by the need to provide an alterative to mainstream media and to democratize media structures and access. These include public access and community access television, community and independent non-profit radio (many under the umbrella of AMARC), the global community networking movement, Indymedia Centres, as well as regional and global information services, such as Media Channel, WETV, Free Speech TV and others, which not only offer alternative media content, but also comment extensively on the media. There is also some evidence that these issues and actions are beginning to emerge in less industrialized countries, which suffer the brunt of some of the worst excesses of media globalization. This augurs well for the future.

The potential impact of NGOs on global governance structures has yet to be tested. But the World Summit on the Information Society (WSIS), held in December 2003 and led by the ITU, provided an opportunity to do just that. Several groups are already organizing to broaden the WSIS agenda to deal fully with issues of information and media and to enable it to play a catalytic role in civil society organization in media and communications. However, an enhanced role for civil society in the global governance of media would also raise issues of legitimacy and representation, just as it does in all other sectors.

A fourth strand that is likely to influence the future of the media landscape is the growing sophistication of the less industrialized countries in relation to their role in multilateral organizations. Over the years, the less industrialized countries have expressed concern at the imposition of external media content and structures and the liberalization of the telecommunications and other communication sectors. Although their motivations vary, many have drawn on genuine concerns and an informed understanding of the long-term risks. The debates in and around UNESCO during the 1980s, with the non-aligned movements playing a central role, for the first time raised a great variety of issues in global debate concerning such matters as media, the press, information and data flows, and the concentration of ownership. The virulent opposition of the United States and the United Kingdom, which in part caused their departure from UNESCO, is an indication of the extent to which these regimes felt their interests threatened.

Recent decades have been more muted. The issues have not gone away, but have been eclipsed by more immediate and pressing needs. Media and communications issues have often been put in the basket of areas that were, regretfully, to be traded off in the WTO, often with very little return. However, some of the larger countries, such as Brazil and India, have their own media sectors and have attempted to negotiate with a view to carving out a niche for their own industries within the overall neo-liberal paradigm.

Nevertheless, there is evidence of the emergence in some countries of a more sophisticated long-term strategic understanding of the role that media and communications can play, not just in economic terms, but also socially, politically and culturally. Reference may be made in this respect to: South African President Nelson Mandela's refusal to simply accept what was offered at the G7 Summit on the Information Society and Development in South

Africa in 1996; the success of a group of West African countries in brokering a deal that kept copyright away from material downloaded from the Web; and the more recent positions and actions of President Konaré of Mali in supporting radio and other media. These suggest a growing willingness to cooperate between less industrialized countries, but also with more progressive industrialized countries, which has been absent for some time.

## Future of Media

The main thrust is for the commercial and liberalization logic to permeate virtually the entire media and communications sphere, nationally and internationally, largely at the expense of their social, cultural and political dimensions. Multinational industry reigns, and the United Nations system is gradually displaced by an ever more powerful WTO, closed intergovernmental clubs of powerful governments and private sector allies. This leads to a contraction of the public sphere and of human rights imperatives, and an extension of the private sphere and the economic rights of those that can afford to exercise them.

At the macro level, this would require the resolution of current struggles concerning, for instance, the WTO and the Bretton Woods institutions, in favour of the neo-liberal approach, with little structural change and the emerging governance needs settled in compliance with the market driven status quo. For the media and communication sector, the structural conditions and regulation of this scenario would include:

— unimpeded global trade in media and cultural products, with no protection on the basis of cultural, social or environmental outcomes;

— a fully enforceable and all-embracing intellectual property regime that principally benefits owners;

— the virtual elimination of universal service instruments in telecommunication, deemed to interfere with competition and the operation of the market;

— heightened commercialization and looser regulation of radio, television and other mass media, and the obligation for public service media to compete in the marketplace;

— the commercialization of spectrum terrestrially and in space, to be sold to the highest bidder; and

— the gradual extension of industry self-regulation in emerging media subsectors.

Were these trends to gain an inexorable momentum, other global stakeholders would face stark choices. The United Nations system would be forced to choose between accommodating the new world order or risking redundancy, being cash-strapped and lacking the internal capacity to devise and enforce an alternative development or human rights based agenda. Less developed countries, similarly, would probably divide between a minority which object, and are therefore sidelined from the globalization process, or perhaps suffer the full rigour of what they have already signed up to, and a majority that believe they have no option but to join in.

Civil society, realizing the dangers too late to mount effective opposition, would find itself more or less excluded from this domain altogether, reduced to a spectator as the global media circus rolls on. The medium-term outcomes of such a scenario might be as follows:

- the number of media channels and sources available grows, especially from international sources by direct satellite broadcast and other means;
- within these, the diversity of programme content diminishes and quality falls;
- public service media disappear or dwindle to niche providers;
- media ownership and content portfolios are further concentrated and centralized;
- support measures for local, community and people's media disappear in the clamour for market sustainability;
- the public domain shrinks, as lucrative parts are hived off to profit-making concerns; and
- infrastructure and new services in telecommunications grow, but are confined mainly to urban and business markets, leading to greater disparities.

Brought to its (unlikely) ultimate conclusion, within a few decades media and communications could be expunged of all voices of dissent and criticism, an entire generation having grown up knowing little else, not just incapable of autonomous political action, but unaware of the concept and practice; the gap between those with access to media and those without accentuating the already great economic inequalities; and media content and information becoming the almost exclusive property of giant corporations controlling creativity and diversity on the short rein of profit maximization.

Most insidiously, the process slowly but surely transforms the very wellspring of ideas and creative capacities, ultimately yielding a self-perpetuating cycle that stifles genuine diversity and is purged of all dissent and non-conformity. The circle is complete. The end point feeds back to the beginning. A consistent and coherent pattern of domination impels media in a downward spiral to a new Information Age Dark Era.

The core weakness of this scenario is the legitimacy deficit that it would generate. Current tensions would intensify and the systematic roll out of this agenda through all media would require such an ever-growing abuse of power that it probably could not be sustained for long. The virtually complete subjugation of the public interest to commercial capital, although possible in individual countries and indeed approximated already in the United States, would encounter sustained and deep resentment and opposition globally.

Many governments, both powerful and less so, would baulk at the prospects of such explicitly one-sided development and its long-term implications. A more credible future for this scenario would therefore require the co-option of major civil society interests and of some governments of less industrialized countries. This would in turn mean a series of concessions in non-core areas that would at least mitigate the outcomes.

### *Multilateral cooperation*

The second scenario represents a decisive shift in the other direction, reinvigorating the democratic core of the media and communications governance structures. A reformed and rejuvenated United Nations system, with mechanisms enabling the participation of civil society, as well as governments, regains the upper hand in media and communications governance. It instates social, economic and cultural rights and the satisfaction of human needs as the core objective, and economic and political structures as the means for their delivery. Social and cultural needs and equitable economic relations are elevated as objectives above the pursuit of any particular economic model.

This scenario would bring some significant regulatory and governance changes:

— a review of the rules of international trade in media products, with priority accorded to cultural renewal and potential social risks, and a range of measures for citizens and governments to influence the impact of external media products, including advertising;

— the promotion of a range of measures for the provision of universal access to telecommunication and media, in rural and remote areas and amongst marginalized groups, even where this significantly impinges on the operation of market mechanisms;

— support for global public service and development-oriented media, perhaps through a multilateral agency, including ongoing funding from a tax on commercial satellite use, on the turnover of the media industries generally or another similar source;

— enforceable mechanisms to halt, and indeed reverse the concentration of media ownership;

— an international agreement on media transmitted across borders that covers issues relating to content quality, diversity and independence, and to freedom from political and other interference;

— the reformulation of intellectual property rights to ensure wider and quicker access to the public domain and to support development goals, while preserving incentives for creativity and innovation in media content; and

— the allocation of international spectrum, as a global public good, explicitly factoring in the social, cultural and development needs of marginalized countries and groups, as well as public service and people's media, and dedicated spectrum at no or reduced cost.

Faced with such a panoply of checks and regulations, in this scenario the transnational corporate sector would find itself forced to roll back expectations and operate internationally for the first time within a regulated environment. Some global corporations might be obliged to split up. Profitability would probably suffer a temporary setback until the sector is reorganized in line with the new rules of the game. Civil society, at least some of the less industrialized countries and marginalized groups in general would see an expansion of media and communications opportunities, by being offered access of which they could hitherto only dream in terms of both participating in media and promoting their diverse views, cultures and ideas.

Medium-term outcomes might include the following:

— a significant rise in non-commercial media, with a mission specifically to contribute to a media environment that puts people at the centre, from the local to the global levels;

— the emergence of well-funded quality public service media globally, and perhaps regionally, alongside the commercial sector;

— a reduction of advertising presence and impact and of the need to maximize advertising revenues, resulting in the alleviation of commercial and consumerist pressures;

— the emergence of public communication spaces for informed democratic dialogue on issues of global concern, and perhaps of a global civil society;

— more equitable access to media services, including telecommunication, reducing the gap between wealthy and poor regions and groups.

Such a scenario could conceivably become a realistic prospect, for instance if it were to be supported by a number of governments of breakaway industrialized countries, collaborating with a majority of less industrialized countries and riding on the back of a wave of civil society lobbying and action at the national and international levels. Realistically, any shift at all in this direction would be (and is currently) opposed forcefully by the United States and some other powerful countries, and by most of the institutions through which these countries cooperate, such as the G8, OECD and WTO. A break in these ranks would be an essential prerequisite. The private sector would use all possible means to oppose such trends.

Global media owners have not in the past stopped short of explicitly deploying their media to protect and expand their private interests, and the threat in this case is probably strong enough to provoke an extreme reaction. Such a radical shift would confront other problems. There are genuine concerns regarding the capacity of current multilateral governance structures to function democratically and effectively. Such a scenario would very quickly face its own crisis of legitimacy, given the generally unaccountable and relatively opaque nature of the United Nations system, with its composition that is almost exclusively confined to governments. To be plausible and gain the level of support that would be required, a reconstructed United Nations system would need greater accountability and transparency and, most important, extended participation beyond governments to embrace other actors, especially civil society and the private sector.

Yet the full realization of Scenario 2, in the absence of a broader move to rethink global governance structures and refocus them on human development, stretches credulity somewhat. A fully fledged Scenario 2 would require entirely new instruments, even agencies in the sphere of media and communications, setting the United Nations system on a par with, or indeed above the WTO in its capacity to enforce agreements; and counterbalancing the WTO trade focus with explicit consideration of social and cultural rights and other economic and sustainability objectives. This is likely only against the backdrop of a much wider movement to reinvent global governance. And a very broad, powerful and robust coalition indeed would be required to wage a sustained campaign to see this agenda through. It would undoubtedly have to incorporate elements of civil society globally, especially in the industrialized countries, and would require concerted action from many governments and courageous stances from the United Nations system.

# 3

# International Broadcasting

Since the early years, the broadcasting media have been very central to the development of national societies and national communities. The media have been implicated in producing and reproducing the national imaginary.This is the kind of topic that often gets linked to the theme from Benedict Anderson about the imagined community, and it is often said that earlier media publishing newspapers were linked to the creation of an imagined community and broadcasting in the 20th century radio and then television have been central in the creation of modern imagined communities, that the television, for example, has made visible to us all of those people who we feel are part of the same national community but whom we would never otherwise generally have seen.

Television has been central in actually producing that community, in instituting that community. This was apparent from the very early days when it was a very conscious strategy of Reith, of John Reith in that period of the formation of the BBC in the 1920s to create a culture in common. The objective was to create a common unified culture within Britain and also to use broadcasting as a means to create a political public space as well. Broadcasting has been central not just to the cultural unity but it has also been central to democratic culture. In many respects we have often come to feel that broadcasting is somehow in its nature a national medium, a national institution. We were for a great period of time through this century unaware in some sense of how the broadcasting system had been constructed, how originally it had been a contested system, and how in some respects it was therefore an arbitrary system, we had come to accept if you like the kind of hegemony of national broadcasting systems.

It is important to recognise that in the early days of broadcasting there were challenges to this national model. First it is important to emphasise that television and radio signals are not in their nature national, means television signals just spread across borders so the development of a national television system was part of instituting a social, political and legal system whereby television could be regulated on a national basis, a medium which one might say in its technology is inherently a transnational medium and had to be regulated as a national medium, and the history of broadcasting is in some respects the history of the development of legal and regulatory systems to try to inhibit that transnational tendency in the medium. The objective, of course, was to promote a national coherence and this led to the attempt to block all sorts of signals coming from outside.

From Radio Luxembourg back in the 1960s, or say Radio Luxembourg earlier than that, and through into pirate radio in the 1960s there was an attempt to create a kind of audio-visual sovereignty within the national culture, and signals from outside were seen as a threat to the integrity of the national cultural life. So that was one sort of dimension of regulating broadcasting on a national basis. The other was that broadcasting also had tendencies towards being a sub-national medium. as well.

In the early days there was a great push for the development of local broadcasting systems, particularly in parts of the north, and also there have been constantly agendas throughout the history of broadcasting in the 20th century for regional broadcasting systems as well. So the national system was also forged at the expense of recognising the diversity of regional and local systems within Britain, to take that particular example. The internal diversity, the differences within the country, the disagreements between different parts of the country, were basically, if you like, suppressed in favour of trying to play up those elements that different parts of the country had in common. The marginalised elements were then designated as minority elements within the culture and dealt with on that basis, so there was a possibility for the regions within Britain to opt out, as the phrase went, to actually leave the national service and to have some programming for their particular region. The important point to notice as well, or to emphasise is that generally the minority interests within national broadcasting were defined in territorial terms, they were the regions, those cultures which had a territory rather than ethnic minorities in the early days.

Television, or broadcasting, came into existence as an imaginary institution articulating a national culture and serving as the communications medium for a national public sphere. A model rooted in the national imaginary. Now to move on from that. Of course what has become clear since the mid-80s really is that this model has increasingly come to be undermined as a consequence of a whole array of economical developments, the unleashing of competition within the broadcasting industry as a consequence of regulatory transformations as national governments came to recognise the inevitability of transnational broadcasting, and thirdly, as a consequence of technological developments, and particularly the development of satellite and cable television. So we have had a real challenge to the national public service regime as a consequence really of a strong corporate push built around new technologies, and a push which national governments have basically had to acquiesce to.

So transnationalisation then began, or appeared to begin, in the 80s as a strategy being brought about by the interests, the profit interests, the competitive interests of large media conglomerates. Companies like Time Warner, News Corporation, Sony and so on have become the figureheads of this agenda and their strategy is clearly to try to get their products to the largest number of consumers that are possible. The imperative is to break down what are now perceived as the anachronistic boundaries and frontiers of national communities, these boundaries are now ones which are seen to impose an anachronistic limitation on the expansion of markets, and are seen as being arbitrary and unreasonable obstacles to the overall objective, which is for these companies to rationalise their business strategies. So through the 80s a whole set of new slogans intended to confront the hegemony, the dominance, of public service. We had the slogans around the free flow of information, the right of companies to market their audio-visual products and services across borders.

In Europe we had the kind of famous phrase of developing television without frontiers. There are some very strong slogans around overcoming old national boundaries and seeking to create what might be seen as the new universal culture of global consumerism.

The competitive market place of ideas, he goes on, and of experience can only bring the world together. So, this notion of the market then against the nation and the market bringing the world together, reminiscent of the kind of coca-cola advertising ideology. With new technologies, says Ross, we can bring services and ideas that would help to draw even the most remote areas of the world into the international media community. So there is this idea of an international media community being created. Ross goes on 'its up to us, the producers and distributers of ideas to facilitate this movement and to participate in it with an acute awareness of our responsibility as citizens of one world'. You see emerging a particular notion of a common agenda, a common set of values that we all as citizens of a shared world, of one world will have.

On the basis of what Ross calls consumers' tastes and desires he envisages then a new order characterised by the interconnection of cultures. Bill Gates talks about the information highway making all communication easier, bulletin boards and other on-line forums allow people to be in touch with each other, one-to-one, one-to-many, many-to-many in very efficient ways. Again this idea of a global conversation, this notion that we are all sitting around on an equal basis with shared ideas and values and so on. So the vision that is being put forward then by Ross, in relation to broadcasting, and by people like Bill Gates, Clinton and Gore in relation to the Information Super Highway expresses a certain aspiration, a certain ideal of creating what might be called a kind of post-national ecuminicism, an new cosmopolitanism, if you like, in the world.

Sceptical about what appears to be rather a banal kind of vision in the end, it's a very commonly heard agenda and people who in fact are claiming to be creating something quite revolutionary and when you hear it, it is actually a very bland and familiar kind of agenda.

Bill Gates promote greater social harmony. So we have there what might be called the ideology of communication which has perhaps in the 20th century almost come to rival the ideology of progress, communication linked to increased intelligibility, linked to mutual comprehension and then to some kind of mutual solidarity and agreement between those people who are communicating. The problematical ideology of communication. New technologies—both media and internet technologies, will bring people closer together and create this global village. In a sense underlying it, lurking underneath the whole thing is a kind of communitarian agenda extrapolated to a global level in which people again overcome the barriers of distance and communicate directly with one another as they would in a face to face community through these new technologies and can thereby come close to each other.

There are certain factors about the complexity and the inertia very often of the real world that make corporate marketing strategies to simply expand markets on a daily basis extremely difficult. First of all we have to recognise the realities of geocultural and geopolitical borders and recognise that many cultures, many national cultures throughout the world are extremely defensive with respect to transborder broadcasting. Another obvious and clear one for most observers is that the factors of cultural difference in the world clearly make global marketing strategies difficult. The fact of religious difference, ethnic and cultural identity issues, the problems particularly of language, the problems of historically evolved taste and sensibility in certain parts of the world is another factor which inhibits the marketing strategy and companies in the 90s have come to recognise this and a whole new kind of corporate speak has begun to emerge about global and local, this has become another very hackneyed pairing.

So we have organisations like CNN having to recognise that once you go down the socioeconomic scale it becomes much more difficult to reach audiences unless you take account of their cultural differences. Similarly Murdock''s strategies in Asia with Star Television have had to recognise regional differences and MTV has had to recognise that it needs to adjust and tailor its programmes for European, Latino and Asian markets. So that's a second issue, a resistance on the basis of culture. In many parts of the world, in Europe for example, have to used this global-local terminology for their own objectives.

There is a campaign almost for regional and small national television which again has operated as a resisting counterforce to the attempts to create a single large market. Again, it is important to note that this Europe of the regions strategy which sounds harmless and quaint is also a strategy which is also very territorially driven. It is to do with those culture which have region or small national territories lobbying for their own national interests and again the ethnic dimension is marginalised. There is a factor of resistance from the continuing importance and perhaps even still centrality of national broadcasting systems. National broadcasting in terms of consumer interest is still extremely important and perhaps in the short to middle term inescapable. There is still a very powerful attachment.

So, there are factors of resistance to the corporate blueprint for a transnational media order but of course this remains a rather defensive strategy and a rather limited strategy. In the case of Levitt, he is talking about simply the preservation of vestiges of the past which he reluctantly accepts and there is a danger that we might persuade ourselves into thinking about how we might preserve the multicultural map. There is always this tendency when thinking about culture to feel all the time that factors are diluting culture or homogenising or standardising, there is a reflex in us so we can think about it we can distance ourselves from it but there is a certain reflex to constantly feel that there is dilution going on and we must try to preserve cultures, preserve national or regional difference and preserve these old imagined communities.

This is a development linked to the development television to Turkish Communities across Europe, an example of this phenomenon of diasporic television. It is now possible for populations in cities like Berlin, Paris, Vienna or Amsterdam to watch Turkish channels. There has been a whole proliferation of new channels within Turkey which are now reaching out, so channels like the state television service TRT are broadcasting specifically to the communities outside of the country. You've got new commercial developments, and again this is commercial television doing this, organisations like show television, interstar, ATV broadcasting to populations in Germany, France and Scandanavia.

## Influence of Convergence on German Broadcasting Doctrine

The Internet offers today what was never possible in broadcasting. From an unlimited supply of information, the user can chose what he is interested in with a mouseclick. Instead of depending on a routine broadcast programming, viewers choose what and when to receive certain content. This form of media use is technically not limited to the downloading of text and still pictures. Also the content of the medium that is known today as broadcasting is increasingly distributed not by the bulk of an unrequested overall 24-hour programming, but by the piece (sliced up television).

In Germany it is the organization of continuously running, well-balanced content under a common editorial control that brought broadcasting under the special regime of the "Augewogenheitspflege" (protection of balance) that was mandated by the German Constitutional Court. On the contrary, sliced-up media content such as videotapes, books or press products has always been treated under the law of ordinary private commercial relationships. If a film no longer reaches its customers as part of an overall programming supply, but as a single product on demand, it should make no difference if it comes to the customer physically on a tape or electronically over the Net.

German Broadcasting doctrine is geared to a situation where -out of technical and economic reasons- the whole range of receivable content was offered by only a few public-law broadcasters. It will be emphasized what problems this doctrine is already creating in a world of multichannel television and how completely useless it is when everybody will put together his or her own "customized channel". The Bundesverfassungsgericht has said that modern developments belong "to the concrete fact situation to which the basic law is related and without whose taking into consideration no interpretation of the freedom of broadcasting seems to be possible that unfolds its normative effects."

The content of the constitutional term of broadcasting "can alter in the light of change within the area of social conduct that is protected by Art. 5 I 2 GG.". Since World War II until the 1980s, broadcasting in Germany was organized solely by public-law broadcasters. Although the Bundesverfassungsgericht never forbade private broadcasting, it was never launched. It was not until the installation of coaxial cable in Germany that the first private broadcasters were licensed - at that point also for terrestrial distribution.

Although the participation of private broadcasting caused the number of broadcasters to increase and extended the diversity of speakers involved in the process of the formation of public opinion, the Bundesverfassungsgericht did not change its requirements concerning the laws that shape Art. 5 I 2 GG. Moreover, its decisions portrayed a deep skepticism as to the contribution that private broadcasters made to the process of opinion formation. But the Court did not shut its eyes completely to the realities of private broadcasting. It's proliferation - besides other reasons - causes the requirement of "well-balanced diversity" to stop functioning absolutely, because private broadcasters were economically unable to fulfill the same standards of minority and niche programming as public-law broadcasters.

Creating the task of "basic supply" for the public law broadcasters, the Bundesverfassungsgericht indicated on the one hand that private broadcasting and broadcast programming from European neighbor countries will increase and on the other hand that these channels cannot be required to offer an equally well-balanced programming structure in terms of content. For the Bundesverfassungsgericht the constitutionally mandated goal is that "the broadcasting system as a whole meets constitutional standards as well as possible." To reach this goal in a "dual order" of private and public-law broadcasting, the Court constructs a twofold condition: As long as it remains impossible during the enlargement of the overall broadcasting supply for private and European stations to reach the "whole breadth of complete coverage, as long the "basic supply" is the duty of the public law broadcasters. And as long as they offer "basic supply" programming, the deficiencies of other channels are constitutionally tolerable.

The introduction of private television in Germany has proven to be a decisive factor for the formation of entrepreneurship in broadcasting. This is a prerequisite for the development of new services that focus on exploiting the economic potential of the distribution of audiovisual content in the most efficient way.

At the beginning of the 1980s an increase of transportation capacity could be expected as a result of the construction of pilot cable projects and the advent of satellite broadcasting. This already had an influence on the dogmatic justification for the notion that the freedom of broadcasting needs further shaping through legislation. In 1981 the Bundesverfassungsgericht abandoned the "scarcity argument" as an important element of reasoning on this issue:

"... The need for additional legislation to shape the Freedom of Broadcasting exists also if in the course of modern development the special situation that is characterized by the scarcity of frequencies and the high financial efforts necessary to broadcast comes to an end. The Bundesverfassungsgericht has always assumed this special situation in its previous jurisprudence (BVerfGE 12, 205 (261); 31, 314 (326)); it has left open what the law should be after its disappearance. Also in this case, the constitutional duty remains to enact legislatory safeguards for the Freedom of Broadcasting. They might be necessary to a greater extend in a situation were broadcasting is inevitable limited to a small number of senders than at a time where this limitation no longer exists. But even then, the necessity remains to secure the guarantee of the Freedom of Broadcasting through statutory precautions..."

In 1981, the Bundesverfassungsgericht dealt only abstractly with the end of scarcity in transportation means. It was not until 1986 that the Court discussed cable and satellite technology explicitly. Again, its judgment is skeptical as to the future proliferation of these new technologies. In particular, the Court seemed to be convinced that because of the high consumer costs cable or satellite reception the impact of these new distribution capacities will me minimal in Germany. In the mid-1990s, over 6% of all German households were connected to the cable network. Over 15.8 million households use cable TV today. These figures are not higher for the sole reason that the costs of satellite reception today only requires a single investment of about 20DM.

In cable 34 channels are delivered today. This limit is not a technical one but a political problem. Out of various reasons DBP / Telekom AG refused for a long time to make available the maximum capacity of its broadband cables. The number of German TV channels from direct broadcasting satellites today is much higher than the number of five, forecasted by the Bundesverfassungsgericht in 1986. In all Europe, 200 satellite channels are available.

These largely enhanced possibilities to reach the TV-viewer create the basis for offering alternative content through alternative services in broadcasting. When the Bundesverfassungsgericht predicted in 1986 that only two or three nationwide private stations would survive depending on advertising revenue it might have been right. It certainly underestimated, however, the fact that a full service program is not the only let alone the most economically desirable way of using a broadcasting frequency.

A major trend in recent years has been the advent and rise of niche and single interest channels. While a full service provider might be willing to serve the viewer with 24-coverage on politics, business, and arts as well sports and entertainment, the single interest programmer has a different goal. He knows that just a small fraction of the audience will follow sports-only programming (in part repeated features) for 24 hours. He wants to supply certain special interest groups at certain times and to build competence in the field of sports coverage.

A fencing tournament, which would receive about two minutes of airtime in a full service program, can be broadcast at full length in this channel because reaching a segmented and wealthy target group (fencing addicts) is attractive for advertisers. Each single program is calculated individually and positioned in the daily schedule. The sequence of the single programs is no longer following some editorial concept that is designed to keep the viewers with the channel but rather attempts to segment the potential audience. The Bundesverfassungsgericht has sustained legislation allowing niche and single interest channels and has welcomed them as broadening the overall program supply.

Present developments in global media are accelerated by a process of technical innovations that enables new economic opportunities and new media services. This process is described as "convergence". It entails the unlimited compatibility of formerly separated technologies, services and user habits. Following recent activities by the EU, this phenomenon receives increasing attention now in Germany. The challenge that convergence poses to media law lies in the fact that the converging of media questions the existing "balkanization of the law".

## TECHNICAL ASPECTS OF CONVERGENCE

### *Digitization*

The digitization of information signals influences the shape of broadcasting. At first, the compression of digital information enables a more intensive use of the existing transmission capacity without the need to build new infrastructure.Digital broadcasting again creates more space for new and alternative services and broadens the options available to the media consumer. Moreover, digitization changes the way in which media products are used. The TV that is supplied with digital signals becomes a switch in a universal distribution network. It thereby offers the same possibilities of information selection and information management as a computer does.

Desktop surfaces and browsers, which yesterday were only known in the world of computers are facilitating the use of a TV set today. In the United States, a debate rages on about the question with which operating system the set-top boxes of digital TV are going to be equipped. A TV set that speaks the language of bits and bytes can be programmed like a computer, can be hooked up to the Internet, or can be used as a video conferencing tool. It can process additional information sent along with the video signal like billing data, it can recognize advertisement and -consequently- is able to block it. It is also capable of automatically choosing the channel on which news is being broadcast at any given time.

### *The Internet*

The Internet speeds up the changes in media usage in two aspects: At first, it functions as an additional delivery medium for any kind of digital information. News coverage, movies or other content elements that are today seen as a part of broadcasting can be packaged and requested over the Internet by any single receiver or by a group of receivers of variable size. Which physical means of transportation is used to fulfill the request, if the signals travel wireless, e.g. via satellite, does not matter at all. A single twisted copper wire is sufficient for the transmission of complete motion pictures. Problems are still being experienced today when it comes to real time distribution of data intensive content over the Internet. This is because real time content depends on the arrival of the data packets in a fixed order at the receiving end.

Structurally, the Internet is not made for a timely, but for a secure arrival of the packets. That is why high traffic rates on the Net, congestion, or the need to pass through bottlenecks can cause delays. Nevertheless, "Webcasting" is already in existence and will spread quickly as soon as these problems are solved. One way to expand the downstream-bandwidth of the Net is the use of ATM. The disadvantage of this particular technology is, though, that it uses a protocol that is slightly different from the well-established TCP/IP. The ATM transfer protocol cannot use the existing routing machines in the Net. Similar progress is envisaged by plans to implement "gigabit"-Ethernet technology, which is a, upgrade of the existing TCP/IP.

Transmission speed is already increased by the use of ISDN-lines and becomes comfortable for multimedia applications through the use of ADSL. While American telcos are currently marketing ADSL technology on a mass subscriber basis, Deutsche Telecom just entered the stage of field tests. ADSL downstream bandwidth of 6 Mbps is sufficient to deliver a high quality MPEG-2 video signal. Even digital HDTV format, normally requiring at least 1 Gbps, can be compressed to fit ADSL capacity. Another solution proposes to broadcast web data in the "vertical blanking interval" (VBI) of terrestrial TV signals. Any PC, equipped with a 10$ tuner card, can filter out the HTML files and store them on a local hard drive or display them directly on the screen. The necessary software is free and only financed by advertising. It is supposed to come with the next Microsoft Windows 98 packet and can thus be expected to flood the market rapidly.

US broadcasters welcome data broadcasting as a new and promising business opportunity. On the whole, "real video" over the Internet is still in its infancy. But "like a dog that is speaking with a lisp, it's fascinating though not yet perfect". Secondly, the Internet imposes a different way of accessing and using media content. In doing so it has a model function for what will occur in the medium that is today called broadcasting. No unsolicited information, no program that just happens to please the "passive" viewer at any given time will be delivered anymore. On the contrary, the user deliberately accesses the information he wants to obtain. Additionally, the distinction between sender and receiver is blurred. The medium allows all users to offer content on demand for others. It is because of these structurally low entry barriers that there is no concentration problem in Internet content supply.

The Internet plays a central role as an alternative, easy accessible and cheap transportation medium for all kinds of media products. It clearly shows the advantages of a worldwide and world accessible data storage unit. With respect to the sort of data stored, no restrictions apply. "Sliced-up" television is obviously an excellent option. While the Internet still offers most of its information for free, meaning without the payment of a fixed amount of money as a condition of use, it can be expected that piece-by-piece programming will only become available at a fixed price.

Technically, conditional access systems can be located at the user as well as at the server end. For both alternatives, solutions are available on the market. As for TV distribution, the first alternative continues to be more commonly used. One reason for this is that TV is still perceived as a "push"-medium and conditional access still means that the individual user can access a stream of data floating by. Another reason is that today, single feature requests are served almost exclusively over the cable network. This tree-structured network has only limited upstream transportation capability.

In most cases, the customer has to place a request over a second network, in most cases the telephone network. This is called a "hybrid solution". In Germany, Deutsche Telekom AG is the only cable network operator. As it will in the future also manage the user based conditional access system for the Kirch/Bertelsmann (and any other) digital television channels, Telekom AG has no incentive to upgrade the cable network to bi-directional capacity and thus to open it to new services and easy Internet access. Finally, the sender will not deliver his product without encrypting it. This means that there has to be decryption software installed somewhere at the user end anyway.

On the Net, most conditional access systems are located on the server side of the connection. Technically, this is the easier solution. Due to the Internet's inherently bi-directional structure, the accessing user can proceed directly from the log-in / access sites to the desired content or he or she can start to download it. As regard to the question of security, problems have been solved by the universal availability of free and standardized encryption software. Consequently, the users can locally decrypt the content they download without being dependent on any special software supplied by the server. The existence of practicable systems of conditional access facilitates the piece-by-piece distribution of movies, documentaries, and other programming on demand no matter what transportation medium is being used.

## Economic Aspects of Convergence

The international marketing of media products becomes increasingly attractive in a world where distances do not matter anymore. Even Germany is beyond the stage where foreign newspapers were only available in station bookstores. Cable networks increasingly transmit foreign language programming, movie theaters increasingly show films with their original soundtracks. With CNN and BSkyB, for the first time truly worldwide television channels are in existence. With increasing mobility, with better knowledge of foreign languages and with increasingly international information habits, direct marketing becomes feasible for content producers.

The Internet and satellite technologies offer excellent possibilities for them to cut intermediaries out of the distribution chain. The only way to market larger amounts of content directly and to tap into the hidden revenue sources that become visible is through on-demand distribution.

### *Profit through Rivalry in Use*

An even greater incentive for direct distribution of single media products is the prospect of creating rivalry in the use of audiovisual media content. The whole market segment of electronic information distribution is characterized by low marginal costs meaning the costs to supply an additional customer with the same content. As opposed to that, profit margins are extremely high if each additional customer can be charged the full price, as for example when selling a movie ticket. So far, this has never been possible in broadcasting.

Larger audiences can only vaguely be transformed into higher advertising revenues. The consequence of this pricing model is that even high-class TV events, like the "superbowl" only generate a revenue of below $ .5per viewer per hour. Even if the costs of specific expensive programs can not be covered entirely by the "issuing of tickets", their supply can be financed by additional advertising that can be sold more expensively due to the presence of a highly segmented audience. The economic potential created by this new form of distribution which was made possible by new technologies and by the Internet as a usage model will not remain unused.

### *Democratic Aspects of Convergence*

Instead of endorsing the passive user habits of a TV viewer, convergent media like the Internet and the "customized channel" require active decisions on selection. The viewer gets bargaining power with regard to every single piece of programming that he selects because he has to pay for it separately. He gains freedom and responsibility with respect to the compilation of his personal TV program. Broadcasting that is "sliced-up" in this way, possesses an even lower function as a "factor" of public opinion formation than an average daily newspaper which is at least composed as a combined product under editorial rules and biases.

Piece-by-piece distribution of broadcast programming lacks this very criterion of broadcasting in a constitutional sense. Through its content itself, this means of distribution will contribute to the market place of ideas in a way comparable to the press or the Internet. But the regulation regime of these media has -neither in Germany nor in the US- been characterized by a "positive order", but by an attempt to secure openness and competition.

National broadcasting to a much lesser extent than some years ago fulfills its integrative function on a national level, let alone on a state level, which would be congruent with the states' legislative power in the area of broadcasting. The driving force of the technological development that is currently witnessed in electronic media is the ease with which distances can be overcome and borders crossed. It has to be taken into account, though, that the capacity of local and regional coverage are not at all diminished but rather improved by the new technologies. Start-up companies in Silicon Valley and local heritage groups in Bavaria benefit equally from the opportunities to offer new services on new channels to new audiences. Both can take profit from the same technology.

One consequence of the considerations mentioned above and the developments already underway, is the "customized channel". The media world of the "customized channel" poses much less of a threat to the elements of the freedom of opinion formation identified by the Bundesverfassungsgericht as protected by Art. 5 I 2 GG than today's multichannel television. In particular, the "prohibition to surrender the means of the media to one group in society" and the guaranteed supply of non-mass-attractive programming are easier to achieve here than in a world of an exploding number of commercial channels.

On-demand television is not only characterized by more international players but also by lower entry barriers due to the availability of alternative distribution avenues. Herein lies the opportunity for the market for audiovisual content to reach a degree of diversification comparable to the press. The press market and its less restrictive legislation regime enacted to secure the openness of entry and coverage, has been deemed appropriate by the Bundesverfassungsgericht in order to fulfill the duties of the mass medium "press" in the process of free opinion formation.

But this opportunity can only be used if the legal treatment of the new services follows the factual changes, i.e. if the individualized broadcasting services are released quickly from the structure of "positive order". The organizational, procedural requirements as well as the content restrictions that the Bundesverfassungsgericht imposes on broadcasters actually impede new entry for small players and promote concentration of the industry. The German broadcasting doctrine is in fact responsible for a major part of the costs of broadcasting that is used to justify this doctrine.

Concentration in the media is extensively criticized in Germany. But this concentration is clearly facilitated by the absence of an open competitive market for audiovisual products. In an open market, the joint control over content production and distribution is not the most effective company strategy. Instead, an open market forces companies to focus more closely on their core areas of competence, a process which can in itself promote the development of a functioning market that creates diversity and variety.

The Bundesverfassungsgericht kept emphasizing the danger to content diversity that results from the assumption that commercial television will only serve the needs of mass audiences and will neglect niche topics because those productions are not commercially marketable. This might be true in an environment where competing full service programmers depend on mass audiences in order to be able to keep advertising revenues high. But such a calculation is already flawed in multichannel television because the decline in shares in the market for eyeballs is inevitable. Broadcasters are not able to reduce advertising prices to an extent that allows advertisers to reach the same audience as in a 4- or 5-channel environment with the same amount of money.

Accordingly, advertisers cannot afford synchronous advertising on all channels in order to reach audiences as in the early 1980s. This simple rationale has encouraged the number of US non-advertising channels to rise as the overall number of channels exploded. On the other hand, the dependence of powerful consumer goods manufacturers on mass audiences continues to prevent the development of an optimal diversity of programming.

In on-demand television mass attraction is not a necessary vehicle for advertisement. Moreover, it is not only possible there to further segment audiences through the creation of more niche and single interest offerings, but also to separate advertisement from program content. Two individuals requesting the same programming can get different commercial messages. Advertising will also change in character. By more accurate targeting, informational advertising will dominate over mere "eye-catchers", because the audience is already interested in the product and does not have to be "seduced" first. Because of the new possibilities of interactivity, advertisers will not primarily try to persuade customers or to create a certain image but to "close" and consummate a deal. Eventually, the customer will be able to control which advertising he or she wants to receive. Some advertisers will pay for the single consumers' attention through discounts, vouchers, or bonuses.

The sufficient representation of national or regional content in an internationalized media world is not just a political claim, but has also entered the jurisprudence of the Bundesverfassungsgericht. The principle of "basic supply" is largely grounded on the rationale that the public-law broadcasters have to supply the audience with local, German or European content. The "customized channel" will urge Hollywood producers to focus less on American culture but more on "western" or "atlantic" traditions in order to be able to market their products directly to a worldwide audience.

When the German broadcasting concept of mandated diversity and full service 24-hour programming will be replaced by individual on-demand purchase of single products, the regulatory state will be faced with a different situation. If in theory everybody (and in practice an unprecedented number of individuals) could become broadcasters, the footprint of the freedom of broadcasting guarantee would broaden tremendously. In this situation, governments would no longer be allowed to shape -under the justification of diversity- the basic right of Art. 5 I 2 GG in a way that only public interest institutions financed by a user flat rate fee or deep-pocketed companies can use it. Instead, governments will have to positively secure access of as many speakers as possible to the distribution media, so that the potential of the new technologies can be fully realized in favor of the goals of the diversity of opinions that Art. 5 I 2 GG wants to reach.

Consequently, the German government should not have permitted the privatization of Deutsche Telekom AG without substantial guarantees that the broadband cable network would be rapidly enlarged and upgraded. Instead, the government should have kept the option to order a "spin-off" of the cable network branch in order to be able to invite private capital into this venture. Furthermore, terrestrial frequencies should be made available to promote wireless competition in the so-called "natural monopoly" cable.

The media ownership provisions in the new media concentration law permit a market share of 3% for single owners. This might prove to be too high. The model provision for this rule, the US Telecommunications Act of 1996, deals with a country in which geographical circumstances require much larger companies and where barriers to entry in alternative media are even lower.

Theoretically, there are two ways, each of which provokes different consequences. On the one hand, one could attempt to include the new forms of media distribution into the constitutional term of broadcasting. In favor of this approach, the argument could be made that also single films, news reports, and shows and not only the whole program of a station has a media-specific influence on the process of opinion formation. On-Demand-TV, like broadcasting streamed over the Internet, would be "broadcasting" and thus -by constitutional mandate- subject to the "positive order" regulations of licensing, surveillance, organization and content.

On the other hand, on-demand content could be separated from traditional broadcasting. Even if the content of single features, one could argue, is the same, this form of distribution lacks the typical editorial oversight, the composition of an overall programming that is typical for the power of broadcasting among other media. Following this line of argument, it has to be decided, if these services that are no longer embraced by the broadcasting definition should become part of a new category in-between individual and mass communication with its own regulatory principles or if they should fall directly into the regime of individual communications governed by the general contract, corporations, and competition law.

The individualization of the consumption of media products that were formerly distributed as broadcasting is presently taking place. Technological changes and economic incentives make it more than probable that in a few years the "customized channel" will be reality. Content that is individually requested from on-line data storage facilities should be treated like individually distributed print products (books) or individually requested content from off-line data storage facilities (videocassettes). Securing openness is here and there sufficient to guarantee an open market place of ideas. The new services have outgrown the confines of their former regime without threatening its objectives and can therefore be released from it without damage.

Offering on-demand informational content bears none of the risks, the Bundesverfassungsgericht mentions as justifications for the special treatment of broadcasting under Art. 5 I 2 GG. It can -on the contrary- be expected that such services will be cheaper and will be able to use many times the number of transmission facilities formerly available, including license-free transmission lines. Both aspects promote diversity and a well-balanced spectrum of opinions, which are elements of the world Art. 5 I 2 GG wants to realize. Both aspects lower entry barriers for small, local "senders" and prevent by themselves the "surrender" of the audiovisual market to one or a few groups in society.

The positioning of on-demand services outside the broadcast realm is also compatible with the Court's statement that public-law broadcasting has to be able to adapt if new services take over "functions of classical broadcasting". Thereby the Court does not subject the new services to the broadcast regime, but merely allows the public-law broadcasters to conduct business in a field ancillary to broadcasting. This is more than justified because it can be said - citing the Court's test for ancillary business by public-law broadcasters - that "especially by them the function of broadcasting as a medium and a factor in the process of free opinion formation is furthered". Currently, the two German public-law broadcasters ARD and ZDF have voluminous Internet presence.

### *Lack of reasonable Characteristics*

Legislative review or constitutional adjudication of the matter will have to consider if the changes in media reality as stated above are reflected completely by only moving on-demand services from the broadcasting regime into the regime of private transactional relationships. Therefore, it is necessary to look at the influence of convergence on the not fully individualized services (e.g. near-on-demand services) and on the remaining portion of classical broadcasting.

Near-on-Demand services are forms of media usage that are not yet fully individualized. They represent a middle category between on-demand services and distribution services. A near-on-demand service is characterized by a sender who sends the same content, e.g. a movie, repeatedly at short intervals, e.g. the movie starts every 1minutes. The viewer can choose the starting time that is most convenient for him. A request in the technical sense from a third-party's data storage unit does not happen. The viewer stills waits for something to come by. He is just not waiting as long as he used to wait. The Bundesverfassungsgericht views these services as broadcasting. The academic literature does not reflect a clear picture. The promoters of a wide broadcasting definition who even want to include on-demand services do so with the near-on-demand services as well (argumentum a maiore ad minus). Some say that the line runs sharply between on-demand and near-on-demand services.

The approach that focuses on the impact of an overall editorially controlled program in which the individual features are embedded, also excludes near-on-demand services from the broadcasting definition, because these services clearly lack an overall editorial program. This seems to be the appropriate approach. Moreover, like in the sphere of on-demand services, it is incomprehensible why the application of different legal regime should follow from the fact that the content distributed is intangible.

### *Classical Broadcasting*

The narrowest approach presented in German legal writing argues that the broadcasting regime will have to be reduced to the business of institutionally organized stations that broadcast programs under a common editorial rationale and thus manage to have a psychological effect on the viewer by preventing him from changing channels and keeping him in something like a virtual world. In the light of the changes in the media world which have been depicted above it is questionable if even these narrow criteria continue to describe a medium today, that bears such risks for the process of public opinion formation that could justify the continued application of classical broadcasting regulation.

It is all but clear at first if even full service stations are able to place audiences under the influence of the fascination of their overall programming. More and more private broadcasters market the single program. Programs are positioned in the schedule with regard to certain target audiences that preferably watch TV at this time. In fact, the daily program plan is composed according to the increase in potential audience over the day, so that the audiences of one program function as the basis for the audience of the following program. But this is more a dream of marketers than a reality because admittedly it is "impossible to reach the same audience over the whole day".

From an economic perspective, this is not even desirable. US broadcasters tend to adapt their programs to a certain, segmented audience, because advertising sells better if you can sell to an even smaller group that has common characteristics. These broadcasters have long given up the goal to "lock the masses in front of the same station all day". Public-law broadcasters even consider themselves to be constitutionally prevented from attempting to reach the same audience all day long. Allegedly, their duties of diversity and basic supply do not allow such programming. A considerable part of their broadcasting is dedicated to various minorities and is not able to keep other groups tuned to the respective station.

To reach the embedding of the viewer in a virtual world, a purposefully designed consecutive order of single programs is unnecessary. For example, well made movies have the same effect. The effect is even emphasized if the movie is not shown on a TV screen, but in a movie theater - a medium entirely different from broadcasting. News or music video channels that run in a way similar to broadcasting can also be managed to create such a "virtual entrenchment". However, they are not reached by the above mentioned definition, because they are not composed of different individual programs, but of constant variations of the same genre. "Media Services State Treaty" does not need a license to operate although it can be organized in the format of an overall running program. This teleshopping service will have a certain "locking effect" on people who eagerly wait for the next product to be presented. Is this effect - that is statutorily tolerated without special safeguards from broadcasting law - significantly increased if the programmer adds "additional entertainment and show elements as well as information content and journalistic forms of presentation that are likely to contribute to the formation of opinions and that are not exclusively related to the presented goods and services". Does this addition justify the sudden switch from a fairly unregulated environment to the much more restrictive broadcasting realm?

Finally it has to be taken into consideration that every possible "locking effect" and thus every alleged justification of the application of broadcasting rules cannot occur independent from the individual way of reception. The user who only logs into a running TV program via the Internet or pay-per-view television for the two minutes of weather forecast can not be a victim of any "locking effect". That means that even the narrowest definition of broadcasting can only be used to exclude services from the application of broadcasting law but not to positively describe the services that remain within the definition.

# 4

# International Communication and International Relations

International communication is vital, and particularly during periods of crisis. It provides us with the opportunity, a necessary opportunity, to gain an understanding of others in this world and furthermore to gain deeper insights into ourselves. Through the academic disciplines of social anthropology and sociology, a succession of phases can be analyzed to explain the process by which people typically react and then adapt to international experiences. These phases can be referred to as:

1. a "touristic" phase;
2. an experience of culture shock;
3. an adaptation, re-orientation.

The boundaries between these three phases cannot be demarcated strictly during the actual experience. Three phases can occur simultaneously, as a person may emerge into the third phase of some aspects of the overall experience while still remaining in the first and second phases in some other aspects. The clear delineation of these three phases is useful for analysis, nevertheless.

## "Touristic" Phase

The initial phase is like that of a tourist, hence "touristic". Interaction with the local population is minimal. Excursions are usually pre-arranged by agents or hosts. The person is often accompanied, escorted. Accommodation and food are provided mostly in hotels or hostels or other temporary quarters for foreigners. While the tourist is the clearest example, this phase is not exclusively theirs. Business people and politicians tend to remain at this level of experience despite the number of times that they may cross international boundaries. They do interact but with select representatives of the other nation. Even during business meetings or political negotiations that may become intense, the interaction is focused on pre-defined purposes and is mediated by agents.

Typically, a businessperson or a politician carries a pre-defined agenda, or purpose, which he or she will project deliberately over the meetings. A tourist does something similar, but indeliberately, subconsciously, projecting his or her own mentality (his or her own expectations and own preconceptions) onto the new experience. Thus, the person assimilates the new, international, cross-cultural experience into his or her own mental categories. In this way, the person continues to live mentally in a world that is known, even predictable. The foreign appears to be more-or-less familiar. The unknown appears to be more-or-less known.

This projection, of one's own mentality onto the new experience, can occur even when one speaks the same language as the local population or a variation of the same language. When a common language exists, one may be lulled even more-so into an illusion that the mentality is the same. One may naively presume that common words will convey the same meanings. Often, common words do. At times, however, they do not. Differences in meaning, and thus the differences in mentality, are not recognized so easily.

In contrast, in a nation that speaks a different language, one will hear a foreign language spoken, one will see a foreign language written, and one will receive many constant, immediate reminders that the mentality is alien to one's own. When variations of the same language are spoken, an illusion of "sameness" may be projected, more-or-less, over the differences. Whether the language is common or foreign, the same propensity exists during this initial phase: It is the propensity to project one's own mentality over the existing reality. Therefore, one's own worldview is not upset during this phase, or it is not upset too very much. Thus, the initial phase is characterized by these elements among other elements:

— a controlled environment

— minimal or superficial interaction with the local population

— and the projection of one's own mentality onto the new experiences.

The experience can be enriching, nevertheless. There is very much to be learned in this initial phase. There is much to be gained by a person for a greater awareness of another nation even during the tourist phase. One learns about other places and other nations even now. This is valuable for the tourist, who does gain a wider spectrum of awareness just by taking the tours. It can be useful for the businessperson or politician, who should obtain at least some experience towards some proficiency among other people. It is the starting point for the sojourner or settler.

## Culture Shock

The second phase, culture shock, commences as soon as the person becomes involved as an individual among the local population. It may be brief, as during a few moments when a tourist ventures into a local restaurant or shop without a guide; or the experience may be prolonged, as when a person visits a place often and interacts intensively. It can become acute when someone remains among the other nation as a sojourner or settler. Inevitably, one will find that some modes of interaction among the local population are different from one's own familiar modes. Some of the ways through which everyday, mundane tasks are accomplished are different from those at home. This occurs through many aspects of the experience. It can occur during practical tasks.

Obtaining either a sack of tomatoes or a plane ticket may be relatively easy for someone at home. The process might become complex elsewhere. Confusion can ensue, and sometimes with absurd consequences. Confusion can occur during interpersonal cross-cultural discourse, also. A contrast between modes of discourse may serve as an example. A person who derives from a nation where the normal discourse between individuals is direct, emphatic, "straightforward", may become confused in another nation where discourse is indirect, subtle, "round-about". This person may not be able to interpret the subtleties in the other nation, where directions are expressed as suggestions, where disapproval is expressed by a question, and where disagreement might not be expressed verbally at all.

As a consequence of this sort of confusion, for example, some Americans will refer to the Japanese as "inscrutable". Inversely, when someone derives from a nation where discourse is "indirect", that person may become offended when directions are given emphatically as imperatives ("Do this, do that"), or when disagreement or disapproval is expressed openly. So, some Japanese will perceive Americans as "rude cowboys". The more one interacts, the more one encounters these sorts of difficulties.

## Adaptation, Re-orientation

The emergence brings us to the third phase in the analysis, adjustment and re-orientation. One may emerge into this phase if one strives to reach it by becoming engaged with the local population, becoming involved. This is easier said than done, particularly if the local population is inhospitable. Earlier in the summary analysis, some customs were mentioned that had been misinterpreted by a sojourner (myself in the example), so that he felt on subconscious levels as if he were disliked by the local population categorically although, in reality, the local population's general attitude toward him was probably no worse than neutral. Now, in contrast, an actual lack of hospitality and an actual distain will become the topic.

On a conscious level, one must deliberately learn about the other nation, its customs, history, worldview. One must learn about the other's differences from one's own. At subconscious levels, one must allow oneself to experience the differences, especially as one will be a minority among the local population. Emerging, one finds, sometimes to one's own surprise, that one can mediate between worlds because one has become fluent in both worlds. Customs, attitudes, and ways of thought that were once shocking have become more-or-less normal now for this person in the other world.

Inversely, the everyday, mundane experiences at home no longer appear to be so normal. Even something as simple and mundane as shaking hands at home may no longer appear normal. One gains an ability to see one's home world, now, through a wider vision, or through new eyes. Ultimately, this person will have gained an ability to cross boundaries and to see.

## Integrating the Press and Media into the History of International Relations

Within this closeted universe, film is at best relegated to the status of mere commercial entertainment for the masses, radio to the ephemeral and television to the trivial. Traditional sources are, of course, essential but my main point here is that they are only part of the mosaic of an activity which has come increasingly to be played out in a public arena that has global parameters. The mass media (that is popular newspapers, radio and film) are almost a 100 years old—as indeed is the profession of the modem historian. The role of the media in history is most certainly not a sideshow, to be dealt with solely by organizations such as IAMHIST, but an integral part of the political process, one to be dealt with by all historians seeking to understand the forces which have shaped the world in which we live.

The role of the media as a determinant of foreign policy is today perhaps greater—or at least thanks to the television more visible—than it has ever been before although there is still a tendency to confuse various aspects of the process by which the media and foreign policy interact. For example, the more tangible and measurable aspect of media opinion is often conflated with the more intangible and less easily measured concept of public opinion. The media certainly, and the press in particular, often represent themselves as the voice of public opinion, whether mass or elite (another important distinction), and cling on to notions of their being a `fourth estate'; this self-defined role gives them their sense of importance and identifies their place in a progressively variegated information society.

Although it may be a role which politicians and officials frequently pander to, it is precisely such people who have also come to recognize the essential distinction between the print media, with its party political traditions, and the electronic media, regulated in such a way as supposedly to overcome those traditions. In this respect, as well as in the simple recognition of the significance of the media's role in mass society, the officials can be said to be ahead of the historians. And so if it struck you as odd to see the separation of the press and the rest of the media in the title on the conference programme, suggesting that the older medium of print is somehow a different type of medium from others.

For the advent of the newer mass electronic media, of radio and television in particular, have come increasingly to provide those in power with an opportunity to bypass the older medium of newspapers and thus address public opinion directly—nationally and, now, internationally—rather than have their views mediated for them by the so-called fourth estate. Even within pluralistic societies, this requires skillful estate management, and it allows politicians the opportunity to set the public's agenda. This in turn has given rise to a host of studies in the area of propaganda, 'the manufacture of consent' and the increasingly sophisticated efforts by social scientists to correlate media output with effects.

Moreover, the broadcast media tend to homogenise public opinion, grouping print journalists and politicians alongside joiners and painters to form 'the audience'. When BBC engineer Roger Eckersley pointed out in 1931 that `from Palace to Slum, people are listening', he saw radio as a great force for democracy, providing a common point of reference for people from different walks of life and backgrounds. Who controlled that common point of reference possessed enormous power to influence national self-identity and thereby reactions to international events.

The press of course remains an important part of the decision-making process by virtue of the inherent longer term process of production which allows for greater contextual analysis and the formulation of (more) considered judgements. The attention lavished by state department officials on senior reporters from the New York Times, for example, may reflect fear, but also rests upon an assumption of its established role in the body politic. Newspapers no longer provide the first draft of history. The electronic media, with their greater capacity for immediacy combined with their increasing power to cross political and cultural boundaries, nationally and internationally, have become no less significant, and perhaps even more so, in the conduct of international relations. Quite simply, communications technology 'interacts with public and private interests to broach political boundaries and develop international audiences'.

A good example of this occurred just over midway into the Gulf War. In the early afternoon (local time) of Friday 15 February 1991, Baghdad radio carried a long statement by Iraq's ruling Revolutionary Command Council in which it appeared that Saddam Hussein was actually offering to withdraw from Kuwait by complying with UN resolution

660. As news spread from Baghdad via an Associated Press wire service flash to Washington and throughout the world via a CNN anchor reading it off the computer screen, the news was greeted with a wave of excitement and relief since it appeared that the war was over.

CNN and ABC reported celebrations in the streets of the Iraqi capital with citizens firing their weapons into the air. Americans on the east coast were waking up to the story and NBC's Today show greeted its viewers with "some stunning news, some very hopeful news' while CBS's This Morning declared that "this war, for a lot of intents and purposes, is over". If A. J. P. Taylor had once postulated the thesis of war by timetable, he would have really appreciated this conduct of war by time zone and media deadlines. As it turned out, the event was a perfect illustration of the dangers of breaking news stories live on air before they had finished—let alone been fully analysed. The global electronic media fed off one another before the rambling statement had even been finished, never mind its translation verified. By the end of the speech it was clear that the offer to withdraw was conditional on Israel withdrawing from the Occupied Territories and the Golan Heights. As one observer noted:

> Once more, TV viewers were hearing the news develop at the same time that government officials and journalists were, and once more balloons were being floated, only to be burst. The problem isn't just that the news reaches the air unedited, it's that it sometimes reaches the air unverified.

Hours later, President Bush, who had been sharing in the general mood of elation as he watched the cheering crowds in Baghdad on CNN, was describing it all as "a cruel hoax dashing the hopes of the people in Iraq and, indeed, around the world". John Major echoed the sentiment, calling it "a bogus sham". Had the media not been (a) so keen to scoop one another, (b) so global in their instantaneous reach, and (c) given the role that they were given by both warring factions, international diplomacy may have had more of a chance. But the reality was that all those factors were present, as they will continue to be as we approach the twenty-first century. This will not always be the case, of course, as the secret post-1982 Argentine-British talks over the sovereignty of the Falkland Islands or even the recent secret Arab-Israeli talks in Norway demonstrate. But these latter examples are more likely to prove the exception rather than the rule in future.

Although we tend now to be increasingly more interested in how the media set the agenda of the politicians, an essential aspect of international communications remains the extent to which, for example, external broadcasting is still so closely related to the diplomatic services. When traditional diplomatic channels break down for whatever reason, the media are often recruited into the service of foreign policy, as when Khrushchev and Kennedy used international radio during the Cuban Missile Crisis. And this is not just a short-term business. Cultural propaganda, or to give it its officially preferred term, `Cultural Diplomacy' or `Public Diplomacy' is designed to serve longer term national interests chiefly through the bringing together of different peoples from different societies, through language teaching, international exhibitions, educational and cultural exchanges.

Public diplomacy is a highly specialized, professionalized and indeed essential adjunct to the everyday conduct of foreign policy. This is especially true for the period since 1945, but its genesis lies in the experience of World War 1. Indeed it was the Foreign Office which decided in 1919 to retain out of the rapidly dismantled wartime propaganda machinery its News Department—the first such peacetime Whitehall press and propaganda office, predating 10 Downing Street's by about a decade. The dual function of the News Department—the representation or projection of Britain abroad and the timely release of information about overseas events to the British and foreign press—was indeed a far-sighted recognition of the growing importance of government publicity to domestic and foreign audiences via the media. As J. D. Gregory of the Foreign Office wrote in 1925:

> The era when it was possible either to lead opinion in foreign politics by mere authority or tradition, or to ignore it from Olympian heights, has long since vanished, and once modem contact, however vulgar, has been established, it is not possible to confine it to an intermittent dispensation of tit-bits of news at the will of one or two minor officials... It has become, and must be, practically a never ceasing intercourse with the publicity world.

Was there a public out there whose increased interest in foreign affairs merited such attention? Even today, the number of people interested in foreign policy is relatively small and the paucity of records relating to public opinion in the days before modem market research techniques, before the likes of The American Institute of Public Opinion in 1935 or Mass Observation two years later, makes it difficult to gauge such matters with precision. There was certainly a public whose role in the survival or destruction of a state was felt to have increased dramatically, a role symboiised by the introduction of mass conscript armies between 1914 and 1918 and by the extension of the universal franchise thereafter. Subsequent developments in weapons of mass destruction, such as the bomber in the 1930s and 1940s or the ICBM in the 1950s and 1960s, made that public increasingly more vulnerable, and therefore susceptible, to involvement in matters of international significance.

And there was increasingly a mass media out there whose role as mediator between government and people needed to be considered not least because it was catering for the information and entertainment needs of populations which were increasingly educated and, thanks to a dramatic and massive expansion in the size of the electorate, increasingly political. In Britain, this sudden and rapid expansion in the size of the electorate after 1918 was regarded by many in power as a necessary but potentially alarming development: necessary because the masses needed some reward for their endeavours during the first total war of 1914-1918 if they were to channel their energies constructively into a pluralistic democracy rather than emulate the example of the workers in the Russia of 1917 or the mass conscript armies in the mutinies of 1918-1919; alarming because of the belief that the new mass electorate was still essentially volatile and irrational and, if it embraced socialism on a large scale, a threat to established institutions.

As Neville Chamberlain put it in 1923: "the new electorate contains an immense mass of ignorant voters, of both sexes, whose intelligence is low and who have no power of weighing evidence". Five years later, Stanley Baldwin echoed similar concerns: `Democracy has arrived at a gallop in England and I feel all the time that it is a race for life; can we educate them before the crash comes?'. And when one bears in mind that a badly scarred population was to experience its second disaster in a generation, the

Great Depression of the 1930s, there were very real fears that Britain might follow the example of some of the more extreme regimes that were springing up around the continent of Europe and beyond.

In so far as broadcasting was concerned, the establishment of a monopoly and the granting of the BBC Charter in 1927 therefore needs to be seen in the light of the hopes and fears that came to a head in the General Strike a year earlier. But the founders of the BBC, personified by its first Director General Sir John Reith, certainly believed that radio could provide an essential element in the democratic system. The Corporation's motto, that Nation Shall Speak Peace Unto Nation', also suggested an internationalist philosophy, and one that was essentially different from that embraced by a Soviet regime which in the 1920s had built the world's largest transmitter to spread the word worldwide, and especially to the `oppressed' occupants of the British Empire.

For Lenin, radio was 'a newspaper without paper, and without borders' and while the British began their Empire Service in 1932 to help foster loyalty to the mother country in the potentially difficult transitional period from Empire to Commonwealth, the phenomenon of 'radio wars' began to appear as a regular feature of international affairs, especially once the Nazis came to power with their theories of 'total propaganda'. For the Third Reich, which was established with a platform to return the Auslandsdeutsche forcefully separated from the fatherland by the Versailles Treaty, radio became an essential arm of its foreign policy process, softening up the target audience like an artillery barrage before the troops moved in.

This internationalization of politics, foreshadowing what would become known as the Global Village, set the scene for the ideological conflict that was the Cold War. But, in the inter-war years, it was every bit as important in what Donald Watt has called the 'European Civil War'. Not untypically, the democracies were slow to respond—the BBC's foreign language broadcasts for example did not begin until 1938. But at home, the response was more concerted if less visible. Its principal instrument was censorship, especially in so far as that other emerging mass medium was concerned, the cinema. With approximately 18 million people attending the cinema every week by the mids, 1930s, mostly working class and young—the very people Chamberlain had feared—the cumulative impact of the messages they were receiving was something no government could ignore.

Cinematograph Acts in 1928 and 1938 attempted to limit the amount of foreign screen fare by the imposition of quotas. Much of the motive for this was economic—a common saying of the times was that 'trade follows the film'. Fear of `Americanization' following in the wake of Hollywood's domination of global screen fare was another factor, and indeed one which was still evident in the 1989 European Community Green Paper, `Television Without Frontiers'. This ever-present fear of exposure to alien ideologies has meant that although a government could take immediate action by banning individual films from the Soviet Union or elsewhere, a policy needed to be in place and indeed in inter-war Britain it was, so much so that in 1937 William Tyrrell, then in his capacity as President of the British Board of Film Censors, could say with some pride that 'there was not a single film showing in London which deals with any of the contentious issues of the day'.

There were, however, several films dealing with the Monarchy, that symbol of national unity so recently rocked by the Abdication Crisis and one of them, Sixty Glorious Years, even had script contributions by the Permanent Under Secretary of State for Foreign Affairs, Sir Robert Vansittart. As John Grierson, the founder of the British Documentary Film Movement who had been employed by various government departments to develop official film publicity put it, the need was to "use the cinema as an instrument of education and propaganda to assist that process of reconstruction which our modem society must undergo".

By the time of the Munich crisis, therefore, a fairly elaborate machinery for what we now call social engineering and national projection was in place. Not only was the BBC transmitting in German and several other European languages, arrangements had even been made to broadcast `black' propaganda into Germany via Radio Luxembourg. But the meeting at Munich meeting was in fact the first international summit meeting arranged with considerable attention made to matters of presentation. British and German newsreel companies collaborated in the coverage, as is evidenced not just by the camera positions in the corteges and conference rooms in Munich; the same was true for Heston airport where American newsreel companies were given pole position to film `Chamberlain the Peacemaker' on his return with his piece of paper. Nor is it widely appreciated that about 20,000 people in London and the south-east witnessed that carefully stage managed event live on television.

This system was, of course, put to its greatest test during World War 11 when propaganda came of age. Not surprisingly, more has been written about the wartime relationship between government, the media and the public than any other period. The postwar period is now coming under increasing scrutiny, especially with reference to the idea of the Cold War being a war of words and images, of ideologies, fought out in the struggle for hearts and minds as well as on the battlefields of Korea or Vietnam or Afghanistan.

During this period, politicians learned to fine-tune the arts of public relations and even press leaks, and much was learned from the demise of Anthony Eden who was crushed by the media over the Suez Crisis. Meanwhile, external broadcasting, whether it be by the BBC World Service, the Voice of America, Radio Free Europe or Radio Liberty, was an integral part of this struggle and War world is seeing the extension of this activity into the realm of television, especially now we are witnessing the arrival of global television services such as CNN. Such services, as we have seen with the 'cruel hoax' example from the Gulf War, have the potential to bypass official public diplomacy channels, indeed creating an alternative to them which is made all the more significant by virtue of their emphasis on live coverage.

Inextricably connected to developments in communications technology which is increasingly more difficult to prevent, can we not start now to examine the relationship between access to alternative news and views, of alternative ways of believing and being, upon the demise of the Cold War? While RFE, for example, was beaming political propaganda into Eastern Europe, can we ignore the impact of such cultural products as MTV or even Dallas in changing attitudes to authoritarian rule with significant consequences for international affairs? How do we measure this? So far, the few pioneers have tended to concentrate on political events.

If we take the relationship between Gorbachev's glasnost and the events of 1985-1991, could we deny the interconnection between media and politics? When the Moscow coup plotters seized the Russian capital's TV stations in August 1991, they failed to appreciate the extent to which Yeltsin could still ascertain what was going on by watching CNN in Moscow or even that Gorbachev himself could do the same under house arrest in the Crimea by listening to the BBC World Service—which ironically he had ceased jamming just three years earlier And when Presidents George Bush and Saddam Hussein began addressing each other via CNN during the Persian Gulf crisis, could we deny the central role played by the media in international affairs today. John Major, for example, has admitted that his proposal for 'safe havens' for the Kurds in the aftermath of the Gulf War was inspired by watching television coverage of their plight in the mountains of northern Iraq.

In Bosnia, the crisis has been peppered with alarming television reports about civilians in cemeteries and bread queues being caught up in artillery fire which has prompted ebbs and flows in the politics of intervention. One wonders whether Beijing would have been a more popular candidate for the Olympic Games in 2000 had it not been for those pictures from Tiannamen Square. Both the leaders of Solidarity and the Polish government are on record as saying that the underground movement would not have existed but for Radio Free Europe.

Contemporary communications technology is indeed dazzling and when an American TV executive said during the Gulf War that "we are the world, we are wired" was he being more realistic than arrogant? After all, history may well judge that the crisis in the Baltic region was of greater long-term significance than the Gulf War that occurred at the same time—even though historians of the future will not have access to the same kinds of media sources for the crisis involving the break-up of the old Soviet empire because the commercially driven television networks chose to make the Gulf its leading story, not the Baltic. The tendency of the media to 'firefight' stories which grab their attention needs to be fully understood before we as scholars can begin to understand why Kuwait and Bosnia receive massive global media coverage while East Timor, Chad and Nagomo-Karabakh do not.

A significant consequence of the preoccupation with politics has been to leave by default the study of cultural forces and their impact to scholars in other fields. Such people can appear cranky to historians preoccupied with empirical evidence and hard data. The rise of cultural studies and media studies, too often dominated by theoretical frameworks and concerns which have no contact with the real world of the media has created a new species of scholar that intimidates and irritates most historians to the point of dismissal—and often rightly so. But once the ideology, the theory and the jargon has been penetrated, is there not something left for us? After all, the examination of the media's role in international relations essentially requires an understanding of the text within the context and even, dare one say it, the subtext.

For example, what is missing in many studies of the popularity of Dallas in just about every country in the world (except, interestingly, Japan) is an analysis of why it was popular at that particular moment in time. It is here that historians have an important contribution to make in a discipline which is increasingly multidisciplinary. If this type of question is not asked now, we can be pretty certain that historians will be asking it in 30 years time. There is one further aspect of all this which directly affects us all. The arrival in the past decade of the domestic video recorder allows us to scrutinize television—provided the record button is pressed—in a manner similar to the print media.

Similarly, during the past decade, the arrival of domestic satellite reception systems enables us access to greater numbers of television channels than ever before without moving from our living rooms. All satellite television broadcasting, even those designed for domestic services, are by their very nature international given that satellite 'footprints' spill over national borders. Indeed, this technology combined provides historians of the next generation with a unique opportunity to study the media and foreign policy. For example, if you wanted to study the press in a bygone age, you would need to read the product—a secondary rather than a primary source—and then go into the archives of the newspapers concerned, to look at the correspondence between editors and proprietors, between editors and journalists, the letters from the public whether printed or not, and so on.

A major problem for film historians has been that much of this type of record material is missing, lost on the cutting room floors of commercially driven film studios or newsreel companies where creativity was expressed on a Steenbeck editing machine rather than on the reams of paper favoured by print journalists and officials alike. But now, for the price of a holiday for two in Florida, an historian can now record on a videotape the size of a paperback book the broadcast output of say a station like CNN. At slow speed, three tapes a day will record for posterity the entire daily broadcast output of a station reaching nearly 200 countries and 300 million people—half the television owning population of the world.

Even more exciting is the fact that, by tweaking the transponders, it is possible to compare this output with the various reports transmitted by satellite of journalists on the spot back to their editors. We can thus compare what journalists as eye-witnesses are saying—the primary sources—prior to the editorial processes, or gatekeeping, which then go to work in shaping their reports into the news bulletins. This is tantamount to having access to the first drafts of history before they are rewritten by subeditors or to finding the bits of film on the cutting room floors before they were swept away by the cleaners.

This is a unique opportunity for the international historian, and one which is being lost with every day that passes without a concerted effort on our part to ensure not just a national but an international archive policy. It is the inevitable consequence of globalization combined with the free-market approach to international media sources by multinational media conglomerates whose concerns are very different from those of our own. As is true for intelligence studies, we have come a long way in the past 20 years to develop a methodology of dealing with the media in the study of international history.

One of the most startling developments has been the emergence of a body of work indicating a degree of control within democracies such as the USA and Britain previously associated with totalitarian regimes. But, if we are not careful and we fail to embrace the challenges provided by the modem international environment and the role therein of the media, we are in danger of pre-empting the future development of international history by quite simply creating a situation for the next generation in which our successors will look back to the twentieth century only to find that our lack of foresight has meant that they are unable to press the rewind button.

## Crystallizations of Media in the Global Revolution

Historically, the discourse of International Relations has distinguished 'international' and 'world' politics, and while the latter has been recognised as more inclusive, the former has been seen as a stronger reality. While, indeed, an 'international society' based on states has been seen as maturing over the three-and-a-half centuries since the Treaty of Westphalia, a 'world society' has been seen as at most weakly emergent. International Relations itself matured as a field, of course, in the shadow of the Cold War.

On the one hand, processes of transatlantic and European integration rendered many old international military divisions redundant, and provided a framework for the emergence of a much freer, fuller world market system. On the other, integration took place in the framework of new inter-bloc military rivalries of states, and depended very much on specifically international, inter-state cooperation within the Western bloc. In addition, integration took place with the clear dominance of one nation-state, the USA, so that concepts of 'national' interests remained strong even as policy was internationalised.

Up to and during the Cold War, media also appeared primarily national in form, and international communication across borders remained secondary. From the point of view of International Relations, media could be seen therefore as components of the 'domestic' order, relating to national politics and public opinion. Media were not seen as signficant components of the international order, except to the extent (generally considered limited) that the domestic affected the international. Increasingly, of course, international theory stressed 'interdependence' between national economies, and the emergence of 'non-state' actors

- such as multinational corporations - in international relations.

By the end of the Cold War period, such processes were seen as breaking down the divisions of 'domestic' and 'international' and leading to 'post-international' world politics. Economic and cultural integration, moreover, was seen as taking the form of 'globalisation' in which borders were undermined. In radical versions of this argument, the proliferation of non-state actors included social movements - including, for example, women's, peace and environmental movements - and was leading towards the formation of a 'global civil society'. This was itself seen as part of a wider movement towards a 'global society'. Curiously, media figured very little in these transformations of the International Relations debate.

International media groups were of course recognised as one variety of the increasingly important multinational corporation, and media were criticised in radical accounts as part of the dominant American hegemony. But the significance of media was often restricted to the interface of 'foreign policy' with 'domestic' public opinion in conflicts, which themselves were often conservatively theorised since war remained mostly a topic in the 'realist' end of International Relations. Because domestic politics too was seen as only an inconsistent, intermittent influence on international relations, it also figured fairly marginally in the field.

Even the growing recognition of cultural phenomena in general in the newer International Relations debates, and the more radical, postmodernist attention to the fusion of cultural forms, brought little attention to the media through which much of these phenomena appear. Specific media phenomena (e.g. CNN, the Internet) have achieved totemic status - the former in discussions of foreign policy, the latter in globalisation debates. However it is fair to say that no systematic, general rethinking of media has appeared in any of the critical debates in International Relations. Media studies retain a cinderella status in all main theoretical schools.

What is at stake is more than adding media as a significant category of 'actor' alongside states and other 'non-state' actors. The idea of 'the media' as a single powerful agent, whether a faithful servant of state and corporate interests or an intruder into their realms, is thebane of serious discussion, and indicates that we have not even reached the beginning of real analysis. What is needed, on the contrary, is a complex conception of media as structure and agency. An indication of the way in which this might be approached can be found in the conceptualisation of the state by the historical sociologist, Michael Mann. He sees the state as both a space, in which a variety of actors operate, but under certain conditions also an actor.

Mann's approach does not adopt the taken-for-granted conception of the state as unified actor, nor does it collapse the possible unity of the state into the multiplicity of interests which battle within it. Against both these one-sided views, it invites us to examine the processes through which, for some purposes and in some situations, states - for all the complexity of their component institutions and the actors within them - may become constituted as relatively unified agents, as well as the obstacles to such processes. Mann also suggests that the 'same' state may 'crystallise' in different ways in different situations - so that the American state appears 'as conservative-patriarchal one week when restricting abortion rights, as capitalist the next when regulating the savings and loans banking scandal, as a superpower the next when sending troops abroad for other than national economic interests. These varied crystallizations are rarely in harmony or in dialectical opposition to one another; usually they just differ. They mobilize differing, if overlapping and intersecting, power networks.'

We might adopt a similar approach to the understanding of media - even if media as social constructs are rather different from states in important respects. Media in general can be seen as social spaces within which individual and institutional actors of all kinds produce representations and communicate to audiences. Journalists and editors both help to reproduce the self-representations of other social actors, and produce their own individual and institutional representations. In this sense, media are both spaces in which many social actors act (including journalists), and can become themselves collective actors, as when for example a newspaper takes an editorial position, or television news and current affairs consistently focus on certain issues.

Media are thus both constitutive spaces of society and distinctive kinds of actor. We need first to take on board the implications of the fact that many individual and virtually all collective and institutional actors relate with each other in important ways through their representations in media. To take the example of states, relations of different centres of state power are represented simultaneously to each other and to mass audiences both within 'their' societies and worldwide, through media. Through theserepresentations - and the ways in which they are consumed, processed and re-represented by institutions and individuals - states like all other actors are surveyed by others.

We can take further the question of the centrality of media through the concept of surveillance. This, Giddens - following Foucault - suggests is a fundamental aspect of modern social relations, and the institutions concerned with it represent one of the four key 'institutional clusters' of modernity. However as an international critic of Giddens maintains, surveillance is not confined to the internal relations of the nation-state, nor is it a one-way process. States survey each other, and they both survey society and are surveyed by it. Although residues of the old geopolitical privacy of states remain, such activity coexists with the surveillance of states themselves by many other social institutions as well as of millions or even hundreds of millions of individuals.

Mass media are clearly central institutions of surveillance in modern society. Their centrality is not merely to do with the quantities of information which they produce. Media's crucial importance is that they are at the heart of the public character of surveillance. As Thompson explains, 'The development of the media has created new forms of publicness which are quite different from the traditional publicness of co-presence.' Because of media, states, social institutions and individuals do not simply carry out discrete mutual surveillance, through their own independent data-collection, monitoring and analysis. Instead, they all have access to a common sphere in which the surveillance function is concentrated and celebrated.

Media produce publicly constituted surveillance processes. Through their consumption of and input to media surveillance, everyone's and every institution's surveillance is related to everyone else's. All actors in the public sphere must necessarily be aware of the most intensive and extensive monitoring of their behaviour, reaching even into previously 'private' arenas. Established institutions - state and non-state - which wish to reproduce or extend their public roles must maintain and manage media attention, and individuals within them who wish to be recognised must adopt strategies for their own media visibility.

Conversely, new institutions and individuals increasingly become recognised as 'public' figures and actors through being picked up in media surveillance. This process applies in such diverse cases as the ways in which marginal political groups become 'international terrorists', or specialist entertainers become 'celebrities'. The means used to attract media attention may vary - from kidnapping and bombs to sex and drugs - but the nature of the process is the same. The contemporary forms of the relations of surveillance reflect fundamental changes compared to earlier periods of modern society.

The early phases of the emergence of modern mass media coincided with the highpoint of nation-states' control over society and the era of acute international conflict between major states. In this era, surveillance was both more national (confined within the state) and one-way (of state over society) than it has subsequently become. In that period, because media were primarily national (or sub-national) in scope, international relations between states were much less complexly mediated. States were often able to exert a great deal of direct control over media, and fashion their relationships with audiences according to state priorities. We can understand much about the roles of media in the Second World War, even in democratic states, in terms of propaganda, and indeed some scholars still see this as the dominant motif of international communication.

States were largely able to monopolise media spaces: individual and institutional action within and by media was largely structured by state strategies. Relations between states involved mutual surveillance of a much less public kind. Although different national media monitored each other and were monitored by states, there was little sense of a publicly mediated sphere beyond the nation-state, and the mutual surveillance of states was less dependent on it. Not only has this particular balance of state-media relationships largely disappeared, but it is no longer helpful to think of media primarily in the national context.

National structuring is only one, even if still a very powerful, context of media. Within an increasingly integrated Western-defined world society, there is a more-or-less integrated global media space within which states like other institutions operate. National media spaces exist as national segmentations of this increasingly common space, overlapping with other elements of structure. Within these mediated spaces, representations are contested by social actors of all kinds. States are the most powerful contesting institutions, but civil society actors, including journalists themselves, often challenge the kinds of representations which state leaders and institutions promote.

Indeed, while it is helpful to consider media as constitutive spaces of the public sphere, in which all public actors - state and civil-society - interact, there is also a sense in which media belong to civil society, and state institutions' self-representations increasingly take the character of interventions in the civil realm. The distinction of state and civil society is a vexed issue. Clearly states and civil societies have developed historically in intimate relationships with each other, initially very much as nation-states and national civil spheres. Civil society, in modern history, can be seen the realm in which the 'nation', as opposed to the state, was constituted, and thus the necessary complement of the nation-state, and this is only now changing.

The public sphere was classically constituted through a range of social institutions which changed through time. Media such as newspapers were part of this process from the eighteenth century onwards, but the national civil society of the mid-twentieth century was already a 'mass society' constituted by mass media in the modern sense - the mass-circulation newspaper, cinema, radio, increasingly television. Although mass media initially consolidated the national form of the public sphere, it is widely considered that the transnationalisation of media has speeded the development of transnational forms of society and politics. 'Nation shall speak truth unto nation', proclaims the motto of the British Broadcasting Corporation, in an enlightened internationalist crystallisation of the classic, mid-century broadcasting remit.

As media markets have become not only international, but transnational and global, the public spaces which they embody are no longer national in the same sense that they were. Broadcasters like the BBC still project national visions, but in a much more complex worldwide market and public sphere. Moreover, it is wrong to counterpose, as so many do, a globalised media - or civil society - to still-national states. It is as well to recall that press and civil society were already partially internationalised in the nineteenth century. Just as the accentation of their national character in the early twentieth century reflected political developments, so did the renewal of international discourse in mid-century.

Clearly the developing media and civil society internationalisation of recent decades has depended on the internationalisation of Western states and civil societies. This also dates at least from the Second World War - in which of course American and British media first developed strong international as well as national roles. The degree of military and political integration of the North Atlantic region after 1945 was itself unprecedented, and has been consolidated in the even more unprecedented development of the European Union as a new kind of polity. With the end of the Cold War and the collapse of the rival Soviet bloc, this conglomerate has attempted to construct a 'global' hegemony, legitimated by United Nations institutions, and partially incorporating the other main centres of state power.

This transformation of the state order has been very much a condition for the development of globalised communications and global civil society (and indeed 'globalisation' in general). The internationalised political order has been increasingly liberal in content, facilitating transnational, and increasingly globalised, communications and culture. It is in these circumstances that press and television have become more and more frameworks for transnationalised and globalised information and ideas. Although many have located the emergence of a global civil society in globalist social movements - environmental, feminist, human rights etc. - the common framework of this emerging form has been the transformed public sphere of mass media.

The development of transnational and global public spheres has coincided with the development of new media technologies, institutions and markets. Mass media have become less homogenous - technologies have multiplied, markets have fractured even as overall they have expanded, and interactivity has increased. However the transformation of the public sphere does not depend solely, or even mainly, on these developments, as the totemic importance of CNN and the Internet might suggest. It is important to emphasise the extent to which historic national media and institutions, such as radio, television and the BBC, have become primary vehicles for transnational and global trends.

Just as state internationalisation has depended on the integration and harmonisation of nation-states' practices, so the transformation of media and civil society has involved interlinked national media. The hugely expanded and speeded-up flow of information and images between media institutions means that core content is increasingly harmonised, even while its framing in public broadcasting retains many distinctively national characteristics. The location of media in civil society is reinforced by the fundamental political transformations of our time.

The movements towards democratisation in Latin America, east-central Europe and the former Soviet Union, and many parts of Asia, Africa and even the Middle East, in the last two decades have had deep significance for the roles of media. However uneven the spread of formal political democracy, and even more of the substance of democratic practice, a historic shift has taken place. Although the weakness of civil society is often seen as an index of the limits of democratic change, and the viability of autonomous civil institutions is still contested in many states, nevertheless there has been a great expansion of the possibilities for an independent public sphere.

Media and journalists are often in the forefront, and at the cutting edge, of transformative processes. Although democratisation and media development often both take specifically national forms, they are greatly dependent on the worldwide integration of both authority structures and media. The embedding of global institutions and democratic norms, however contested, and the creation of global media networks, go hand in hand to transform the character of media. Certainly, global media industries centre on markets for entertainment commodities, and corporations which dominate them may try to block the kinds of news coverage which challenge their authoritarian state partners.

However, the diffusion of information through increasingly global media cannot be contained within bounds which even the most powerful state leaders would prefer. There are powerful processes of change which are transforming the relations of states and societies and leading to the creation through global media to the constitution of a global public sphere, which is a crucial part of the infrastructure of an emerging global civil society. Any analysis of these trends needs however to emphasise their contradictory character and the contested character of all the movements involved.

### *Media as Sites and Actors in Global Politics*

The Iraqi wars of 1990-91 present a considerable paradox in contemporary international relations. On the one hand, the (Persian) Gulf War appears as something of a limiting case, the first clearly interstate conflict after the Cold War to have involved the Western powers as direct protagonists rather than war-managers. It is therefore a standard against which other 'new wars' are measured, and only the Kosova war of 1999 has matched it. On the other hand, the Kurdish refugee crisis has been taken as a paradigm of a new form of 'humanitarian intervention' in which states use military power for ends distinct from the classic pursuit of strategic interest. Despite the obvious links of these two emblematic episodes, they have been studied for the most part separately. Moreover, despite the contrasting media roles which were central to the two cases, no attempt has been made to theorise the linkages between these experiences.

The crisis originated in the war with Iran and the genocidal repression of the Kurdish people in the 1980s. In 1990-91, it involved four distinct phases of war: the Iraqi army's invasion of Kuwait; the UnitedStates-led coalition's campaign against the Iraqi state; the Shi'ite insurrection in the South of Iraq and its crushing by the Iraqi state; and the Kurdish insurrection in the North and its defeat. In these wars, there were three principal kinds of military actor: the Iraqi state; the coalition of the United States, Kuwait, Saudi Arabia and over thirty other states, which fought under the United Nations; and the Shi'ite and Kurdish insurrectionists. There were however other, non-military, participants - and to a large extent, victims - within the zone of conflict: notably the civilian populations of Kuwait, both citizen and non-citizen (who were attacked and forced to flee by the Iraqi army), and of Iraq.

It was clear to all, of course, that the war was heavily mediated. The postmodern sociologist Beaudrillard even opined that the Gulf war did not take place: the war was a phenomenon of the media.Communications researchers briefly turned their attention to international politics, and international researchers to media, in larger numbers than ever. In neither case, clearly, was attention sustained. The most important studies confirmed the success of the principal coalition states' governments and armed forces in managing media coverage, to reinforce the military campaign. There was little detailed attention to even this issue as it affected the Arab world.

And almost all academic media studies ceased at the point at which George Bush attempted but failed to end the wars, with the coalition ceasefire of 28 February 1991. There was therefore very little close attention to the role of the media in the insurrectionary wars and their aftermath, the huge and desparate exodus of refugees from the repression of the Saddam Hussein regime. This is extremely curious given that the totemic role of CNN, which arose first from its coverage of the coalition assault on Iraq, became identified in subsequent debates with the role of media in the Kurdish refugee crisis and the genesis of the Anglo-American-French intervention to create 'safe havens' in Kurdistan.

The term 'CNN effect' - as emblematic of the media's role in international politics today as 'Vietnam syndrome' was in earlier days - means the ability of dramatic television pictures of suffering to force Western governments' hands in the way they are presumed to have done in the Kurdish case.

# 5
# Responsible Communication

In recent years researchers have pointed out that there are huge differences in people's ability to obtain and act on information. This is causing concern, with experts arguing that a fundamental split is developing between the information haves and havenots throughout the world. The information rich have good access to information-especially online, but also through more traditional media such as newspapers, radio, television, and books-and can plan their lives and react to changes in circumstances on the basis of what they know or can find out.

The information poor don't have such access and are vulnerable to all kinds of pressures. Though the information rich are mainly in the industrialised countries and the information poor are mostly in the developing world, similar splits are obvious between prosperous and disadvantaged groups inside industrialised countries. The Internet has ushered in the greatest period of wealth creation in history. It's rocked the way we deliver and receive information and the way we do business. And so, for many, it is easy to accept euphoric claims - like those of Vice President Al Gore - that the Internet is also bringing about a brave new world replete with an "electronic agora" and "online democracy". It's not.

More than 80% of people in the world have never even heard a dial tone, let alone surfed the Web. And the gap between the information haves and have-nots is widening. In a speech this week at Telecom 99 in Geneva, Switzerland, UN Secretary General Kofi Anan warned of the danger of excluding the world's poor from the information revolution. "People lack many things: jobs, shelter, food, health care and drinkable water. Today, being cut off from basic telecommunications services is a hardship almost as acute as these other deprivations, and may indeed reduce the chances of finding remedies to them," he said.

The hype for everything online obscures the reality about how technology is changing life at the end of the 20th century. From Manhattan and Madrid, the Internet has fundamentally changed work, recreation - even love. But in Malawi and Mozambique, life remains very much the same. More than 80% of people in the world have never heard a dial tone, let alone sent an email or downloaded information from the World Wide Web.

The statistics on the basic building block of connectedness - that is, phone lines - are stark. According to the latest UN Human Development Report, industrialised countries, with only 15% of the world's population, are home to 88% of all Internet users. Less than 1% of people in South Asia are online even though it is home to one-fifth of the world's population. The situation is even worse in Africa. With 739 million people, there are only 14 million phone lines. That's fewer than in Manhattan or Tokyo. Eighty percent of those lines are in only six countries. There are only 1 million Internet users on the entire continent compared with 10.5 million in the UK.

Even if telecommunications systems were in place, most of the world's poor would still be excluded from the information revolution because of illiteracy and a lack of basic computer skills. In Benin, for example, more than 60% of the population is illiterate. The other 40% are similarly out of luck. Four-fifths of Websites are in English, a language understood by only one in 10 people on the planet. The lack of resources in poor communities can't explain the technology gap alone. In the developing world, there is still resistance to the idea that technology is a quick-fix. Internet will be virtually global in five to seven years. But for that to happen infrastructure must be put in place, which means a lot of money - and fast. The Net may be the wave of the future but age-old problems still apply.

In East Palo Alto, the area bordering the tech-rich Stanford University campus and the corporate HQs of multi-billion dollar companies such as Yahoo and Oracle, more than 17% of the population lives in poverty. Only 14% have a four-year college degree and less than one out of five families has a computer in the home. Even in America the digital divide is wide. But as technology increasingly becomes a part of everyday life, and the political debate, a new awareness is emerging that the benefits of technology will not filter down by themselves.

"It's taken a while for mainstream culture to understand how it would make their lives easier - and what their lives would be like without it," said Magda Escobar, the Executive Director of Plugged In, a community project that aims to bridge the digital divide. "It is also a very sexy issue. And it's politically advantageous for everyone - liberal or conservative - to focus on it." Plugged In is leading by example in East Palo Alto. The non-profit organisation offers residents state-of-the-art computers and courses to build their literacy and computer skills, work on their CVs or make money as Web designers.

Plugged In Enterprises, a teen-run Web page design business, is one of the centre's most dynamic and talked about programmes. Each year 36 teenagers learn cutting-edge business skills and earn money working on projects for real clients including Hewlett-Packard and Sun Microsystems. PIE, as it is known, is run by John Mireles, a 17-year-old from nearby San Jose. Formerly a graffiti artist, John's own projects include transferring his own highly-charged images into digital form and pushing the medium to its limits. His goal: to earn a good living that leaves him plenty of time for his own art.

Plugged In also runs a programme called Community Kids which hosts 55 children each day after school and involves them in hands-on arts and crafts and computer projects. The Plugged In Community Technology Centre, a mixture of a café, copy shop and library, is a resource for teenagers and adults to work on their CVs or get career advice. But there is still much work to be done. The latest report from the US Commerce Department, Falling Through The Net, reports that the digital divide widened between 1998 and 1999. Black and hispanic households are approximately one-third as likely to have home Internet access as households of Asian/Pacific Islander descent, and roughly two-fifths as likely as white households, according to the report.

The disparity does not only follow racial lines. Even at the lowest income levels, those in urban areas are more than twice as likely to have Internet access than those in rural areas. "We need to keep up the pressure to keep up with the technology," says Ms Escobar. "There's a risk that people will just dump equipment into poor areas. This is a long process."

One of the most basic models of the communication process begins with a simple triangle: sender, message, receiver. Somebody has to talk, something has to be said, somebody has to listen. Today, masses of information are being generated, more information every day, more than the world has ever seen before. That's not exactly wrong, but its not totally right, either. Too much information is unavailable, even to the information rich like Theo Schoeman. We're missing something.

Similarly, information transmission problems are now a thing of the past. After all, we have optical fiber and satellite delivery systems. But is that all it really takes? If laying fiber means information now flows everywhere, what is Negumbo Johannes' problem? And what about us as information receivers? Even if untold quantities of new information were suddenly available and delivered free to our door, would we know what to do with it? Where's the evidence to support that assumption? If information is doubling every three or five or seven or ten years, where has all that information gone? Is the world really awash in information? And if it is, is that the end to all the world's problems?

We are counting articles and pointing to large numbers, but not looking closely enough at the information being generated. We are talking about bandwidth as a solution to information flow without looking carefully enough at how information really moves from one place to another — and why it often can't move at all. And we seem extremely arrogant about our own abilities to handle information despite endless examples of our frailties. If we are going to take advantage of developments in information access, we have to begin by being honest about the kind of information that is available, the ability of information to move, and our own ability to process it.

Over the past decade or two there is an information explosion. We are told we now live in an information age. If we want to start discussions of an information explosion, and define this as the information age, it would be helpful if we would begin by at least defining the term "information." Toffler defines information as "data that have been fitted into categories and classification schemes or other patterns." That's not a bad beginning. It implies that information is something that has been worked on — "fitted" into patterns or other larger structures. But it is still very vague. For instance, it doesn't tell us where we might go looking for information, or what forms we might find it in.

Michael Buckland at UC-Berkeley's School of Library and Information Studies takes a look at the forms of information. He focuses on "information-as-thing". This is a very practical approach for a librarian to take. In essence he asks, where is this stuff and how much room will it occupy? His answer is that information comes as

1. data -.records that can be stored on a computer.
2. text and documents - papers, letters, books, that may be on paper, microfilm, or in electronic form. Spoken language in any medium
3. objects - dinosaur bones, rock collections, skeletons
4. records of events - photos, news reports, memoirs

Such a definition is both insightful and practical. It reminds us that information can come in many forms. Information is not a neutral object to be discovered and counted, like atoms or zebras, but an expression shaped from the very beginning by the creators of that information. In short, information comes from somebody, and that somebody determines from the beginning how much information there will be, what form it will take, and even if it will exist at all. If you want to understand information, go to its source.

How many sources are there? In one sense there are billions — each of us who has ever occupied our planet. Five of them are shown below.

— Public Information

— Personal Information

— Organizational Information

— Professional Information

— Commercial Information

These five don't exhaust all the information sources we may encounter, but they represent major sources. By examining each, we will see how much information is really out there, what form it takes, and how good it is.

### Public Information

The rush to examine all the new opportunities made available by technology, much of the information people have still comes from very traditional sources — television, movies, radio, newspapers, and books. It is true digital information is supplementing and even supplanting these earlier forms, but it hasn't totally replaced them and won't any time soon. But while these traditional sources of information are still important, they aren't always accessible.

For instance, CNN is nice, but to see it you not only need a television, you need an electrical outlet to plug the TV into. That may not be a problem in the US where they have 850 TVs per 1000 population. But it seems to be a problem in countries like Bangladesh (5 TVs per 1000) or Kenya (9 TVs per 1000). Books are still a critical resource for information, but some countries have virtually no publishing industry, with the entire continent of Africa producing just 2% of the world's book titles.

Besides availability, there is the question of origination. There are lots of movies circulating through the world, but they come from very few countries. Developing nations occasionally complain about this cultural dependence, and even formed the New World Information and Communications Order, but there is no sign of real change here. In the meantime, not only do some countries struggle under the weight of foreign culture, exporting countries like ours have almost no opportunity to hear other voices or see other perspectives. The information flow is all one way.

### *Personal Information*

"It's not what you know, it's who you know," is cynical, but it is accurate. It might be even more accurate if rephrased, "Who you know determines what you know." The value of personal contacts may be more difficult to calculate than the number of scientific articles published or the band width of optical fiber telecommunications networks, but it can be seen in the success rate in job seekers networks and in the conscious effort being placed on creating mentorships, especially for women and minorities.

While personal information access is a central process for many people, it poses several problems. The first is the possibility of conscious abuse. Many women's network were set up specifically as a response to the perception that "old boy" networks were creating an unfair advantage for men - men talked to each other, helped each other, in ways that were closed to women.

A second problem is less visible, but may in fact be a more difficult problem to overcome. The problem is cultural.

Some cultures interact while others are more aloof. College calculus, may serve as the best, if most unlikely, example here. Uri Triesmann tried to determine why oriental students at U. C. Berkeley were able to pass calculus while Black students almost always failed. Both groups had been stars in high school - getting into Berkeley isn't easy - yet Blacks just couldn't pass the course.

Some might respond to those results with racial slurs or attacks on Affirmative Action. Triesmann moved into the dorms and studied how both groups spent their days. What he discovered is that Asian students began each quarter setting up study groups. These weren't just groups for grinds - they had their pizzas and social evenings, too, but most of their time together was for studying. Blacks had social groups too, but these groups were strictly social. When it cam time to study, each Black student went back to his dorm room, closed the door, and studied alone. That was their culture, and it was a cultural trait that was destroying them.

Cultures of isolation aren't the only problems of personal information channels. Since these channels are largely invisible, they can be filled with myths, lies, hatreds. Few outsiders even know what is being said, nor do they have opportunities to correct even the most egregious errors. Yet error-prone or not, these are important channels that supply much of the world's information.

### Organizational Information

Whether organizations are businesses, or universities, or government agencies, they seem to be conflicted over information. Internally, organizations seem more willing to share information with members and employees. Externally, organizations seem unwilling to tell the world what is going on, and seem very willing to lie. Internal organizational communication is based around an ideal and a reality. The ideal is that organizations function best when employees know what is going on. Maybe they have been asked an opinion, maybe they have played a role in forming policy, maybe not. But at least they know what the organization is trying to do.

The reality is that information flows within a context. We can put in new email systems and create a system that is theoretically capable of letting each and every worker have electronic access to the CEO. But that doesn't mean the CEO will ever read the email coming in. Nor does it mean that all workers will be thrilled with new opportunities to communicate with an organization they may have tangential relations to at best. An area of information flow that may be even more challenging is the new flows being created between organizations.

Electronic data interchange (EDI) systems connect companies and government agencies in ways never attempted before. The computer systems needed for this new interchange may be daunting, but they are nothing compared to the ethical and legal challenges on the horizon. Then there is the question of how organizations communicate with the rest of the world. Whether the organizations are public or private, large corporations or small proprietorships, information is withheld from outsiders as a routine measure.

### Professional Information

A major source of information is professional bodies. And there are lots of these bodies. The last decade has seen a major growth here in the US.

| | 1980 | 1992 |
|---|---|---|
| Scientific, Technical, and Engineering Associations | 1,039 | 1,365 |
| Trade, Business, and Commercial Associations | 3,118 | 3,851 |
| Health, Medical Associations | 1,413 | 2,290 |
| (US Census, 787) | | |

With over 7,000 professional associations in existence in 1992, it would appear every occupational group or subspecialty had some organization they could turn to to push their professional interests or communicate professional information. How much information do they generate? One calculation says there have now been a million papers published in the mathematics field, half within just the last ten years. Without question, professions are producing in volume. The problem is whether the large number masks areas that are being left empty. Professions tend to have specific biases — who they will let in, who they will listen to, what they will say to the public, and how they will relate to each other. Each bias curbs the kind of information that professions produce and the kind of information available to members of the profession.

### Commercial Information

Information can be sold. We are long-used to credit bureau's selling information about our purchasing and payment histories. Now those bureau's are being joined by thousands of businesses who's entire inventory consists of information in a database. Their competitive advance is based solely on the size and contents of that database. Universities are entering the information business in a big way, selling not just collections of other people's information, but original research. Join any of their research consortia and you too can get the latest data months, or years, before your competition.

Is this information industry matures and grows, we begin to see that it will not only be a major force in the economy — an employer of thousands, maybe tens of thousands — but it will be like any other industry. It will produce products for which there is a market. The names of the fifty most credit-worth individuals in your zip code may be available from many sources. The phone numbers of the federal programs an immigrant may turn to for temporary help, may be less easily accessed. Universities may have new sources of funds for building material science research centers. They may have less money available to pay visiting poets. The commercialization of information has commercial consequences. Profitable information is available from many sources; nonprofit information struggles to survive on handouts. Each of these five information sources shapes information, with some of the "shapes" looking more and more like distortions.

### Availability of Information

If the amount of information available is somewhat less than our hopes, at least we can easily get to information now, right? We have all these satellites and optical fiber networks now. Information access isn't supposed to be a problem. Naisbitt even divides American history along the fault line of information access. "The following year — 1957 — marked the beginning of the globalization of the information revolution: The Russians launched Sputnik, the missing technological catalyst in a growing information society. The real importance of Sputnik is not that it began the space age, but that it introduced the era of global satellite communications.

With satellites in the air, information flow seems sure to follow. And any measure of data traffic makes it clear huge amounts of information are in fact moving through space. Some, Toffler among them, have looked at the data traffic and remarked on the global linkages that seem to be following. As capital flows electronically across national borders, zipping back and forth from Zurich to Hong Kong, Hong Kong to Norway, Norway to Tokyo, Tokyo to Wall Street in milliseconds, information traces equally complex pathways. A change in U.S. T-bill rates or the yen — deutsche mark ratio is instantly known around the world, and the morning after the big event in Los Angeles, youngsters in Ho Chi Minh City discuss the latest Grammy winners. The mental borders of the state become as permeable as its financial frontiers.

Toffler and the others are obviously right. Information does flow more easily to many places. Who can help but be impressed by the ability to send email around the world in minutes, the chance to access libraries and databases in other nations, the transportation system that gets across continents in hours. We can get to far more information far more easily than ever before. At least some of us can. In our excitement to explore the new opportunities before us, we may over look a few things.

Despite all the satellites we put in the sky and the cellular phone networks we build along our interstates, there is some information we can't get. If this really is an information age, those barriers need to be examined, and ultimately they need to be removed. There are three barriers — transmission problems — not because they are the only barriers information faces, but because they represent the kinds of problems that will preoccupy our efforts to make all information available to all people. These are the problems:

— Information Exiles

— Tyranny

— Information Criminals

### *Information exiles*

Information is like any other commodity in that it is not evenly distributed across the world. Some people live in the midst of gold fields; many others can barely find coal. Some of the information vacuum we instantly recognize. For example, no one expects the Bushman of the Kalahari to walk around with cellular phones. Other isolates are less obvious. The growing army of people living in neigborhoods (or countries) too dangerous to visit certainly qualify. In either case, the number of people totally removed from the information infrastructure is huge.

What happens to these people in the information age? As subsistence farming and handicrafts persisted through the industrial age, will the disconnected continue on, barely feeding themselves, producing the primitive and quaint for middle class coffee tables? Early indications are that the disconnected will fare far worse than their predecessors in previous revolutions. The gap between the rich and the poor, the knowing and the ignorant, will be larger, the room along the margins far smaller.

### *Tyranny*

While previous revolutions created classes of haves and have nots, the information age is already showing that it will be complicated by the "wills" and "won'ts." For a huge number of people, you can bring the optical fiber to Johnny, but you can't make him connect. There are no shortages of examples to prove this assertion, but let's take a contemporary example - satellite dishes. In one week's time in late 1993 three distinct corners of the world showed just how arbitrary our species can be.

The week began in China with an announcement the sale and manufacture of satellite dishes was now banned. Too many comrades were using the dishes to bring in "decadent" news and entertainment shows. Decadent information might lead to decadent ideas and then to decadent actions. So the government stepped in and satellite access ended. The news from Algeria was more bizarre. Islamic fundamentalists decided it was no longer enough to cleanse Algeria of Western influences by murdering women tourists caught shopping in street malls. Now they had turned their attention to neighbors who had satellite dishes. Since the dishes were pointed to Europe rather than to Mecca, it was obvious Western ideas were entering the country. The response was attacks on dish owners.

But for pure cussedness, no one beats the South Africans. In 1993 with majority rule in the offing, the South African Broadcasting Corporation elected a new board of directors, including Blacks. The response of the Christian right was to refuse to pay their TV license fees and ask SABC to fix their TV's so they could no longer get public television. To these Christians it was obvious SABC was now a communist agency and would begin giving air time to Blacks and other Atheistic forces. They would rather have no television at all than risk the possibility of an occasional Black face flickering across their living room. China, Algeria, South Africa - all places where people are deciding whether they will or won't listen, view, read or discuss. The same decision - to include or exclude - to listen or turn away - to read or ignore - is being made individually the world over.

### *Education*

Assuming we can find some way to get the optical fiber to Johnny, and assuming that Johnny won't be shot if he hooks up, what if Johnny can't read? A world of information may be physically and politically available to people, but it may be no more useful to them than a library is to illiterates. Some totalitarian governments figured this out long ago. It was the stated public policy of South Africa to limit the education of non-whites. People who believe in equality are not desirable teachers for the natives.

Education must train and teach people in accordance with their opportunities in life, according to the sphere in which they live. That such words could be uttered in public says much about the tragedy of South Africa. Unfortunately, South Africa is not the only place where education has been used to control, to limit. Education is a ready weapon demagogues are ready to wield. Even for those with some connection to basic human values, education is a problem. In the developing world where fewer than half of its citizens may make it to the sixth grade, information resources are inaccessible resources. Barely able to read, what difference does it make that they can review scientific articles from around the globe?

### *Psychology*

Brilliant, well-educated, well-connected people can also miss most of what is happening in the world. In fact it is quite likely that they will. All it requires is that they take a part of the world and explore it to the exclusion of everything else. An example often given is the railroad industry. Creating railroads is no small matter. These are complicated systems that were the technological and political extremes of their time. Leaders of the railroad industry can be forgiven for being preoccupied with getting lines built, designing locomotives that were powerful and reliable, and getting trains out on time. These were not foolish people. But they were hypnotized. By focusing exclusively on railroads they missed out on larger opportunities in transportation.

How could they and countless industries since them make such an obvious error? The information was there. Why didn't they use it? If we are to prepare for the free flow of information, one place to start working is on our own perceptions.

### *Noise*

Neil Postman's Amusing Ourselves to Death is a lengthy indictment on contemporary American culture. It takes only an hour or two of prime time television to fully agree. The print media follow suit. How could our founding fathers ever believe that the First Amendment would be used to protect the right of newspapers to print Elvis sightings, Lady Di's appointment calendar, and conversations with extra-terrestrials. Were we always so silly? Will the information age cause us to finally come of age and end this terminal adolescence that seems to control the US? Maybe not. For one thing, the sheer volumes involved leave plenty of room for trivial pursuits.

The typical CD-ROM drive now being built into many home computers holds 600 million bytes of information. This is somewhat in excess of 300,000 pages of text. After you put all the great books of antiquity (meaning any book on which the copyright has expired) on one disk, what do you put on the others? Articles about Elvis sightings, and Lady Di's activities, and... Suddenly the much vaulted information highway has become silly street. Maybe that's what we want. Maybe the noise we hear is the noise we crave.

### Fightfor Information

While it would be lovely if the nature of the world suddenly changed and we were all suddenly awash in information, as the examples above illustrate, we still live in a world where information is restricted. The limits come from institutions that reveal and pursue only information that meets their needs. The limits come from tyrrants who have already learned how to clamp down the Internet as effectively as they cut off satellite communication and television. The limits may be our own as we routinely ignore or distort information that doesn't match our prejudices. The limits are there, overwhelming satellite launches and trenches full of fiber. If we want information, we will have to fight for it.

Why fight? An increasingly common question is "Is all this really necessary?" For the tired executive who spends all day in meetings, uses audix and email by the hour, stares at endless computer print outs and then goes home to a pile of mail and thirty channels on her cable TV, the answer might appear to be "no." Another eighty or hundred channels, yet another computer network, yet another club or association, yet another conference call, is like giving someone already eating three thousand calories a day another three or four thousand calories. They are just as likely to be sick as grateful.

According to a report circulated by Human Rights Watch - Africa in early 1994, slavery still persists in Mauritania. While the practice is officially banned, Human Rights Watch believes there are over 100,000 slaves in the country. The government of Maaoviya Ould Sid'ahmed

Taya is apparently making no effort to stop slavery or to stop cruel punishments of slaves. It is reported that the punishment for attempted escape is as follows: "the victim is seated flat with his legs spread out and buried in sand up to his waist. Coals are placed between his legs and lit, slowly burning the legs, thighs, and genitals of the victim." Since the country is so obscure few seemed aware of the atrocities being routinely committed.

The report by Human Rights Watch Africa was picked up by the wire services and carried widely throughout Africa. There was no immediate response from Mauritania, and certainly no indication that the country had suddenly decided to free its slaves. But the publicity still mattered. To the enslaved of that nation at least the possibility of freedom now exists. As long as their treatment was unknown to the rest of the world, there was no reason why their treatment might ever improve. True, just shining the light of day on vermin doesn't instantly solve the problem.

When St. Louis was being gradually drowned by the Mississippi in the summer of 1993, the publicity drew thousands of spectators who stood and watched while people's homes went under. But the publicity also drew thousands of volunteers who worked in the heat and the mud to fill sand bags to save other people's homes. Both groups were out on the levees. Both groups walk the Earth. A human tragedy reduced to a five minute segment on late night TV may be ghastly entertainment to the twisted, but it can also be an alarm bell to the many who will risk everything to help. And there are people who will help when they know about a problem. To believe otherwise is to believe oneself a member of a very sad species. Information makes the invisible visible. It will bring hope. Ultimately it will bring help.

All is not a struggle for jobs and food and safety and housing. There is still poetry and sunsets and music. There are also people who help. One of the world's blessings is the millions of these kind souls. One of the world's torments is the difficulty often encountered in using this help well. One study by the World Bank found less than one project in three was successful. Many were clearly failures even in the early years when they were receiving substantial funding. Others collapsed the minute external funding dried up.

Helping isn't easy. Good intentions lie in ruins world wide. One cause is that people seem to know too little about the problem they are trying to solve. Whether the problem is homelessness, teen pregnancy, or starvation in the Sahel, problems are always more complicated than people originally think. It is especially difficult where problems are only half seen. Getting the necessary information may involve leaving the office to actually talk to the dirty, the sick, the powerless, or it may take sneaking TV cameras past the local junta's soldiers, or getting the international accountants past the doctored books, or reading the books or articles some would rather censor. Learning comes before helping. But learning isn't easy.

There are some who are concerned that nations will be marched from one crisis to another by the power of TV images — governments and aid agencies putting out the fire-of-the-week based on the latest CNN broadcast. A bigger problem may be the quality of the images and the quality of other information sources. For too many of the problems of the world, the necessary information just isn't coming through. We have the people and right intentions. What we often don't have is a good sense of how to use them.

So, what are the stakes? For many, the stakes are life and death. The technical, personal and social requisites to the information age are substantial and need to be recognized, but the benefits are real. Large-scale, multi-level access of information by trained citizens does not guarantee that people will suddenly drop their prejudices, stop making stupid decisions, or have the courage to act on the data before them, but it certainly gets us closer to that time than we are now. So whatever the current problems of information creation and transfer, those problems need to be solved.

# 6

# Newage Communication

Global flows of news and information were the subject of intense debate in international fora in the 1970s. News gathering and reporting has been controversial, both within nations and between nations, as long as mass media have existed, but never - neither before nor since - have information flows been debated with such passion as in the 1970s. The United Nations, and UNESCO in particular, were the prime arenas where these issues were thrashed out. In the decades immediately following the second world war, the media debate was mainly a protracted trench battle in the Cold War, where the West rallied around the principle of "free flow of information" and the Eastern bloc iterated the need for state control. Although this East-West dispute was by no means resolved in the 1960s, the situation changed with the addition of a North-South dimension in the 1970s.

Besides the opening of a new front, the focus of the dispute was broadened to include flows of other media products besides news, flows which were assuming increasing importance in international relations. A new perspective on the principle of "free flow of information" came to light. These developments had their roots in the dramatic changes in world politics that took place in the 1960s. Numerous colonies gained independence from the colonial metropoles. With independence came demands for recognition of the countries' national sovereignty, not only in political terms, but economically and culturally, as well. The undertones in these demands often harmonized with those of the Eastern bloc.

At the same time, the newly liberated countries were in dire need of development assistance from the industrialized countries. "Development", the process of evolution toward a modern society, occupied centre stage. Scholars and development experts assigned mass communications a central role in the development process. In the Cold War era the newly independent countries of the third world were of strategic importance to both East and West. Development aid was an important factor for "winning the hearts and minds" of developing countries.

New patron-client relationships emerged; old, established ones evolved. The successes achieved by the oil-producing countries in OPEC in the 1970s strengthened the position of the third world as a bargaining partner. A set of demands that would result in a New International Economic Order was put on the agenda; demands for reform of existing patterns of news and information flows - in short: a new international information order - were soon to follow. But a new international information order, in the sense its authors intended, was not to be. After some brief years of debate, the issue disappeared from international agendas.

More general theories of development that recognize the role of media and mass communication in processes of socioeconomic development and cultural and economic globalization guided the examination of how emerging media relate to communication systems and policy objectives. The framework of the study is inspired by the work of Anthony Giddens, particularly his work on a social theory, and modernity. Giddens sees the social structure as a dynamic entity that structures social action while at the same time being constituted through social action. As a consequence of this view, no relationship between the media and society can be presumed a priori; rather, the relationship has to be explored in its historical context.

Contextual factors are all-important. In Giddens' view, the process of globalization follows from modernity; modernity is inherently globalizing. Four dimensions of modernity which tend toward globalization are identified:

1. the development of world markets;
2. the rise of the nation-state system;
3. the emergence of military blocs; and
4. industrialization.

## Mass Media in the Development Process

The issue of a new international information order is bound up with ideas about the role of communication in the development of societies, on the one hand, and the relations between developed and developing countries, on the other. The purpose of development is to improve the living conditions of the members of a society. Development is at once a process and a goal. What is needed to bring about development, and what constitutes "better living conditions" have been bones of contention ever since the days surrounding national independence from the colonial powers, starting in the late 1950s, and continuing into the 1970s.

National development arose as an issue in the wake of the second world war, and the issue made its entry onto the international agenda in the 1950s. It was introduced by the USA, now a world power and interested in exporting its model of society. The Marshall Plan (economic and technical assistance for the reconstruction of Europe), and the Truman Doctrine (mutual defence against aggression by third parties) played key roles in this regard. In addition, there was the founding of the United Nations and its specialized agencies, among them UNESCO, the United Nations Economic, Social and Cultural Organisation. Initially, 'development' was mainly a question of economic growth, i.e., a steady and lasting increase in productivity and per capita income. There was an unshaken faith in technology and 'know-how'. Two different schools of thought developed.

The more dominant of the two envisioned "the passing of traditional society", in favour of a modern, Western-style nation-state. Gradually, 'development' came to include political, social and cultural spheres, as well. The other school took its starting point in the model of socialist societies in Eastern Europe, China and Cuba and aimed, with assistance from the Soviet Union, to create nation-states with planned economies. Here, the motor force was not the market, but political decision-making. These models of development coincided with the emergence of nationalist movements in many colonies in Asia and Africa.

Modernism was part of the legacy of the colonial metropole, and the idea of a nationstate met strong and widespread resistance. At independence, however, European models of the nation-state prevailed. The new countries were in great need of assistance to combat poverty, illiteracy and unemployment. Concepts of development were therefore paramount in politics and the economic sphere. Thus, the world of the 1960s was polarized along two dimensions: capitalism vs communism, and developed vs underdeveloped. These two dichotomies produce four worlds, but the third and fourth of these worlds, i.e., the underdeveloped countries adhering to capitalist and communist/socialist ideologies, respectively, melded and came to be referred to as the 'third world'. Their shared history and social and economic situation were more dominant than any differences that may have arisen after independence. The countries of the third world were all characterized by low degrees of industrialization, low per capita income, high rates of infant mortality, poor standard of public health, illiteracy, and extreme inequality.

The development process became a prime focus in the contest to win the third world countries over. The role of mass media also assumed prominence in this process, not least due to technological advances. Scholars who have studied development in the postwar period up to the 1970s have identified phenomena and precepts that form two separate paradigms of development:

— *The modernization paradigm*: theories relating to modernization, political and economic development and technology transfer, and

— *The dependence paradigm*: theories relating to imperialism and underdevelopment and revolution and liberation.

Where the modernization school saw the problems of developing countries as the result of characteristics inherent in the history of the territories, the dependence paradigm pointed to underdevelopment as the result of capitalism and its expressions, colonialism and imperialism.

The concepts of 'development' and 'communication' are both partly normative; they stand for desirable forms of social change. As a consequence the modernization and dependence paradigms are normative. In the modernization paradigm, communication is seen to facilitate or hasten progress toward a modern, as opposed to traditional, society. In the dependence paradigm, it is rather a question of media imperialism.

The modernization paradigm is essentially optimistic, whereas the dependence paradigm is essentially pessimistic about development in the countries of the third world. But the two paradigms also express ideological standpoints, if by ideology we mean a system of ideas, political-economic, about the nature of the world, what it should be, and how best to go about achieving the goal. Ideology consists, in other words, of the following components:

> An ideology is a belief system by virtue of being designed to serve on a relatively permanent basis a group of people to justify in reliance on moral norms and a modicum of factual evidence and self-consciously rational coherence the legitimacy of the implements and technical prescriptions which are to ensure concerted action for the preservation, reform, destruction or reconstruction of a given order.

The Cold War polarized ideological debates into two camps, a classical Liberal and a Marxist. The polarization is reflected in the two paradigms of development. Liberal features of the modernization paradigm are, for example, the norm of individual freedom and a preference for social change by consensus. The focus rests on the nation-state, and on internal dynamics in the development process. The dependence paradigm, on the other hand, is well aligned with Marxist theory, tending philosophically toward materialism and emphasizing social equality as a norm. Its approach to society is essentially conflict-oriented, and analyses focus on world capitalism as a system and on centre-periphery dynamics in the development process.

The modernization paradigm was dominant in the 1950s and 1960s, and the views that characterize that paradigm largely coincide with the approach to development, with a decided emphasis on development assistance, that was embraced by the UN and UNESCO at that time. But when exponents of the dependence paradigm, who were critical of the modernization approach, demanded a change in policy in the 1960s, it marked the start of a 'war of ideas' in the international arena. In fora like the UN and UNESCO, each national representative had access to the floor and could air his views. It was here that the non-aligned states formed an alliance to demand a new international information order. Thus, it was these two competing paradigms of development and their ideological components that constituted the fundaments for the ideas expressed in the debate on a new international information and communication that took place on the international plane, namely, in UNESCO.

## Issues in Information and Communication

The concept of "free flow of information" was formulated in the USA in the final throes of the second world war. No national frontiers should be allowed to hinder the flow of information between countries. Before the war, Europe and the USA had shared control over the international news market. The USA was, however, excluded from the extensive territories under the control of colonial powers Great Britain and France, who controlled the flows of information in their colonies. Even while the war was still raging, it was apparent that the USA would emerge from it as a world power. The U.S. saw before them a world without colonial ties, a world that lay open for an expansive economy in the U.S.

The information sector was a key factor in paving the way for economic expansion. People everywhere were tired of the propaganda and censorship that were part of the war effort and welcomed the thought of 'free flows' warmly. The idea of a 'free flow of information' was spread over the world. Newspaper publishers in the U.S. and representatives of the news agencies Associated Press (AP) and United Press (UP) travelled around the world, preaching the gospel of 'free flow'. It was particularly important to win support for the concept in the United Nations and especially its specialized agency, UNESCO. Thus, UNESCO came to be the main arena in which information and communication issues were debated in the postwar period.

UNESCO is often associated with development assistance, and in its first years the organization was indeed primarily an aid organ. There was a great need for reconstruction within UNESCO's sphere of activity after the war, and UNESCO did what it could to muster expertise and funding for the reconstruction effort. The emphasis on material assistance was reinforced when colonies began to free themselves from colonial metropoles and became nations in their own right. UNESCO, like the UN as a whole, came to be regarded as a system for the transfer of resources from rich countries to poor countries.

The assistance UNESCO provided in the 1950s and 1960s was guided to a large extent by the faith American researchers had in the positive role mass media played in the development process, not least in promoting literacy. UNESCO assistance mainly focused on technology transfer, both hardware and software (radio and TV programs). It was UNESCO's goal to ensure that every country had at least 10 copies of a daily newspaper, 5 radio receivers, 2 television sets and 2 cinema seats per thousand inhabitants.

A second major role for UNESCO was fact-finding. UNESCO collaborates with numerous organizations and arranges meetings and conferences on a variety of subjects. These result in books and reports. UNESCO is one of the largest publishing houses in the world. Innumerable reports the field of mass communications have been issued, with a marked peak in the late 1970s and early 1980s. The volumes report research findings, current thinking and opinion pieces, conference proceedings, and statistical compendia. This role doubtless contributed to UNESCO's becoming the principal arena of debate concerning systems of information and communication between nations and regions of the world.

Finally, UNESCO also has a norm-setting function that is founded in international law. Like many other bodies within the United Nations organization, UNESCO drafts and adopts international agreements between member nations. Whereas neither UNESCO nor any other UN body is invested with legislative powers, they have been instrumental in bringing about numerous international agreements. Today, the UN institutions have acquired such stature that they tend more and more to be considered legal entities. The UN Charter contains clauses that require member nations to observe the Charter's legal force and to adapt national legislation accordingly (Article 104). Thus, procedures for building up a body of law have been elaborated within the UN system.

A certain interplay between the UN General Assembly and, for example, the UNESCO General Conference may be observed. Issues are discussed within UNESCO and are then forwarded to the mother organization and the General Assembly. Flows in the opposite direction also occur. Some documents in international law have binding force for the signatories, and each must adopt and ratify the agreement individually. Most such documents are either treaties or conventions. UNESCO and similar institutions are highly instrumental in bringing such documents into the world. The Charters of the United Nations and UNESCO are, for that matter, examples of such treaties.

Declarations and resolutions lack the binding force of a treaty. Nonetheless, they are of juridical significance, playing a major role in the development of international law in, for example, the preliminary work on treaties and conventions. Declarations have higher rank than resolutions, and declarations and resolutions adopted by the UN General Assembly rank higher than declarations and resolutions adopted by specialized agencies like UNESCO. The term 'declaration' applies to documents, the purpose of which is to establish legal principles; in formal respects a declaration is similar to a convention. A resolution sets out policy for the organization that adopts it. A resolution may subsequently evolve into a document of international law. Researchers are agreed, however, that both resolutions and declarations adopted by the UN

General Assembly must be taken into account when determining whether a given principle of international relations is to be considered part of the body of international law. From the start, both the UN and UNESCO have had an explicit commitment to norm-setting in the field of information and communication. The statutes of both organizations contain injunctions to act to protect and promote freedom of expression and freedom of information. Article 1.2 of the UNESCO Constitution states, for example:

> ... collaborate in the work of advancing the mutual knowledge and understanding of peoples through all means of mass communication and to that end, recommend such international agreements as may be necessary to promote the free flow of ideas by word or image.

This commitment was acted on as early as 1948, when the United Nations convened an international conference on information. International law in the area of information and mass media started with the founding of the UN and UNESCO. From the start, the work on information and the media was closely related to the organizations' work on human rights. A rapid pace of technological development in communications raised the need for international regulation, e.g., with respect to the use of space for communications satellites. As a consequence, information issues were politicized, a development that had a significant impact on UNESCO's subsequent work relating to the sector.

In its early years UNESCO experienced obvious tensions and some friction between industrialized and developing countries. The former emphasized UNESCO's norm-setting function, whereas developing countries emphasized the organization's assistance programs. Development assistance was directly related to the development process as practiced according to the modernization paradigm. Thus, it was natural in the late 1960s and early 1970s for critics of the modernization paradigm to voice their criticisms in connection with discussions of assistance. It was, however, UNESCO's norm-setting function that subsequently provided the venue for discussions of the principles of a new international information order.

### International Agreements Relating to Information and Communication 1945-1979

International agreements, treaties-conventions, declarations and resolutions relating to information and communication that were adopted by the UN General Assembly and UNESCO General Conferences make up an important part of any history of the strivings for a new international information order. No less than 41 conventions and declarations saw the light of day in the postwar period up to 1980. They focus on the legal status of various elements in mass communication and specify objects for regulation on a multilateral basis. They may be seen as attempts to establish a certain order concerning the roles of information in the international political system.

More precisely, the 41 documents comprise eight treaties and conventions, six declarations and 27 resolutions. Two out of three were adopted by the General Assembly. It was not until the 1970s that UNESCO made its debut as a setter of norms. The texts deal with seven topics: rights and freedoms with regard to information; free flow of information; communications satellites; development of third world countries; peace-security-propaganda; discrimination; and a new world information and communication order. The largest number of agreements were adopted in the areas of rights and freedoms, peace-security- propaganda, development of third world countries, and free flow of information.

The documents issuing from the United Nations tend to focus on international legal aspects, whereas the resolutions emanating from UNESCO tend to focus on measures intended to promote a free flow of information. Three conventions have their origins in agreements arrived at during the period: the Declaration of Human Rights of 1948 led to two conventions in 1966; a resolution on "false and distorted reports" was incorporated into the convention on "international right of correction"; and resolutions on peaceful uses of outer space in 1961 and 1962 were incorporated into a declaration in 1963 and, ultimately, the Outer Space Treaty of 1967. Major efforts were made in the 1940s and 1950s to bring a convention on freedom of information into being, but agreement on the issue remained out of reach. On the whole, however, we see the rudiments of a body of international law pertaining to information and communication emerging during the period. One may also classify the agreements chronologically:

— 1945-1959: freedom of information and development assistance

— 1960-1969: new communications technology prompts regulation

— 1970-1979: prevailing principles are challenged.

Many of the documents contain elements that portend the subsequent demand for a New World Information and Communication Order.

### *1945-1959: Freedom of Information and Development Assistance*

Issues relating to freedom of information and 'free flows' of information predominated in early years. The concerns were mentioned in the Charters of both the United Nations and UNESCO. Both issues are expressions of the East-West confrontation known as the Cold War, which of course obstructed progress in the area, despite numerous draft conventions. Development assistance to third world countries and the evils of propaganda received a lot of attention in this context.

The agreements that were reached in these years were imbued with the views of the industrialized, primarily Western, parts of the world. Two factors explain this. The UN had 50 charter members, UNESCO had 20. This clearly influenced the norm-settting function. Secondly, if it is surprising that such documents as the treaties of Beirut (1948) and Florence on the free flow of information could have originated in UNESCO, we should recall that the Soviet Union did not participate in UNESCO until 1954.

### *1960-1969: New Communications Technology Prompts Calls for Regulation*

The decade witnessed significant developments in communications technology, particularly communications satellites. There was a widely perceived need to regulate the technology on an international plane. In the span of seven years, the General Assembly was able to adopt two resolutions, a declaration and, finally, a treaty on the use of outer space. Issues relating to satellites also gave rise to heated debates relating to the free flow of information between East and West in UNESCO in the late 1960s, but without resulting in an agreed document. The UN extended its role as aid donor vis-à-vis the poor countries of the world. The documents are formulated from the wealthy countries' perspective. Another issue that surfaced during this period was racial discrimination; a convention on 'the elimination of all forms of racial discrimination' was adopted in 1965. All seven texts from this period were adopted by the UN General Assembly.

### *1970-1979: New Perspectives and Challenges to Prevailing Principles*

The principle of 'free flow' was debated more and more. The world had changed quite dramatically since the end of the war. Many former colonies were now independent nations. In the span of roughly a decade in the 1950s and 1960s no less than 85 countries were born. The fledgling nations were anxious to protect their national and cultural sovereignty, which represented a new perspective on the issue of free flows of information. Meanwhile, new technology - not least satellite communication — changed the nature of world communication itself.

The 1972 UNESCO General Conference adopted a resolution proposed by the Soviet Union on setting out Guiding Principles on the Use of Satellite-Broadcasting for the Free Flow of Information, the Spread of Education and Greater Cultural Exchange. The vote was 55 in favour and 7 opposed, with 22 abstentions. The USA, which opposed the resolution, found itself outvoted. Thereafter, the focus of the debate in UNESCO shifted to media and cultural imperialism and its consequences. The debate swelled and may be said to have preoccupied UNESCO through the 1970s. In this period, the West frequently found itself in the minority as newly independent nations often sided with the Eastern bloc. The UN and UNESCO produced four declarations and sixteen resolutions during the period.

Nearly half of them emanated from UNESCO General Conferences, a testimony to the emergence of the organization as a forum in the area of information and mass communication. No treaties or conventions were forthcoming, however. The Cold War continued, but was modified on some issues by a new North-South dialogue. West and East were no longer the only actors on the stage.

Representatives from developing countries coordinated their activities and were able to influence both the content of documents and agreements and the number of agreements reached. Seven of altogether nine resolutions on development in third-world countries between 1945 and 1979 were adopted in the 1970s.

'Decolonialization', in both political-juridical and economic and cultural senses, had supplanted 'development assistance' as the focus of debate. In other words, earlier documents were seriously challenged. New principles and views were put on the agenda. The confrontations were innumerable, particularly in the work on a mass media declaration, which after much anguish, was adopted in 1978. This work on media issues occupied UNESCO nearly a decade. In early 1974, UNESCO's Director-General called on twelve experts to put together a preliminary draft of a declaration on mass media, more precisely, a Declaration on Fundamental Principles concerning the Contribution of the Mass Media to Strengthening Peace and International Understanding, to the Promotion of Human Rights and to Countering Racialism, Apartheid and Incitement to War. The aim was to formulate overall guidelines for the role of mass media in the international system. When the draft came up for discussion in the Fall, the confrontation between the USA's commitment to 'free flow of information' and the Soviet Union's commitment to state control came to a head.

At the same time, several of the developing countries criticized the concept of 'free flow', characterizing it instead as a 'one-way flow' and an expression of imperialist ambitions. Here, the East-West conflict was displaced by a confrontation between North and South. Treatment of the Declaration on Fundamental Principles was postponed. Efforts were also made to establish the concept of a 'right to communicate'. The idea was to establish an overarching principle, under which problems relating to mass media might be analysed and corrective measures proposed. Sweden introduced the concept, coined in 1969 by Jean d'Arcy of France in the context of new communications technology, at the UNESCO General Conference of 1974. After lengthy discussion and numerous amendments a resolution on the 'right to communicate' was adopted.

The General Conference of 1976 also failed to produce a declaration on mass media. At one point several Western delegates left the meeting in protest. Newly appointed Director-General Ahmadou-Mahtar M'Bow was instructed to work out and present a revised draft to the next General Conference, in 1978. Mr. M'Bow worked hard to formulate an acceptable draft, as the impasse had brought nearly all other work at UNESCO to a halt, but the draft proved unacceptable to most member countries as it included an argument for state influence over the media. The draft went into committee and emerged in a markedly diluted version that could, finally, be adopted. The feature of the resolution was a frank qualification of 'free flow of information'; the phrase was replaced with "a free flow and a wider and better balanced dissemination of information". The resolution also affirmed that the General Conference was

> [c]onscious of the aspirations of the developing countries for the establishment of a new, more just and more effective world information and communication order (Declaration on Fundamental Principles Concerning the Contribution of the Mass Media to Strengthening Peace and International Understanding, to the Promotion of Human Rights and to Countering Racialism, Apartheid and Incitement to War, 28th November 1978, UNESCO, Paris).

Thus, the decade ended with documented acceptance of a fundamental rethinking of the principles to govern information and communication on an international plane. When third world countries lodged their demand for a new international information order in the international arena, it was in the light of the role UNESCO played as a source of development assistance and as a setter of norms in the economic, social and cultural sectors. UNESCO was an instrument in a concerted reform effort. At the same time, the developing countries were dependent on UNESCO's assistance, for literacy training, education and development of the media sector.

## Demand for a New International Information Order

The non-aligned countries tabled their demand for a new international information order in the mid-1970s as an extension of already voiced demands for a new world economic order. Although the non-aligned countries could hardly be considered a unit in terms of ideology or political-economic systems and as a group had leanings toward both of the major blocs. The geopolitical changes that took place in the 1950s and 1960s when many former colonies attained their independence led to the emergence of a third force alongside the capitalist ('first world') and socialist ('second world') blocs. The concept of a 'third world' was coined in 1955 at the milestone Bandung Conference (Indonesia) of some thirty Asian and African states.

The conference adopted several resolutions of historical significance: on the abolition of colonial rule, on the realization of democratic self-determination, on disarmament, and on economic and cultural cooperation. The Bandung Conference was the first joint manifestation under-taken by the new countries of Africa and Asia, and from it issued a movement of non-aligned countries that aspired to be 'a third force to act as a buffer between capitalism and communism'. What the non-aligned countries meant by a 'new international information order' can be extracted from the documentation of the movement's meetings from the period between 1973-1980. The documents from the meetings that concern information and communication have the character of political 'position statements'; they resemble statements of foreign policy and doctrine that we find in the field of international politics.

They are generalized, declare a definite point of view or posture in relation to the issue at hand, and an explicit world-view. At the same time, the statements form a sort of bridge between ideology and concrete action. It is sometimes difficult to discern specific policy objectives, guiding principles concerning how to go about realizing those objectives, or proposed solutions. What we have to work with are discussions of the role of mass media and information in the development process, national media structures and media policies versus international media structures and international regulations/ policies, which touch on regional aspects and flows of media products as well as the third-world countries' relations with the industrialized part of the world.

The non-aligned countries discussed issues relating to mass media for the first time at their conference in Algiers in 1973, i.e., some years before they formulated and raised their demand for a new international information order. That the demand for reform of the world communications system arose out of the non-aligned camp was hardly sheer chance. A prime factor was the tumultuous change that was taking place in the world oil market. Oil flowed primarily from the third world to the industrial world, and the prosperity of the industrialized world depended heavily on the third world. Still, companies based in the USA, Great Britain and The Netherlands controlled the world oil market.

All this changed when the third-world countries whose oil reserves were exploited began to act in concert. The 'OPEC Crisis' or 'Fuel Crisis' of 1973, which brought a sharp rise in the price of petroleum products, broke a position of near-total dominance that the USA had enjoyed for over a century and won the non-aligned countries an unprecedented bargaining position. The countries of the third world had already voiced demands for a new world economic order at the start of the decade. It was in their interests to reform the structural factors that caused economic imbalances and injustices in the international system, yet up to now the countries had not been able to coordinate their efforts. Only after the success of OPEC (Organisation of Petroleum-Exporting Countries) and with the acquisition of greater diplomatic finesse were they able to form and maintain a more or less united front.

### *The Declaration on the Establishment of a New International Economic Order*

In 1974, the United Nations adopted The Declaration on the Establishment of a New International Economic Order. In it, the prevailing order was characterized as one of "inequality domination, dependence, narrow self-interest and segmentation," whereas the new order would be founded on the principles of "equality, sovereign quality, interdependence, common interest and cooperation among states, irrespective of their economic and social systems". The declaration may be seen as a frontal ideological challenge to the status quo, that was generally termed 'liberal'. A new international economic order presumed a reorganization of the international economic system. National independence from the colonial powers was a strictly political-juridical matter; it was with the demand for a new economic order that the countries called attention to the neo-colonialism of the prevailing world economic system and demanded reform.

In practice, the countries demanded fair terms of trade, economic assistance, and access to Western technology. Information was first brought up in the context of a 'new international order' at a meeting of the non-aligned countries in Tunis in 1976:

> Since information in the world shows a disequilibrium favouring some and ignoring others, it is the duty of nonaligned countries and other developing countries to change this situation and obtain the decolonization of information and initiate a new international order in information .... .

At a minister-level conference some months later in New Delhi, the Ministers of Information of the nonaligned countries put it this way:

> The Conference ... stressed that the de-colonization of information is essential for these purposes and that the establishment of a New International Order for Information is as necessary as the New International Economic Order. ...

The demand for a new international information order was an outgrowth of third-world resentment of the imbalances in international news flows, as summarized in the phrase, 'one-way-flow'; the lack of respect for third-world peoples' cultural identity that such imbalances reflected, the monopoly positions of transnational communications corporations, which were perceived as a threat to the countries' national independence; and the inequitable distribution of communications resources in the world. These complaints were hardly new, but having achieved nationhood, the countries could now act to protect their national sovereignty and cultural identity.

Numerous academic studies carried out in the 1970s confirmed these complaints. News flows between the industrialized parts of the world and developing countries, or as many expressed it, between north and south, were far from balanced. International systems of communication were designed to serve the interests of the industrialized countries, and developing countries had no alternative but to use them. A handful of transnational corporations controlled the markets for news and communications technology. National media systems in the developing countries were poorly developed; many were state-controlled. Generally speaking, the media were weak and could neither supply their own countries with national news nor gather news from abroad. As a consequence, they were heavily dependent on international news services. The news these services carried was primarily commerce-oriented or reported events of a transient nature in personalized and dramatized renditions.

The documents relating to mass media and information that emanated from the meetings of nonaligned countries in the latter part of the 1970s indicate that the concept of a new international information (later also communication) order implied far-reaching reforms of the existing order, including all kinds of information - political, social, economic and technical; all the media - press, radio, TV, böcker, film, data banks, etc.; and all kinds of communications technology: communications satellites, cable-TV, telecommunications, including the price and rate control. That is to say, the proposals covered far more than content and the direction of flows and extended well into the organization and control of structures in the sector.

Four cornerstones emerge out of the material; they were referred to as 'the four Ds'. They represent themes that recur time and again in the discussions of the new order.

1. News flows are castigated as "one-way flows", and measures to ensure a more equitable balance of news flows between countries are demanded (Democratization).
2. The 'one-way flow' and misrepresentations are interpreted to reflect a lack of respect for the countries' cultural identities, a matter of great importance to the nonaligned countries (Decolonization).
3. The monopoly status of transnational corporations in terms of communications technology is perceived as a threat to national independence (Demonopolization).
4. The vital role of mass media in the development process is underlined, and the nonaligned countries join together to demand a more just distribution of communication resources in the world (Development). Thus, the demands were broad and fluid and partly overlapping; they describe different aspects of the problem complex.

Several of the documents of the non-aligned countries contain lists of recommendations as to how the countries should go about their work, on national, regional and international levels, to achieve a new information order. A systematic study of the documents in relation to 'the four Ds' reveals the implications of the new international information order, from the point of view of the non-aligned countries.

*1. Democratization*

This first cornerstone is the most comprehensive. Four central demands can be discerned:

— The right of people and individuals to acquire an objective picture of reality by means of accurate and comprehensive information as well as to express themselves freely through various media of culture and communication.

— The right of every nation to participate, on the governmental and non-governmental level, in the international exchange of information under favourable conditions in a sense of equality, justice and mutual advantage.

— The responsibility of various actors in the process of information for its truthfulness and objectivity as well as for the particular social objectives to which the information activities are dedicated.

— Guarantees for and the necessary protection of journalists and other factors of information in the performance of their mission, and the responsibility of journalists in the performance of this mission.

These four points are closely related to the then on-going debates in UNESCO on 'free flow of information' and the conditions under which journalists operated. They are phrased with reference to the international situation, while democratization on the national level is largely glossed over.

*2. Decolonialization*

The second cornerstone consists of two subthemes. First, we have passages that highlight self-determination, national independence, cultural identity, and so forth:

— The fundamental principles of international law, notably self-determination, sovereignty and non-interference.

— The right of every nation to protect its national sovereignty and cultural identity.

— The right of each country to the observance of its interests, aspirations, and its political, moral and cultural values.

These texts refer to international law, and some concepts resemble the rhetoric of the dependence paradigm. Cultural identity is also assigned key importance. Second, we have themes that invoke the demand for a new world economic order. Here, too, the rhetoric is reminiscent of the dependence paradigm. In more concrete terms, it has to do with the assignment of radio frequencies, access to frequencies on geostationary satellites, and telecommunications infrastructure.

### *3. Demonopolization*

The third cornerstone refers to another prime topic of debate in UNESCO of the 1970s, namely, the operations of transnational corporations:

> The right of every nation to develop its own independent information system, in particular by regulating the activities of transnational corporations.

This item might well have been included under the preceding heading, but the emphasis put on 'demonopolization' in the documents merits a heading of its own. That emphasis also reflects the degree of influence the dependence paradigm exerted. The issue was discussed both on the international level, through the demand for a new world economic order, and on the national level, through proposed regulation of transnational corporations in third-world countries.

*4. Development*

Central features of the fourth cornerstone are the following three items:

— The right of every nation to develop its own independent information system.

— The imperative of a more equitable distribution of information media.

— Adequate professional training for journalists including those working in indigenous languages.

The documents are most specific in relation to this theme. Here we find numerous exhortations directed to the industrialized countries: "adoption of national communication policies," "define a new concept of news not based on sensationalism...," "multiply exchange agreements among the countries of the third world," "consolidate and develop the infrastructures of information," "promote national agencies and POOL," "creation of regional information systems," "creation of centres for the training of journalists in the developing countries," etc.

Key elements are the necessity of national communication policy, the development of infrastructures, the establishment of national news services and regional news exchanges, journalism education, technical collaboration between regions and, not least, a will to "use horizontal cooperation, aid and solidarity between developing countries as the main instrument of the independence in information". Mass media, news media in particular, and most of all the press, are accorded a central role in the development process. The measures mentioned in the documents all refer to conditions in the third world, but the question acquires international scope because of the countries' need of development assistance from international organizations and the developed countries:

> ... the obligation of the international organizations to assist the nonaligned countries towards the emancipation and developmet of their national information systems ...

All in all, the content of a NWICO is formulated on the level of abstractions. The demands are not specified beyond a few key sentences under each cornerstone. This reflects how difficult the countries found it to agree on concrete measures. Yet the documents leave no doubt that the goal is a truly new international information order. Decolonialization is paramount and, ultimately, radical changes in global power relationships are implied.

Many of the themes are formulated on the macro level. We find many more references to "the right of every nation" than to individual rights and freedoms. Issues relating to mass media and news flows take priority over other forms of communication. A number of problems are elevated to the international level, although they actually concern issues of a national character. They are discussed in an international context. The key passages noted here clearly indicate the desired direction: a rejection of the modernization paradigm in favour of self-determination, national independence, cultural identity and democratic flows of information between nations.

Thus, the documents of the nonaligned nations represent the contours of a new third view of development, having four main principles:

1. Development based on self-determination and cultural identity,
2. The recipient's control over development assistance,
3. International perspectives, and
4. Regional cooperation.

The demand of the nonaligned countries for a new international information order in UNESCO brought tensions to a head at the organization's General Conference in 1976, where the formulation of a declaration on mass media topped the agenda. The nonaligned bloc were partly successful, but no declaration was forthcoming from the conference. Instead, a commission, The International Commission for the Study of Communication Problems, known as the 'MacBride Commission', was appointed to study all manner of problems of communication in the world. One of its chief tasks was to

> analyse communication problems, in their different aspects, within the perspective of the establishment of a new international economic order and of the measures to be taken to foster the institution of a "new world information order".

UNESCO used the concept of a "world information order" rather than an "international information order". The change in wording was made on the initiative of the Western countries, who wished to make the connection to the demand for a new economic order less explicit. The word "international" connotes relations among nations, whereas "world" prompts associations to global cooperation more generally, with concepts like "the global village" and "world government".

## MacBride Commission

The phrase, "new world information order", which was used in the terms of reference of the MacBride Commission, was rather short-lived within UNESCO, being used only two years. In the final text of the mass media declaration that was adopted in 1978, the wording is "a new, more just and effective world information and communication order". One might interpret the change as a further adaptation to the position of the Western countries in that the new wording may be taken to mean not a totally new order, but an improvement of the status quo ante.

The Commission perceives corporate dominance to be a consequence of the postwar doctrine of 'free flow of information'. Furthermore, the report baldly describes international information flows as one-way and vertical (top-down). Long-term measures to improve the availability of international news are discussed in terms of the working conditions of journalists, professional skills and attitudes, and the views of governments.

A section entitled "The Technological Dilemma" discusses issues relating to new technologies. Here, the Commission did not report a single, unequivocal view. The commercialization of information is harshly criticized, as is the expansion of advertising markets. The Commission stressed the importance of the social function of information. An important theme in the report throughout is, for that matter, an emphasis on the societal roles of information and the need for democratization of communication flows. The sharp differences that had characterized the discussions throughout the 1970s were also present in the MacBride Commission.

MacBride Commission suggests that the third world's critique of the prevailing order was heard and gained some measure of acceptance with regard to the pattern of information flows and the dominance of transnational news and media corporations as a threat to cultural integrity and national independence. But it is only when we analyse the Commissions conclusions and recommendations that we can truly assess the degree of acceptance the third world's views on international information and communication attained.

## *Recommendations of the MacBride Commission*

### *An Approach*

Fundamental to the demands of the nonaligned countries for a new international information order was the idea of greater regulation of the media system on an international level. The task of the MacBride Commission was to study the problem area and consider solutions.

### *1. A Communication perspective*

The MacBride Commission was asked to study all forms of communication on the level, including developments in communications technology. How do the recommendations reflect this? How does the Commission interpret 'communication'? To gain a clearer idea of what aspects of the prevailing order the MacBride Commission sought to change it is interesting to examine the links in the communication process that the Commission emphasizes. Where are changes called for? Here it is useful to distinguish between the media institution, meaning "the principles, laws, conventions and instruments for regulation that society has at its disposal", that is to say, the media on a societal level; the media organization, which executes the production and distribution functions, i.e., the media companies within which production takes place; and media audiences.

*2. A development perspective - the roles of mass media in society*

The starting point here is theories of the role of information and communication in the development process and the ideas in the third-world countries' demands for a new international information order. On the basis of theories of the social purposes of the media, the following five functions are identified: information, interpretation, continuity, entertainment and mobilization. Some functions overlap; the first and fifth have to do with change, whereas the middle three concern integration.

*3. A third-world perspective*

Here the focus rests on 'the four D's'. To what extent do the recommendations of the Commission support the demands for Development, Democratization, Decolonization and Demonopolization? These demands call for measures not only in the developing countries but, perhaps even more so, in the developed countries. Where does the Commission call for changes? Is it conditions in the developing countries, in the developed countries? Or, are the issues discussed in a global perspective? Are any actors specified? Ultimately, it is a question of the extent to which the recommendations call for national, regional or international solutions.

*4. A practicability perspective*

To what extent are the recommendations practicable? The

following categories indicate different degrees of specification and action orientation: 1) systems level (overarching, general goals, indicate general direction); 2) strategic level (action-oriented, but general); 3) implemantation level (application, concrete solutions, outlined step-by-step, specified actors).

The measures the MacBride Commission recommended to bring about a "new more just and efficient world information and communication order" may be described in four points:

1. *The development of third-world countries so that they become truly independent and self-reliant and develop their cultural identities.* Proposed means to reach these goals include: tailoring national communications policies to suit the conditions in the country, building infrastructure, equitable distribution of common global communication resources, limits on the activities of transnational corporations, preferential treatment of non-commercial media, balanced flows of technical information.

2. *Better international news gathering and better conditions for journalists.* The Commission recommends ethical rules for the practice of journalism, improved journalism education, multiple news sources, observance of the Helsinki Agreement and the Geneva Convention.

3. *Democratization of communication (access and participation, the right to communicate).* Important measures here are guarantees of human rights, acceptance of 'the right to communicate', abolition of censorship, editorial independence, limits on media concentration and monopolization, limits on the influence of advertisers on editorial policy/media content, attention to the communication needs of

women, children and minorities, and facilitation of horizontal communication.

4. *Furtherance of international cooperation*. The measures in this last category aim to effectuate previous proposals through international cooperation: development assistance, support of regional fora and collaborative projects, e.g., NANAP, collaboration between professional organizations and within the research community, an international centre for research and planning of information and communication.

The recommendations of the MacBride Commission with the aim of bringing about a more just and efficient world information and communication order focus almost entirely on conventional mass media. This, despite the fact that the Commission's terms of reference were much broader in scope. The importance of traditional communication is referred to in the introductory remarks accompanying the recommendations, but none of the recommendations concern traditional forms or channels of communication. Media technology is the only aspect besides mass media to be considered.

The recommendations are highly structure-oriented; most of them concern media institutions and media organizations. Fewer than a handful treat media content (advertising and news), and not many more than that concern media audiences (education in the development process, horizontal communication, the special communication needs of certain groups). In a number of the recommendations the Commission assigns the media specific functions. The mobilization function is stressed in relation to development, the continuity function in relation to cultural identity, the information function with respect to news gathering, and both information and interpretive functions in relation to democratization of communication. Elements of both change and integration are present.

The document largely bears the stamp of a development perspective. The greater part of the recommendations treat conditions in the third world, and taken together, most form a third paradigm of development. When it comes to measures relating to communication technology, the picture is more mixed and somewhat contradictory. Several of the recommendations fit in with a modernization paradigm, but a couple are more in keeping with the dependence paradigm. Neocolonialism confronts decolonization. On the whole, however, it is clear that the third-world countries receive more support for their four demands, the 'four Ds' than in any previous international document. Most support is expressed for development (national communication policy, building of infrastructure, journalism education) and decolonization (cultural identity), but there is support, albeit in more general terms, for democratization (just flows of information, the allotment of radio frequencies, satellite capacity, telecommunications) and demonopolization (regulation of transnational corporations), as well. A lot of emphasis is put on the right to communicate, defined as "the right to be informed, the right to inform, the right to privacy, the right to participate in public communication" at all levels - "international, national, local and individual".

The Commission regards these issues as national, whereas the non-aligned countries applied an international perspective. The Commission's proposals are nearly all national in focus. Furthermore, there are far more references to what developing countries should do than to what developed countries should do. At the same time there is, in the fifth part of the recommendations, an emphasis on development assistance and organs of international cooperation as sources of support to the third world, which strengthens the document's leanings toward a development perspective.

Most of the recommendations are formulated on the strategic level. Some are quite concrete, but few specify any actor. The actors specified are international organs, etc., that already have a regulatory framework. Thus, the key question of who should undertake the recommended measures remains unanswered. The forms of international cooperation outlined in the fifth part are not sufficiently specific. All in all, then, the extent of implementation is weak, which definitely limits the prospects of bringing about a new information and communication order. Some recommendations are formulated on the systems level, and these are unfailing indications of the areas in which the Commission was unable to resolve its differences. Examples of this in the second part concern limiting the commercialization of media and strengthening cultural identities, while all of the recommendations in the fourth part, on democratization of the media, have this character. These are also the object of the most reservations on the part of individual commission members.

### MacBride Report at the UNESCO General Conference of 1980

The report of the MacBride Commission, Many Voices, One World, was one of the main points on the agenda of the 21st General Conference of UNESCO, held in Belgrade in 1980. As at the two preceding General Conferences, Nairobi in 1976 and Paris in 1978, mass media issues dominated. This was the first time, however, that UNESCO would debate the concept of a 'new world information and communication order', a NWICO. How would the international political system respond to the recommendations of the Commission? Would it prove possible to change the structure of world communications by means of political decision-making? In the following we shall consider the findings of an analysis of the debates and resolution that followed upon the report of the MacBride Commission.

The general feeling before the General Conference was that the debate concerning the MacBride report would be heated and the confrontations many. This was not the case, however. Compared to previous debates on the subject, the discussions at the 21st General Conference were both constructive and open, even if no major changes of position were to be noted. A majority of the speakers in Programme Commission IV Culture and Communication, where the MacBride Commission was debated, received the report favourably, which is not to say that there was no criticism. The political differences between East and West, North and South had not diminished.

The non-aligned countries pursued their agenda of a NWICO and criticized the dominance of the industrialized world in the area of communications and the marked imbalance of exchanges of information between countries and regions. The power of transnational corporations over the communication of ideas, messages, etc., and the threat that power implies for the countries' cultural identities were stressed. Many speakers from third-world countries spoke of the role media play in the development process. In this connection they supported the principle set out by MacBride Commission, that national communication policy should strive toward the same goals as the country's development policy. The non-aligned countries also lauded the MacBride Commissions support for the idea of democratization of the media. Many stressed the importance of developing the use of "small and local media".

The Eastern states emphasized the responsibility of mass media and their role in combatting racism, colonialism, imperialism and so forth. These speakers found the MacBride Commission too West-oriented. The delegates of the Eastern countries were remarkably restrained in this debate, compared to previous General Conferences. The Western countries continued to stress freedom of information and freedom of expression and the rights of individuals. They expressed the hope that the MacBride report would be used "to promote democracy and freedom of communication, diversity and plurality of news production and access to a broad spectrum of sources". The strongest criticism of the MacBride Commission was raised by members of the Western 'bloc', with the USA and Great Britain the most outspoken critics. These two countries saw the document as militating against a free flow of information.

An emphasis on practical measures was widely supported, and many spoke in favour of a project proposed at a UNESCO Intergovernmental Conference in Paris the preceding Spring, namely, "a project for the establishment within the framework of UNESCO, of an International Programme for the Development of Communication". Nearly all the delegates were agreed as the need for greater communication capacity in the third world and that international cooperation was needed to develop infrastructures in the third-world countries. These were the aspects of the MacBride report that received the most attention.

To the surprise of many, Director-General M'Bow's document on the findings of the Commission were quite cautious and general. The passage, "no need for immediate actions at this stage," clearly signaled that the recommendations of the Commission would be let go by the boards, that no implementation would be forthcoming. But a majority of the speakers agreed that the Commission had fulfilled its task and regarded the report as a milestone in continued international discussions. There was also general agreement that the recommendations, while far from definitive, could be used as a framework of the construction of a new order.

In his closing remarks, the Chairman of the General Conference underlined the need of assistance in the field of communication. He also expressed the view that the debate had demonstrated the need for UNESCO to play an active role with regard to communication. He hailed the MacBride Commission report as a step along the way toward a new international information order that must be founded on 1) the "elimination of domestic and external barriers," 2) "pluralism of information," 3) "freedom of the press," and 4) the "free circulation of information, ideas and persons".

Finally, the Chairman announced that a working group would be appointed to draft a resolution on the subject. Three drafts had been tabled: one from each 'bloc'. After protracted and difficult negotiations, consensus on a draft resolution was reached. Several countries, including Great Britain, the USA, Canada, Australia and Japan, asked that the reasons for their vote be recorded in the minutes. These largely revolved around the definition of 'a new world information and communication order'.

### A Draft NWICO

The preamble of UNESCO Resolution 4/19 on the International Commission for the Study of Communication Problems is reminiscent of Article 19 of the Declaration of Human Rights and of Articles 19 and 20 in the International

Convention on Civil and Political Rights. The first part of the resolution acknowledges the contributions of the non-aligned countries in the area of information and communication:

> Noting the increasing attention devoted to communication problems and needs by other intergovernmental organizations, both regional and international, notably the Movement of Non-Aligned Countries which, in the Declaration of the Colombo Summit, stated that "a new international order in the fields of information and mass communication is as vital as a new international economic order' and, in the Declaration of the Havana Summit, noting progress in the development of national information media, stressed that "co-operation in the field of information is an integral part of the struggle for the creation of new international relations in general and a new international information order in particular," ... .

It was the first time such an acknowledgment was made by an international organ such as UNESCO. Several clauses referred to the work of the Mac-Bride Commission, which is lauded as a valuable contribution to the study of problems relating to information and communication. Many problems were seen to have been defined, analysed and constructive solutions to them proposed. The recommendations of the Commission, however, were deferred and filed among the preliminary documentation for UNESCO's Medium-Term Plan 1984-1989.

Some features of the recommendations are included in the resolution. Certain phrases in paragraph 10 highlight the need to develop information and communication: the drafting of national communication policy, developing infrastructure, democratization of the media. These three points are the most concrete points in the resolution. They refer primarily to the recommendations listed in the

MacBride report under the heading, "I. Strengthening Independence and Self-Reliance" and the portion of "IV. Democratization of Communication" that pertains to human rights. Paragraph 13 of the resolution also refers to the recommendations (40 and 46) of the Commission concerning "improved international reporting". The resolution calls for the need for UNESCO to help enhance journalists' knowledge of other cultures and the economics and politics of other countries.

The essential content of the resolution is to be found in paragraph 14, where a couple of points outline the content of a conceivable new world information and communication order. The paragraph consists of three parts, a)-c). The first contains eleven points that provide a conceivable framework for a new world order; the second states that the new order shall be founded in international law; and the third points out that different countries will choose different solutions, according to their social, political, cultural and economic traditions and circumstances. This latter point was empasized in the MacBride Report, as well.

It is quite clear that it was difficult to midwife the resolution, and particularly the catalogue of possible 'fundaments' of a new world order in paragraph 14, into being. One sign of the power struggle is the phraseology that introduces the eleven points in part a). The use of "could" instead of "should", as in b), is a sure sign that a NWICO is a process that the authors of the resolution have agreed to continue working on and one that may be based on the fundaments set out in the resolution. Thus, the resolution assumed more the character of recommendations than calls to duty on the part of the signatories.

The fundaments outlined in paragraph 14 are even more general than the recommendations in the MacBride report. All eleven points in part a) may be traced back to the 82 recommendations of the Commission, but the language has been modified. The level of abstraction and the rhetoric both reflect the amount of diplomatic effort that went into forging agreement on the draft and, not least, of the lukewarm reception of the MacBride recommendations on the part of Director-General M'Bow -which countries like the USA and Great Britain greeted with some satisfaction.

Development, strengthening of independence and self-reliance, cultural identity, democratization and the right to communicate were key concepts in the recommendations of the MacBride Commission. Of these key concepts, only 'development' and 'cultural identity' were included in the text of the resolution. The fundaments included in the resolution may be grouped according to their thematic content.

— First, there are incitements to remove various hindrances and negative effects .

— Secondly, freedoms (of information, the press, journalists' rights and responsibilities, multiple sources).

— Third, a couple of more concrete points concerning development and third-world countries' need of development assistance.

— Finally, the concluding points are about cultural identity, the right to participate in international flows of information, the right of access to sources of information, etc.- all in all: aspects of the 'right to communicate', albeit the phrase is absent from the resolution. On that point no consensus could be reached.

The concluding paragraph of the resolution (§ 15) expresses a sense that UNESCO has hereby affirmed:

> ...its willingness in its short-term and medium-term activities to contribute to the clarification, elaboration and application of the concept of a new world information and communication order ... .

In all probability no resolution would have been forthcoming, had the Director-General insisted that the resolution be based on the 82 recommendations of the MacBride Commission. An emphasis on 'development' may be the factor that made consensus possible. Development and development assistance were also in focus in the creation of the International Programme for Communication Development (IPCD), which may be counted among the indirect results of the work of the MacBride Commission's work. The terms of reference of the IPDC were set out in a separate resolution, the preamble of which states:

> ....this international programme, aiming to increase co-operation and assistance for the development of communication infrastructures and to reduce the gap between various countries in the communication field, must form part of the efforts for the establishment of a "new, more just and more effective world information and communication order"....

Otherwise, the resolution consists of statutes, procedural rules, scope of activity (purpose). The tasks of the IPDC are set out in 14 points. These fall into four categories:

1. *Development assistance* - analysis of needs, planning and development of a national communication sector, development of infrastructures, assistance in using communication in the development effort in economic, social and cultural spheres;

2. *Coordination* - to facilitate cooperation between actors in international communication development, to strengthen the cooperation between UNESCO and the International Telecommunication Union, to promote regional cooperation, e.g., between news services in the developing countries;

3. *Information* - to gather information about needs and resources in the field of communication, to evaluate cooperation between developing and developed countries; and

4. *Funding* - raising the financing necessary to carry out assistance, coordination and information activities.

Many delegates expressed their satisfaction over the institution of the IPDC. Delegates from the third world were particularly pleased. The draft from the DEVCOM meeting in Paris in early 1980, which preceded the IPDC resolution, was included in the resolution of the General Conference. It is a more far-reaching document than the MacBride resolution, viewed from the point of view of the nonaligned countries. It contains rhetoric like 'safeguarding national sovereignty and cultural identity,' 'situations of dependence,' 'state of dependency of developing countries in the field of information and communication,' 'democratization of international relations in the field of information,' a 'need to establish a new information and communication order,' 'the fundamental contribution that the information media and mass communications can make to the establishment of a new economic order' - rhetoric that is much more in keeping with that of the non-aligned countries than either the MacBride Commission or the Western countries. Although the USA had advocated donor control and limited authority on the part of UNESCO at the DEVCOM meeting, the text emanating from the meeting was adopted in consensus, to the surprise of many observers.

## Information and Communication Order in the Era of Globalization

The face of world politics changed drastically in the first years of the 1990s with the disintegration of the Soviet Union and the fall of communist governments in Eastern Europe. A far-reaching restructuring of markets worldwide ensued, and the past decade has witnessed the successive commercialization, deregulation and privatization of many sectors. Globalization, particularly of markets, has permeated the public sphere and many aspects of our daily lives. National markets are becoming integrated into a global market structure. National frontiers are fading in many other respects, as well. Not least in the media system, where technological innovation and deregulation, particularly in the field of telecommunications, have accelerated the process. A new political and economic world order has brought changes in the information and communication order, too.

The contrasts between North and South have changed little since the 1970s, when the issue of a NWICO was raised. This is made abundantly clear in Human Development Report, published annually by the UN Development Programme, UNDP. On the whole, underdevelopment and poverty have declined since the 1950s. Freedom from colonial rule brought improvements with regard to education and health care and a more rapid pace of economic growth. But the development process has proven a rocky road. To mention but one example: globalization creates tensions that have increased or threaten to increase poverty. Every fourth person in the world today subsists on an income of less than one U.S. dollar a day.

UNDP not only forecasts a low rate of economic growth and stagnation for the developing countries, but goes on to identify a number of stumbling blocks to development such as political conflicts and war, slower progress in fields like food security, and the spread of HIV/ AIDS. Properly structured, globalization can lead to a more just, peaceful and secure world. Globalization holds the promise of reducing inequalities and poverty through trade, technology diffusion and the exchange of knowledge, and through greater consciousness of shared values such as democratic rule and human rights.

The globalization we see today, however, is not always global. In some respects the world is more fragmented today than perhaps ever before; there are sharp divisions - between rich and poor, between the powerful and the powerless. Thousands of millions of people lack access to the mutual interaction that globalization makes possible. Exclusion is the plight of the poorest countries of the south, yes, but also of the poorest in the richest countries. Virtually every country of the world knows the problems and conflicts this gives rise to: widening income gaps, poverty, environmental degradation, ill health, ethnic conflict, racism, inequality of men and women, discrimination, intolerance, etc.

Exclusion is more than a question of material assets — it is also a question of access to knowledge and culture, i.e., the fundaments of social development. Unless the cultural diversity inherent in society is acknowledged and represented in the public sphere, no positive political, economic or social development will be possible. For many people, globalization has meant that the world is shrinking. Cultural frontiers are being transcended and a great diversity of actors are active on the global stage. But there is a down side, as well; globalization may also lead to homogenization, to the extinction of uniqueness, of definitive cultural idiosyncrasies.

The institutions and companies that control globalized culture today tend toward standardization; commercial interests steer, and there is a risk that the interests of the wealthier peoples of the world, consumers, will prevail. At the same time, the world seems in some respects to be becoming less accessible. Everywhere in the world there are people who feel a need to defend their cultural identities. As a consequence, the frontiers between nations, cultures and religions are being turned into 'front lines', locally and internationally. Transcendence and lines of defence are two simultaneous phenomena in the same globalization process.

Mass media play a decisive part in what we call the globalization process. Without the media and modern information technology globalization as we know it today would not be possible. Access to various media, to telephony and digital services are often held forth as crucial to our political, economic and cultural development. Free and independent media are also vital to the survival and development of democracy. Meanwhile, a good share of the people of the world lack electricity and access to telecommunications and are thereby condemned to marginalization.

The development of innovative information technologies and the ongoing processes of deregulation and concentration of ownership have spurred the pace of globalization. Particularly communications satellites and digitalization - not least the Internet - have had an enormous impact. These innovations have opened worldwide markets for media products such as television programs, films, news, games and advertising. They have been a sine qua non for the formation and proper functioning of global enterprises and flows of information across national frontiers. The production and distribution of media products are highly concentrated branches, with respect to both content and ownership. Meanwhile, traditional distinctions, between information and entertainment, between hardware and software, between product and distribution, are blurring.

Much of what could be only vaguely discerned on the horizon back in the 1970s is now upon us in full force. The relationships between the rich countries and the poor countries of the world that the MacBride Commission described at the end of the 1970s seem to prevail, essentially unchanged. Issues relating to mass media have been marginalized within UNESCO, and the world today is far too fragmented for an issue like 'the right to communicate' to gain acceptance. In sum, there is no basis in reality for a political discussion of how to regulate the international media system, as was done in the 1970s.

### *Global Actors in the Media Market*

The international wire services were pioneers in the development of a global network. Having started up in the early 1850s, they were the first transnational media systems, products of modernity. They defined political and economic news, thereby creating a product that was sold, in different packaging, to political and economic elites, either directly or via mass media, at home and in other parts of the world. The wire services developed information technologies so as to improve the global communications networks. Today, they distinguish themselves from other acctors on the global market in that they both contribute to globalization and consolidate their own countries.

Contemporary news flows differ from those of the 1970s through a much larger volume and through greater diversification. But interest in using other sources than the major wire services is limited so that they have retained their privilege of defining what constitutes news. They, particularly market leaders AP and Reuters, also supply Internet services with news copy. Here there is a natural link to the main sources of news film. The news market today is highly diversified and segmented into a number of subgenres: business news, sports news, entertainment news, medical news, and the Internet facilitates further development, both in terms of geographical extent and volume.

But the content the services carry does not seem to have evolved to any notable extent. When CNN 'stole' a sizable share of the global market in the mid-1990s, the dominance of the USA in news reporting worldwide was the target of criticism, and researchers found that 'the news seen on World Report is the same old news of the world'. Otherwise, use of third world sources is no more than sporadic. Less than four per cent of the material carried by EBU's news exchange, EVN, in 1991 originated in regional collaboration with third world news organizations. To some extent, the sparse representation may be attributed to a scarcity of material that is of relevance to EBU's viewers. Hjarvard analysed the obstacles and disinterest that collaboration has met on the national level and comments that collaboration seems to occur despite, rather than as a result of, national policy. Interest resides among journalists, not governments. But even if regional collaboration has not brought about any major changes, regionalization of news reporting has developed, particularly in the Arab world.

The news service, Al jazeera is a case in point. But this is not to say that Al jazeera is a major news source outside the Arab world.

Critics of the status quo in the 1970s took the concentration in the media branch and the threat to diversity that it posed as cause to demand some form of international regulation of media markets. Since then, media corporations have grown considerably. Back in the 1970s, the objects of concern were the major wire services and, above all, film studios that operated on the international market, e.g. Columbia, Warner Brothers, Twentieth Century-Fox, United Artists - all based in the USA. Indeed, it is among these companies that we find the germ of many of the transnational corporations (TNC) that dominate the media market today. Some of these companies have taken advantage of deregulation and privatization in vast regions of the world and purchased and fused with other companies to become global media conglomerates.

The TNCs operate on multiple levels, global channels spread the same message, regional channels in local languages are established, and technical systems are made available. A few transnational media companies, most of which are based in the USA or Europe, dominate the spread of media products. Their cultural presence is considerable on virtually every continent. Lately, they have begun to establish themselves in the developing countries. Together with the World Wide Web, the expansion of media TNCs also has increased the paramountcy of English. Most of these companies are primarily involved in television and entertainment, but several also deal in news gathering and distribution. All control more than one medium and are thus able to advertise and sell their products in one medium via one or more others.

Both of the two transnational corporations in the third world are to be found in Latin America. They are Globo in Brazil and Televisa in Mexico. Globo is the larger with a volume of roughly USD 3 billion. Having started out in the newspaper branch, the company now has expanded into television, pay-TV, music publishing and book publishing. The media have become increasingly commercialized over the past few decades. Market shares are worth a great deal of money. How economic transactions are organized and the degree of concentration of economic power in various branches play a decisive role in the globalization process. A country's place in the global pecking order is a function of its ability to compete on the world market. Competitive strength is not only a question of efficiency or economic rationality; many factors - political, social and economic - play in. Samir Amin points out five different monopolies that the dominant actors make use of to maintain and strengthen their hold on the market and that together form the framework in which globalization takes place.

The five monopolies relate to technology, finance, natural resources, media and communications, and weapons of mass destruction. In the case of the media and communications, Amin gives the following motives:

> [The media and communications] not only lead to uniformity of culture but also open up new means of political manipulation. The expansion of the modern media market is already one of the major components in the erosion of democratic practices in the West itself.

The issues of cultural identity and the right to participate in international flows of information is related to both national media structures in the developing countries and the countries' links to the global system. Several countries in the third world still lack adequate infrastructure for modern mass media. This hinders the countries' development, while it also blocks their access to the international news and media system. The lack of electricity and telecommunications in much of developing countries' territory is one key problem. Other hindrances reside in the realm of national media policy. Those who can change the situation are not always motivated to do so; those who want to change the situation are not always in a position to.

An examination of existing international statistics in the communications sector shows some improvement in the countries of the third world since the 1970s, in some countries more than others. For example, the density of radio and television receivers has risen, as has newspaper circulation. Particularly the broadcast media have expanded. In the mid-1960s UNESCO recommended that each country should have at least 20 TV sets, 50 radio receivers and 100 newspaper copies per thousand inhabitants. In 1980, the MacBride report notes that 100 countries of Africa, Asia and Latin America had not reached these minimum standards by the mid-1970s. Ten years later, five countries were still below the three standards, and an additional 55 were below at least one of them.

African countries predominated among these least developed countries with respect to the media. Ten years further down the line, the figures have further improved - in some countries, but not others. Again, the poorest countries of Africa lag behind. In several developing countries, the pace of progress in the media sector has been quite slow, particularly in rural areas, where a majority of the people live. In the world as a whole, it is estimated that there is about 250 television sets per thousand inhabitants, a considerably greater share than have a telephone.

In less than a decade, from the mid-1980s to the mid 1990s — the number of television channels in the world doubled, as did average viewing time and the number of TV sets in households. Satellite television is accessible worldwide; transnational satellite channels have vastly increased the volume of programming available, and numerous niche channels carry specialized content to various target audiences - not least young viewers. In developing countries, which have experienced rapid deregulation, many Western-style radio and television channels now serve urban areas. Feature films, serial drama, talk shows and music predominate. Still, not everyone has access to television. In the poorest countries the estimated density of television sets per thousand people is no more than 23.

Radio is still the medium that reaches the most people. The fact that a good share of the third world still lacks electricity makes radio crucially important outside urban areas. Between 1970 and 1997, the density of radio receivers in developing countries increased from 90 to 245 per thousand inhabitants. In the interval 1970-1997, newspaper circulation in the developing countries doubled, from 29 to 60 per thousand. Circulation nearly doubled in the least developed countries, as well: from 4.5 per thousand in 1970 to 8 per thousand in 1997. The Internet is generally considered the cardinal example of "the digital revolution".

In 2002, an estimated ten per cent of the world population had access to the Internet. More than three-quarters of today's Internet users are to be found in the wealthiest (OECD) countries, which have 14 per cent of the world population. Only one per cent are located in Africa. Thus, we find a huge gap between different parts of the world - 'the digital divide' is as wide today as it ever was.

Most prognosticators say that the new information technology will make a tremendous difference in the future, but that a majority of the people of the world will not have access to the Net. The lack of telecommunications infrastructure in regions of Africa, Asia and Latin America will keep many people in the margins.

Internet is known to be the younger generation's medium par excellence. But in Africa, South America and a good part of Asia, the share of children and young people who have Internet access is only a couple of per cent. Meanwhile, roughly 80 per cent of Swedish children have Internet access at home. Children and young people in the wealthiest countries of the world are a truly multimedia generation, whereas many of the children in the world cannot watch television, and books are in short supply. The IPDC was inaugurated to accelerate the expansion of mass media in the third world. But, after twenty years, the results of the program are modest, to say the least. In some instances support made possible through the IPDC has significantly contributed to regional news exchanges, and to some extent the IPDC may be credited with having facilitated news gathering. But all too often, national media policy has stood in the way of international news exchange and news gathering across national frontiers.

IPDC operations have been criticized widely, and in 1995 reforms designed to make the program more efficient got under way. But at the same time it is difficult to see how the IPDC can help to create functional media structures. The establishment of modern communications infrastructure is much too costly for any one development program. Deregulation in the third world has opened the door to competition, privatization and foreign ownership, but this route to development often implies new dependency relationships. The conditions found in the third world in the 1970s are largely unchanged in the 100-odd countries that have experienced a slow pace of development and are still politically and economically dependent on other countries. In these countries, the situation described in the MacBride Commission's report still applies.

The new world information order, as formulated by the nonaligned countries, was clearly linked to the dependence paradigm, particularly the elements, decolonization and demonopolization. But the documents also contained an indication of a new position in the countries' quest for their own paths toward development and communication; it had to do with independence, self-determination and cultural identity. The demand for a new international information order may be seen as a reaction to the modernization paradigm. The MacBride Commission was clearly influenced by the nonaligned states' ideas. Self-reliance and cultural identity were key principles in the Commissions recommendations. Concepts like access and participation were made explicit.

The Commission also introduced the local level and horizontal communication into thinking about development. There was also a hint of the idea that the causes of underdevelopment might be found in the developed and the developing countries alike. This 'new' view was also expressed in the IPDC resolution of 1980. The MacBride Commission's recommendations were hardly unequivocal, however. The ambiguities were particularly apparent in the Commission's treatment of communication technology and technological development. Here the Commission's thinking alternated between the modernization and dependency paradigms; the concept of neocolonialism confronted decolonialization. But, above all, the recommendations suggested a third, alternative concept of development.

In the early 1980s, some scholars and development experts began speaking of 'another development', a term first coined in 1978 in Development Dialogue, the journal published by the Dag Ham-marskjöld Foundation. Here, key concepts are cultural identity and self-reliance and access and participation. This third approach may be characterized as a reaction to both the modernization and dependency paradigms. Universal models, which of necessity are always simplistic, are rejected in favour of an emphasis on the characteristics and needs of each individual country and the conviction that development efforts must start with specific conditions and needs.

Social, economic, cultural and religious components of development are identified; and the focus rests more often on local conditions than on the nation or international relations. This is not to say that relationships of international interdependency were ignored. An oft-cited phrase was, "Global problems, local solutions". Adherents of this approach also regarded traditional values as an important factor for fostering a sense of identity and meaning and a source of continuity in the face of social change. At the same time, democratic processes and regard for human rights were kept in focus.

In most recent decades, much of the work on 'another development' has focused on the concept of multiplicity, a concept introduced by Jan Servaes in the late 1980s. The principal features of 'the multiplicity model' may be summarized in five points:

1. All nations are interdependent in one sense or another. Internal as well as external factors can therefore influence the development process.

2. Development should be considered in a global context, in which both Centre and Periphery, as well as their interrelated subdivisions, are taken into account.
3. There is no generally applicable model of development; each country must devise its own development strategy.
4. Development comes of self-reliance and cultural identity.
5. Development requires access to and participation in local communication systems, that is to say, horizontal communication.

# 7

# Communication and Print Media in the Information Era

With the advent of the web and internet, the future has arrived. The dream of an interconnected planet where physical labour becomes minimally important and knowledge creation becomes the source of value and wealth appears to be here. For cyber-enthusiasts, the new information and communication technologies increase our choices. Bill Gates believes "it will affect the world seismically, rocking us in the same way the discovery of the scientific method, the invention of printing, and the arrival of the Information Age did." Author of Being Digital, Nicholas Negroponte writes that "while the politicians struggle with the baggage of history, a new generation is emerging from the digital landscape free of many of the old prejudices. These kids are released from the limitation of geographic proximity as the sole basis of friendship, collaboration, play, and neighbourhood.

Digital technology can be a natural force drawing people into greater world harmony." Douglas Rushkoff believes that computers are creating a generation gap between the "screenagers" and others, with screenagers having the most important skill of all-multi-tasking, choosing and doing many things at the same time (of course, forgetting that women have always had to do many things at the same time-taking care of the home and children as well as other types of formal and informal work). In any case, ICTs are creating a new world, an interactive, truly democratic world.

For proponents, the new technologies reduce the power of Big business and Big State, creating a vast frontier for creative individuals to explore. "Cyberspace has the potential to be egalitarian, to bring everyone into a network arrangement. It has the capacity to create community; to provide untold opportunities for communication, exchange and keeping in touch." Cybertechnologies will allow more interaction creating a global ecumene. They create wealth, indeed, a jump in wealth. The new technologies promise a transformational society where the future is always beckoning, a new discovery is yearly.

Critics, however, argue it is not a communicative world that will transpire but a world of selves downloading their emotional confusion onto each other. Far from creating a community based on consensus, the information technologies could easily create states of alienated and atomised individuals, glued to their computer terminal, terrorising and being terrorised by all those whose values conflict with their own. Social scientist Kevin Robbins is not convinced that our lives will be meaningfully changed by the information revolution; rather, he believes the information and communication technology (ICT) hype merely replaces the classical opiate of religion and the modernist idea of progress.

Indeed, for Robbins, the new technologies impoverish our imagination of alternative futures, particularly our geographic imagination. Focusing on distance, Robbins quoting Heidegger reminds us that the end of distance is not the creation of nearness, of intimacy, of community. "We are content to live in a world of 'uniform distancelessness,' that is, in an information space rather than a space of vivacity and experience." There is the illusion of community-in which we can create virtual communities far and away but still treat badly our neighbours, partners and children.

But, writes Robbins, more than destroying the beauty of geography, techno-optimists such as Bill Gates, Nicholas Negroponte and others take away space for critical commentary (personalising the discourse by seeing critics as merely imbued with too much negativity), that is, for the creation of futures that are different. Critical commentary, however, is not merely of being pessimistic or optimistic but a matter of survival.

Earlier it was Comte's positive science that was to solve all the problems of religion, of difference and now with the end of the cold war, it is liberal democracy. Michael Tracey writes that it is not an accident that just at the precise moment " the planet is being constructed within the powerful, pervasive all consuming logic of the market, there is a second order language, a fairy tale... that suggests in Utopian terms new possibilities, in particular, those presented by the new alchemies of 'the Net." What was once the cant of progress is now the cant of cyberspace-from love to democracy, from evil to poverty, all will be delivered, all will be redeemed-virtuality is "here".

Thus, while the internet helps connect many people (especially those in the North) and supplies much needed information (especially important in the South) it also represents a specific form of cultural violence. While it intends to create a global community of equals, making identification based on age, looks, race, (dis)ability, class or gender less relevant, it also, through promoting, enhancing and cementing current ways of communicating, silences billions of people.

Some of the excluded are non-English speaking nations, "irrelevant" nations and peoples, national, religious and ideological minorities, poor in poor countries and poor in rich countries, the majority of women, most old and disabled, and almost all children (although certainly not Western screenagers). In the 21st century most of the world's population will still be silenced. Reality will still be that of the strongest and most powerful. The new communication technologies will further enhance differences between poor and rich, between women and men, and between the world and its narrow part defined as "the West". And once poor, if the world and women catch up with the dominating forces, it will be on their terms and it will be in their language.

## Women and Global Conversations

Before crying for our lost battle, we (women, non-English speaking people, not so technically-oriented individuals) can start thinking in terms of what exactly is silenced, and what can we do about it. How can we engage in global conversations while not losing our own identities, our own understanding of reality, our ways of speaking, or our own language? How can we use the Net without being used by it? Women and others do not necessarily have to be disempowered. Women have proved they can speak the language of their "enemy" (as has the South of the North). After all, that is what women learn in schools, gather from books and from all the other print media: someone else's history, someone else's perspective and someone else's knowledge.

Most feminists agree that in order to achieve this women had to either became bilingual (some successfully and many through the destructive process of othering their own selves) or to abandon their own traditional language. While it is not so clear what this traditional language might be, obvious differences between women's and men's ways of speaking are found to exist. Research, in general, shows that women ask questions while men make statements, that women talk about people and feelings while men talk about things, that women use more adjectives, more modal forms such as "perhaps", "sort of", "maybe", and more tag questions and attention beginners. It is often stressed that language not only reflects but also perpetuates and contributes to gender inequality, and that through language hierarchy between genders is "routinely established and maintained".

Feminist researchers find that men are more likely than women to control conversation while women do "support work" being some sort of "co-operative conversationalists" who express frequent concern for other participants in talk. The main solution for the transformation of current conversational division of labour between sexes cannot be only in the area of language because even the most "neutral" terms can always be appropriated by the dominant culture (like the meaning of the word "no" can be at time constructed to mean "maybe" or "wait a while"). Susan Ehrlich and Ruth King write: "Because linguistic meaning are, to a large extent, determined by the dominant culture's social values and attitudes, terms initially introduced to be non-sexist and neutral may lose their neutrality in the "mouths" of a sexist speech community and/or culture".

The organisation of words and ideas into knowledge was similarly done in a context of masculine power where women were made invisible, their existence either denied or distorted and their ways of knowing and issues of interest labelled irrelevant. While many feminist linguists are attempting to reinvent language and support women's emancipation through linguistic interventions, it is clear that this has to be done simultaneously with political, economic and cultural transformations in the areas of knowledge, language and the written word. The question is: can the Net become a site for this reinvention? Can women's and others' ways of knowing and speaking find space and voice on the Net? Can we escape the tool-centric approach of the new information and communication technologies to create a softer, listening future in which we co-evolve with nature, technology, the spirit, and the many civilizations that are humanity? Can the Net be communicative, in the widest sense of the word?

While it is obvious that women can and do use the most dominant language, it is also claimed that women would rather use "softer", more intuitive and face-to-face approaches. In a future controlled by women, oral tradition, body language, sounds, dreams, intuitive and psychic ways of communicating possibly would be equal with the written text, or at least not so much suppressed. Maybe, in such a society where women would participate at all levels and in all spheres it wouldn't be necessary to introduce "dressing Barbie" video games in order to make girls more interested in new computer technologies.

Maybe new software would be more interactive and more user (women/other) friendly and maybe new communication technologies would look completely different. Maybe they would not be so individualised, and maybe, netweaving would be done in a context of community or friendly groups and not in a context of alienated individuals. Priorities would certainly be somewhere else: where the quality of life of majority of people would have the highest value. Thus, there are, and can be even more so, progressive dimensions to the new technologies. As Fatma Aloo of the Tanzanian Media Women's Association argues, "They are a necessary evil." Women and other marginalised groups must use and design them for their own empowerment or they will be further left out and behind. Without being part of the design (the "knowledge ware") and use process, they will further have to other themselves when they use the ICTs.

What is needed then is the creation of a progressive information society. It would be a world system that was diverse in how it viewed knowledge, appreciating the different ways gender and civilization order the real. It would not just be technical but emotional and spiritual as well and ultimately one that used knowledge to create better human conditions, to reduce dukha (suffering) and realise moksa (spiritual liberation from the bonds of action and reaction). The challenge then is not just to increase our ability to produce and understand information but to enhance the capacity of the deeper layers of mind, particularly in developing what in Tantric philosophy is called the vijinanamaya kosa (where knowledge of what is eternal and temporal is touched).

Certainly, even though the web is less rigid than a library, it is not the liberating information technology some assume-spiritual energies and shamanistic dissenting spaces cannot enter. Of course, underlying an alternative view of an information society is a commitment to prama or a dynamic equilibrium wherein internal/external, "male/ female" and spiritual/material are balanced.

We need to imagine and help create social spaces so the new technologies participate in and allow for the coming of a real global civilization, a prama, a gaia of cultures; one where there is deep multi-culturalism; where not just political representation and economic wealth are enhanced but the basis of civilization: the epistemologies of varied cultures, women and men, how they see self and other, flourish. To begin to realize this, we need to first critically examine the politics of information. We need to ask if the information we receive is true; if it is important, what its implications are, and the who is sending us the information.

We also need to determine if we can engage in a conversation with the information sent-to question it, reveal its cultural/gendered context, to discern if the information allows for dialogue, for communication. We thus need to search for ways to transform information to communication (going far beyond the "interactivity" the web promises us), creating not a knowledge economy (which silences differences of wealth) but a communicative economy (where differences are explored, some unveiled, others left to be). To do so, in addition to engaging critically with the assumptions beyond the information discourse, we also need to expand the limited rationalist discourse in which "information" resides. What we learn from other cultures such as the indigenous Indian Tantric is that the new electronic technologies are just one of the possible technologies creating world space. Indeed they just act at the most superficial materialistic levels.

As important as cyberspace is microvita space or the noosphere being created through our world imaginations, through our increasingly shared collective consciousness. Certainly while the reality of the information era is one of exclusion, the potential for shared communication futures remains. To do so will require far more communication-sharing of meaning-than we have ever known and at far greater levels, in light of the many ways we know and learn from each other. While we have highlighted the structures of power that create colonization, we also need to acknowledge personal agency; we particularly need to be far more sensitive to how we project our individual and civilizational dark sides on others.

The information era will further magnify our assumptions of self-innocence and other-as-guilty unless we begin to reveal our complicitness in soliloquy posing as conversation. If information can be transformed to communication, the web then can perhaps participate in the historical decolonization process giving power to communities and individuals in the overall context of global human, economic, environmental and culturally negotiated universals.

## Information Age and the Printing Press

We are in the midst of the "Information Age." Pundits have proclaimed it for years; articles in the popular press have plumbed its implications for every imaginable enterprise; businesses are enamored with it; on-line and print magazines are devoted to it; government is wrestling with it, movies have been made about it; people are talking about it--can there be any doubt? It is both important and difficult to see where the information age might lead.

Important, not least, because gargantuan fortunes are there to be made for those who see the future clearly. Important also, because information is affecting a wide variety of human enterprises in significant ways (businesses are "flattening" and globalizing; people are buying faxes, cell phones and computers; schools are wiring themselves in anticipation; governments are scrambling to handle information age problems, etc.).

It is difficult to see where the information age is leading primarily because the technologies fueling it are still being developed and at a furious rate. It is difficult also because of the breadth of the impact of information technologies to date. With so many areas of society being affected, many effects are transitory, many are insignificant, some are contradictory and some are even undesirable. Because or perhaps in spite of both the importance and difficulty of addressing the future of the information age, there has been no shortage of attempts to do so. These attempts break down roughly into three categories.

The first contains those who would project from the capabilities generated by information technology where the information age might go. Let's call these people technologists. Prominent in this category would be Microsoft's Bill Gates. His best-selling book-The Road Ahead-is a good example of suggesting how technological advances might affect our lives in the years ahead. Other examples in this genre include Nicholas Negroponte's Being Digital and Michael Dertouzos' new book, What Will Be: How the New World of Information Will Change Our Lives.

The second category of people addressing the future of the information age contains those who would "invent" rather than try to predict the future. These are the inventors. These include people who are looking for "killer applications" or hardware breakthroughs that will yank the future of information onto a whole new trajectory. In the third category are those who try to divine the future by drawing on parallels with the past. These are the historians.

Chief among these in the popular literature would have to be the Tofflers who argue the information revolution is following the agricultural and industrial revolutions as important "waves" in human history. Also included here are the works of colleagues Carl Builder-who argues information technologies could bring down the power of the nation-state in the same way the printing press helped bring down the power of the Catholic Church in the Middle Ages, and David Ronfeldt-who argues that the network is next in the progression of societal forms from tribes through hierarchies and markets.

The parallels between the printing press era and today are sufficiently compelling to suggest:

— Changes in the information age will be as dramatic as those in the Middle Ages in Europe. The printing press has been implicated in the Reformation, the Renaissance and the Scientific Revolution, all of which had profound effects on their eras; similarly profound changes may already be underway in the information age.

— The future of the information age will be dominated by unintended consequences. The Protestant Reformation and the shift from an earth-centered to a sun-centered universe were unintended consequences in the printing press era. We are already seeing unintended consequences in the information age that are dominating intended ones and there are good reasons to expect more in the future. Thus, the technologists are unlikely to be accurate and the inventors may neither have their intended effects nor be the most important determinants of information age progress.

— It will be decades before we see the full effects of the information age. The important effects of the printing press era were not seen clearly for more than 100 years. While things happen more quickly these days, it could be decades before the winners and losers of the information age are apparent. Even today, significant (and permanent) cultural change does not happen quickly.

— The above factors combine to argue for: a) keeping the Internet unregulated, and b) taking a much more experimental approach to information policy. Societies who regulated the printing press suffered and continue to suffer today in comparison with those who didn't. With the future to be dominated by unintended consequences and a long time in emerging, a more experimental approach to policy change (with special attention to unintended consequences) is soundest.

This is speculation of the highest order. We are essentially saying the Internet era is very similar in important areas to the printing press era, and, because the printing press had broad and profound effects on its age we should expect similarly broad and profound effects from the information age.

### *Technological Breakthroughs*

It is here we want to return to the question of what the information age really is, for that is at the heart of our thinking. In fact, the basic argument can be stated as follows:

— As the first true many-to-many communications medium, the networking of computers is the defining characteristic of the information age,

— There has been only one comparable event in the recorded history of communications-the printing press. It was the first true one-to-many communications medium, and no change since has been as dramatic as networked computers,

— The impact of the printing press on its era was profound in breadth and depth, and was directly related to its one-to-many communications capability,

— It is thus that we argue the many-to-many capability enabled by networked computers will play a role in similarly broad and deep changes in the information age.

Networked computers that define the information age. Other definitions of the information age are much broader, encompassing other information technologies such as faxes, cellular phones, non-networked computer applications, few-to-few intranets, and so forth.

### *Future of Networked Computers*

While profound cultural changes are generally slow in developing, the same cannot often be said of technological changes that propel them. The printing press spread quickly (for its time) from Gutenberg's first press in Mainz in 1450 throughout Europe by 1500. In that time, as many book copies were printed as had been produced in the previous millennium by scribes. The technology, though it continued to evolve, was largely in place after 50 years. The impact of the change was not clearly seen for another century or so, but the capabilities of the technology were seen reasonably clearly early on.

We are not yet to the point we can see the capabilities of networked computers. Their growth has been no less dramatic in our time, but we are still on the "steep part of the curve" from the technology standpoint. Since ARPANET first went on line in 1969, the growth in networked computers has been exponential. The growth rate has slowed recently, but is still doubling every 12-15 months. We are also still on the steep part of the curve for the capabilities of the computers themselves. If the parallels between the print and network eras are to be useful, some measure of the "eventual" characteristics and capabilities of networked computers as a communications medium must be known.

The enthusiastic projections that accompany any new technology usually overestimate actual progress, but can vary wildly in their prescience on either side of the eventuality. Projections of electronic computer usage were laughably understated, while those of dirigibles were just as laughable in the opposite direction. Since we are still at the growth and hype stage of networked computers, where can we turn for prescience? The eventual impact of a technology is at least weakly dependent on its ubiquity; the more widely spread the greater the likelihood and magnitude of impact.

The typical new technology is very expensive or esoteric and, thus, is initially restricted to a small segment of the population. Some technologies, such as space travel, languish there indefinitely. Others, such as books, stay in the province of the elite for some time, and eventually make their way throughout the populace. Still others, such as calculators and televisions, start out expensive and enjoy a steady drop in price and a concomitant rise in circulation. Where exactly are we with networked computers and where might we wind up?

Reaching pervasiveness depends primarily on access to networked computers being affordable and on people's interest in having that access. Affordability, in this case, depends on the affordability of both the networking and the connections to the network. Due to its peculiar history, networking itself has been relatively inexpensive since its inception. A crucial element of the Internet dates back to

1962 at RAND when Paul Baran developed the concept of packet switching as a means to maintain connectivity of the military command and control network in case of nuclear attack.

In 1969 the Advanced Research Projects Agency funded the first large-scale test of this concept. In the fall of that year the first node was installed at UCLA (RAND was the seventh node). Because of the decentralized structure of the ARPANET and a telephone network in place to support it, expansion was easy and the net grew rapidly. In 1983 ARPANET broke off the military part (which became MILNET) and the non-military part grew into what is known today as the Internet (with ARPANET officially closing down in 1989).

If one has a computer, connecting to the Internet costs little or nothing, since each node is independent, and has to handle its own financing and its own technical requirements. While the price of connecting to the Internet has been historically low, it still requires a computer. Though computers continue to drop in price, they still cost several hundred to several thousand dollars new. On the other hand, computers have enjoyed the longest stretch of uninterrupted exponential growth of any technology known to man. A plethora of available projections show continued uninterrupted exponential growth in performance and exponential decreases in cost, size and power requirements for several more generations. But decreases in cost are usually figured on a performance-per-dollar basis.

The price of a new generation of computers is about the same as that of the previous generation. However, there are other options for connecting to the Internet. If one were not afraid of swap meets and minor begging, one could start from scratch and connect (with generations-old equipment) to the Internet today for under $200 initial outlay and $10 a month. Another option is the "set-top" box. This is a computer designed specifically to hook up to the web using an ordinary TV set as the monitor. Today it can cost as little as $100 and $15 a month, and there is growing competition in this market.

As far as the interest in networks today, Joel Birnbaum would say we are in the third of four stages for a pervasive technology-where it has become well known and commonplace, but is used directly by only a rather small portion of the population. The fourth stage is where the technology becomes integral to daily life. Best estimates today say there are at least 19.5 million computers connected to the Internet in 241 countries. One respected estimate says in the United States 40.6 million people over 18 have used the Internet in the last year. At these rates, worldwide saturation would be achieved before 2010. We know not to trust the timelines of such simple projections, but is there evidence we are headed for saturation?

Anecdotal evidence provides some provocative snippets at this point. Win Treese, for example, writes that 25% of all Australian households have a personal computer, 16% of Estonian elementary and secondary schools are connected to the Internet, and two daily newspapers in Iran have websites.

### Computer Technology

What will be the situation when the exponential growth of both networking and computers has finally tailed off? It is the many-to-many nature of networked computers rather than the specific technology. For that reason, but realizing that the ubiquity/availability question is an important one, we will use very conservative estimates of the capabilities of networks and computers when they "stop growing exponentially."

The computer projections are based on currently-used lithography technologies (primarily the 150 nanometer electron-beam lithography in development at IBM). Lithography can arguably be pushed down to the 5 nanometer range, and more exotic methods based on different phenomenology (Scanning-Tunneling Microscopy, molecular machines and self-assembling systems) hold promise for making even more remarkable advances. To put these numbers in more graphic terms, a computer of 2010, in a size no bigger than portable computers today, would have the computational power of today's supercomputers, and it would cost about the same as today's portables. Lesser capabilities would be available at lower costs in much the same way they are today.

The network capacities of 2010 are less than an order of magnitude away from NREN, the National Research and Education Network, which was approved by the US Congress in the Fall of 1991, as a five-year, $2 billion project to upgrade the Internet "backbone." NREN will allow the electronic transfer of the entire Encyclopedia Britannica in one second. Projections are for networks worldwide to feature 3-D animated graphics, radio and cellular phone-links to portable computers, as well as fax, voice, and high-definition television. The NII (National Information Infrastructure) or "Information Superhighway" is intended to be even more capable, but the more conservative projections above will be sufficient to make the case.

Uses of networked computers. What about the uses of the Internet? Again, we will depend on today's uses. To review, the current primary functions supported by Internet are four: e-mail, discussion groups, long-distance computing and file transfers. E-mail is electronic mail that is similar to FAXs. It is global in scope with more than 240 countries accessible today (up from 137 in 1993). The discussion groups, or "newsgroups," are a world of news, debate and argument generally known as "USENET." Sterling describes USENET as "rather like an enormous billowing crowd of gossipy, news-hungry people, wandering in and through the Internet on their way to various private backyard barbecues."

There are some 2800 separate newsgroups on USENET, and their discussions generate 400,000 articles and 800 megabytes of data traffic a day. The variety of subjects discussed is enormous, and growing. Both USENET and e-mail are widely available, even outside the high-speed core of the Internet itself. News and e-mail are easily available over common phone-lines from Internet fringe-realms like BITnet, UUCP and Fidonet. The other two Internet services, long-distance computing and file transfer, require what is known as "direct Internet access"-using TCP/IP (Transmission Control Protocol and Internet Protocol). As above, long-distance computing was an original inspiration for ARPANET and is still a very useful service for some.

Programmers can maintain accounts on distant, powerful computers, run programs there or write their own. Scientists can make use of powerful supercomputers a continent away. File transfers allow Internet users to access remote machines and retrieve programs or text. Many Internet computers allow anyone to access them anonymously, and to simply copy their public files, free of charge. Internet file-transfers are becoming a new form of publishing, in which the reader simply electronically copies the work on demand, for free. One aspect of file transfers is the latest rage on the Internet, and embodies an important computer software technology that will figure in the speculations below. That aspect is the World Wide Web (WWW, or "Web").

As with packet switching, the WWW was developed (by physicists at the European Particle Physics Laboratory) for a narrow, specific problem (creating a unified hypertext markup language (HTML) network for high-energy physicists working in a variety of locations internationally). It is leading to is a "point-and-click" way of browsing through the entire Internet. With browsers such as Netscape Communicator or Microsoft Explorer, the user can "surf" the Internet in a more user-friendly way. Further, making current Internet documents compatible is easy: "Using a relatively simple set of commands, World Wide Web users can turn their documents into hypertext: nsert the proper bit of code, and a word becomes a link;...nearly any InterNet document-text, picture, sound, or video-can be retrieved and viewed on the World Wide Web." WWW services are currently growing by 60% per month.

At this point let us draw a very conservative picture of a networked computer system in the year 2010. The network will have a wide variety of computers connected to it, including personal computers with the memory and processing capabilities of today's supercomputers. About 50% of the households in the U.S. will have computers (up from 28% today) and 30% of households will be connected to the network (up from 11% today). A disproportionate percentage of computer ownership and network usage will be in White and Asian households, in the upper quartile of income and belonging to college graduates. The network will be based on something like hypertext with browsers bringing "point-and-click" friendliness to WWW interactions containing text, pictures and videos.

At least three of today's network functions will still be popular: discussion groups, e-mail, and file transfers. Most major domestic and many foreign libraries, universities and governments will be accessible through the network with direct access to millions of individual documents. As to where we are on the "curve," We will get "that far" before the curve starts to tail off. More importantly, "that far" is critical mass in terms of making the system permanent. It may not yet be pervasive in the sense the Birnbaum uses it, but it will be at least as pervasive and permanent as books were in their early history.

### *Impact of the Printing Press*

While the history of the printing press has been studied voluminously, its effects on society have received little attention. Elizabeth Eisenstein's book, The Printing Press as an Agent of Change, was the first and is still the only comprehensive attempt to study the impact of the printing press. Before the publication of her book in 1979, historians generally conceded the role of the printing press in weakening the power of the medieval church, but gave it little credit beyond its assist to Luther and his Protestant Reformation. Eisenstein persuasively implicated the printing press in the Renaissance and the Scientific Revolution as well, magnifying both the breadth and depth of its impact. Her latter views are more controversial.

Eisenstein's work was provoked by Marshall McLuhan's similar (less carefully researched) notion that the printing press was an important watershed and her book created a stir among her fellow historians. While several reviewers found parts of Eisenstein's work problematic, D.W. Krummel echoed the sentiments of many in writing: "...just as Western civilization was never again the same thanks to the invention of printing, so our understanding of the invention of printing will never again be the same thanks to Eisenstein's scholarship."

Eisenstein argues that the printing press changed the conditions under which information was collected, stored, retrieved, criticized, discovered, and promoted. Change is multi-causal, but argues that-as an agent-printing had important causative effects on the Reformation, the Renaissance and the Scientific Revolution. Wewill leave significant details to the section on the changes enabled by the technologies, but before then, a general discussion of the causative effects of printing is in order.

Eisenstein, better than anyone, recognized the difficulty in trying to establish the impact of the printing press. The first century of printing produced a bookish culture that was not very different from that produced by scribes, and one must wait until a full century after Gutenberg before the outlines of new world pictures begin to emerge into view.

" As Rosaldo said in a way that might echo more strongly today: "...roughly during the first century after Gutenberg's invention, print did as much to perpetuate blatant errors as it did to spread enlightened truth. Putting scribal products into print resulted in a cultural explosion. Never had scholars found so many words, images, and diagrams at their fingertips.

And never before had things been so confusing with, for instance, Dante's world view achieving prominent visibility at the same time that Copernican views were making their way into print. Nonsense and truth seemed to move hand in hand with neither made uncomfortable by the presence of the other. Though many have discussed Renaissance culture's playful spirit, love of many-sided accomplishment, or lighthearted indifference to historical fact, Eisenstein more prosaically says that things simply had not yet been sorted out."

This long delay between cause and "sorted out" effect is not surprising when the effects are cultural and profound. It does, however, complicate establishment of the cause-and-effect relationship. Given the difficulties, the strength of Eisenstein's work is her careful argumentation about the connection between a given cultural change-seen clearly only many decades after the invention of the printing press-and the more tangible changes brought about by printing.

Eisenstein's arguments about the impact of the printing press on the Reformation are aptly summarized by Kingdon: "Scholars have long recognized the essential role of the press in spreading Protestant doctrine. Luther himself, in fact, claimed that the invention of printing was a gift from God to reform His church. But Eisenstein argues that print did more than spread the Protestant Reformation: in an important sense, print caused the Reformation. Without access to the printed editions of biblical texts and church fathers, and the worrisome variants on crucial dogmatic issues they contain, Luther might never have been stimulated to develop his revolutionary new theology. And without accessibility to print, Luther might never have spread his ideas not only in the Latin of the scholarly community but also in the vernacular German of the lay community."

Eisenstein argues that, while the medieval Catholic church was a prolific user of printing, the changes it wrought were outside the control of the church. The proliferation of different biblical texts eventually cast into doubt the existence of a single infallible text. This led to alternative interpretations such as Luther's, but the ability to publicize those interpretations by the same means of printing kept them from being crushed as were earlier heresies.

As for the Renaissance, it began well before the invention of the printing press. Historians credit Petrarch with its origins in the mid-fourteenth century in Northern Italy. The "renaissance," or "rebirth," refers to a return to the humanism of the classical Greeks. To argue the causative effects of printing, Eisenstein divides the Renaissance into pre- and post-printing phases. "Rebirths" of humanism were not uncommon in the medieval period. Two of the largest were the Carolingian in the 9th century and one in the 12th century.

Eisenstein points out that the Italian renaissance differed little from earlier ones until the printing press "fixed" it and helped spread it north of the Alps. "Typographical fixity" refers to the preservative power of print. Ideas recorded in only a few manuscripts were always in danger of being forgotten or lost by the intellectual community. Put those same ideas in hundreds of identical printed copies, and they were much more likely to spread and endure. Eisenstein suggests that before the printing press, the fall of Constantinople (and its extensive collection of classical texts), in 1453, would have been disastrous for humanism.

Another argument applies to all three of the major events of the printing press era, but perhaps best to the Scientific Revolution. This is the idea that the printing press changed attitudes towards the past. As Mander puts it, "Scribal culture revered the ancients because they were closer to uncorrupted knowledge-that is, knowledge not yet corrupted through the process of scribal transmission... Print culture, because it allows for cumulative advance of knowledge, views the past from a fixed distance."

Eisenstein argues that this change in attitude led to a willingness to question the ancients and to consider new ideas; fueling both the rise of humanism and Protestantism. In science, the notion of cumulative and progressive knowledge was absolutely revolutionary. "Scientific data collection was born with printing" and new contributions became part of a "permanent accumulation no longer subject to the cycle of rapid decay and loss." Copernicus compared the ideas and data of Ptolemy, Aristotle and others; noted their errors and inconsistencies; and published "De Revolutionibus Orbium Coelestium" in 1543-starting the Scientific Revolution. This change in culture is captured neatly in: "the reversal of meaning undergone by the term "original." In its old meaning it meant closest to the origin of things, to the initial creation of the cosmos. In the first truly typographical culture it increasingly meant "novel," a break with precedent."

These summaries do little justice to the case Eisenstein builds for the impact of the printing press. While not all historians share her enthusiasm, there is a general concession that the impact of print has been under-researched and, thereby, underestimated. The printing press was not the only change taking place in the period from 1450 to 1650, (just as networked computers are not the only change taking place today). Nonetheless, Eisenstein's research is clear evidence that the printing press had a profound effect on society during the time Europe was making the transition from a medieval to a modern world. The stage is set, then, to draw parallels between the change-producing capabilities enabled by the printing press and those enabled by networked computers.

### Manipulation of Knowledge

The one-to-many nature of the printing press had important

effects on several fronts relating to the manipulation of knowledge. These effects are seen in retrospect. The printing press will be "responsible" for the change from the capability in the scribal era to that in the print era and networked computers will be responsible for the change from the capability in the print era to that of networked computers.

### Preserving, Updating and Disseminating Knowledge

The printing press didn't create the book, it changed or redefined it. In the scribal culture, books or manuscripts were produced laboriously by scribes, each slightly different from other copies of the book. Errors in one manuscript were propagated to the next copy of that manuscript, and new errors were typically added. The knowledge or thought that resided in a manuscript was available to very few to read or to own. "Wandering scholars" were a primary source of feedback and dissemination. As they read a given manuscript, their marginal notes added any corrective or additive thoughts they may have.

As scholars wandered, they carried the knowledge from the manuscript with them and could offer it to others. The paucity of manuscripts and wandering scholars made the preservation of knowledge precarious at best. The effects of the printing press on this situation were enormous. One cannot doubt its impact on the preservation and dissemination of knowledge. Thousands of copies of a single manuscript virtually assured both its survival and spread. Even if restricted primarily to the wealthy, the sheer numbers of available books made them much more available to the general public.

Updating the knowledge in books had a more subtle and interesting history. In the early stages, printed books still contained and propagated errors, but their wider availability slowly had a dramatic effect. A printed book, unlike a handwritten manuscript, was a standardized product, the same in its thousands of copies. It was possible for publishers to solicit corrections and contributions from readers who, from their own experience, would send back a report-and this was common practice.

Eisenstein (and others) argues that this feedback reversed the slow degradation of recorded thought and ushered in the era of accumulation of thought upon which the Scientific Revolution was built: "The advantages of issuing identical images bearing identical labels to scattered observers who could feed back information to publishers enabled astronomers, geographers, botanists and zoologists to expand data pools far beyond all previous limits...The same cumulative cognitive advance which excited cosmological speculation also led to new concepts of knowledge. The closed sphere or single corpus passed down from generation to generation, was replaced by an open-ended investigatory process pressing against ever advancing frontiers."

The many-to-many communications medium of networked computers enables the process of preserving, updating and disseminating knowledge to be carried one or two steps further to the immediately available, instant feedback, constantly-updated, "3-dimensional" (non-fiction) book. There are two important aspects to this. The first relates specifically to the updating of knowledge. A well-documented book can do a creditable job of addressing all the knowledge and thought up to the time of its publication, but can't address even the reaction to itself, let alone the thoughts it provokes. Subsequent editions are used to correct this "problem," but are rarely published less than a year (more commonly 3-12 years for reference works) after the original. At that point, parts of the first edition are obsolete, but there is no good way to so indicate on a first edition copy.

A good example of the changes enabled by networking is the FAQ (Frequently Asked Questions) found in the discussion groups of USENET. After a group (such as sci.math) has been in existence for a while, users new to the group will begin asking questions that have been discussed at length earlier. At some point, a regular user will offer to generate a FAQ-a list of frequently asked questions and answers that represent the author's concept of the group consensus. The FAQ will then be posted to the group and recommended changes can be discussed and incorporated (the many-to-many part in action).

The resulting FAQ is then archived (and posted periodically in some groups), to be referred to when one of the questions is brought up again and to be updated as necessary (again taking advantage of the potentially wide readership and discussion capabilities). The sci.math FAQ, for example, was a useful place to look recently to keep track of the status of Andrew Wiles's proof of Fermat's Last Theorem. More generally, any "official" site can be the location to check for the latest on an unfolding situation. A recent example is the NASA site and the Mars explorer. Literally millions of enthusiasts could stay as current as they wished in a way previously available only through 24-hour coverage by traditional broadcast media.

Another activity that takes advantage of many-to-many feedback capability is on-line journals. The Association of Research Libraries (ARL) counted 74 peer-reviewed electronic journals at the beginning of 1994, and 142 a year later. As of July 1996 there were 1688 electronic journals, newsletters, and newsletter-digests accessible through the Internet. These generally publish articles that have been refereed in the usual way, but make available to a wide readership the potential for ad hoc discussions of articles that appear.

The second aspect of change with networked computers is that of hypertext linking and relates more to how knowledge is disseminated. From the printing press era, encyclopedias do a good job of providing pointers to other reference material on a given subject. With hypertext linking, this referencing becomes immediate. If the reader has an interest in further information, a click on the hypertext link will take the reader to that information. This capability opens the book into a new dimension with immediate accessibility to definitions of words, alternative means (say, more visually-oriented) of understanding a concept, active discussions of a given topic, further research on the subject, alternative interpretations, etc.

The dissemination of knowledge is importantly changed by the immediacy of this new referencing capability. It takes important advantage of the many-to-many capabilities of the Internet both in the sense of the interconnectivity with data from all over the network, but also in the sense that building the individual pieces of an "Internet book" can-and from an efficiency standpoint, must-be done by a large group of people. Ironically, both the FAQ and hypertext capabilities work best with a single copy of a work that is accessible by anyone on the network. Further, there is nothing particularly new in the capabilities enabled by the network: books are widely available; feedback (e.g., reviews) on books and incorporating feedback into subsequent work/editions are both common; references can be discovered and obtained from any library.

The same was true of manuscripts in the scribal culture. What makes the two communications breakthroughs important are the quantum increases in the ease and speed with which knowledge could be promulgated; feedback could be received and incorporated; one could find up-to-date knowledge and one could be put in touch with a wide range of materials on the topic. On the other hand, anyone who would argue there will be little impact must argue that the same kind of jump increase in speed and ease of updating and disseminating knowledge that led to dramatic changes in the printing press era will not have much of an effect in the networked computers era.

### *Retrieving Knowledge*

In the scribal era, the ability to retrieve information was largely dependent on an individual's recall capabilities. There were numerous mnemonic devices to aid the individual memory. There were authorities available for consultation, but for instant recall, the individual had to rely primarily on his/her own memory. The ability to retrieve information took a significant jump in moving to the print culture. Indexes to books existed in the scribal culture, but were not systematically enforced. Before printing...the task of indexing a book was up to each manuscript's owner. Manuscripts with a detailed index bravely begun for A and B but faltering later in the alphabet are familiar to medievalists...'La naissance des index'...elegantly surveys the contrivances that medieval readers used to find their way around manuscripts: ingenious bookmarks, lists of chapter headings, concordances, marginal glosses, arcane symbols, numbered lines and columns, alphabetically arranged epitomes.

With the generation of hundreds of identical copies of a book, 'more complete and better arranged' indexes became a selling point for printers in the late fifteenth century. But indexes were just the iceberg tip. The printed book brought a variety of changes that led to a more orderly, systematic approach to the printed word: title pages, regularly numbered pages, punctuation marks, section breaks, running heads, tables of contents, etc. All of these had their obvious and subtle effects.

Eisenstein says of title pages: "Most studies of printing have, quite rightly, singled out the regular provision of title pages as the most significant new feature associated with the printed book format. How the title page contributed to the cataloguing of books and the bibliographer's craft scarcely needs to be spelled out. How it contributed to new habits of placing and dating, in general, does, I think, call for further thought."

Bibliographies, book catalogues and encyclopedias flourished thanks to these systematic changes brought about by the printing press. These, in turn, contributed to the retrieval of and critical reflection on published works and the accumulation of knowledge that characterized particularly the Scientific Revolution. In fact, cataloguing of all kinds became popular. "Medieval botanists knew some 600 varieties of plant, essentially not many more than in the ancient world. By 1623 some 6,000 varieties had been catalogued."

The ability to retrieve information has taken another significant jump in the age of computers. Eisenstein says of the printing press, "Until the recent advent of computers, has there been any other invention which saved so many man-hours for learned men?" Typical word processing programs have the ability to search through entire documents at high speed for phrases, words, or partial words. Ordinary algorithms can search hundreds of pages in seconds. Oft-searched documents-such as dictionaries or encyclopedias-can be formatted so that similar searches take fractions of a second. Specialized routines can search for word patterns (such as all five-letter words that start with "b", followed by two consecutive vowels). This is a powerful "indexing" capability that doesn't rely particularly on the many-to-many nature of networked computers.

Encyclopedias on CD-ROMs permit quick retrieval of widely disparate entries that contain specific words or phrases. Few users of a CD-ROM encyclopedia will go back to a multiple-volume book version. On the other hand, for several years, libraries have had the capability to electronically search for words or word combinations in the titles or keywords of documents in a wide variety of remote databases. Further details on the "hits" could be accessed as well. What networked computers enable is the combination of these two capabilities. Anyone connected with the network can become a "super librarian," searching remote databases via full-text search for any combination of words imaginable.

Colleague Jim Gillogly tells of writing a document recently and wanting to include a half-remembered quote from "Little Women." He accessed a distant electronic library, downloaded "Little Women," used full-text search to find the quote, and copied it into his document; all in a matter of minutes, without leaving his chair. In the same way that indexes were only a part of the retrieval revolution in the printing press era, full-text search is part of a wider computerized search that is changing the way people access knowledge. A good example here is the variety of "search engines" for the Internet itself. Developers of these engines are busily trying to outdo each other in the ability to find information on the Internet.

A recent personal communication about a young woman who found her estranged father through the

Internet suggests the breadth of information retrieval capabilities that such search engine developers could hope to provide. Such "data-mining" tools are still in their infancy in the network culture, but are sure to be as significant as their counterparts in the printing press culture. Libraries will undergo tremendous change in the network culture, as librarians are well aware.

### *Owning Knowledge*

Before printing there was little "ownership" of intellectual property. The Bible is a classical example. Who wrote the Bible? Many parts that are attributed to specific authors are various rememberings of what the author actually wrote or said. The same is true with other ancient manuscripts attributed to single authors-including those of Socrates, Plato, and Aristotle. It wasn't until the printed book that the notion of literary property rights developed. In fact, the first rights were "privileges" and were granted, not to authors, but to printers. A landmark in the history of literary property rights...came in 1469 when a Venetian printer obtained a privilege to print and sell a given book for a given interval of time.

By 1500, legal fictions were already being devised to accommodate the patenting of inventions and the assignment of literary properties. Upon these foundations a burgeoning bureaucracy would build a vast and complex legal structure. Eisenstein suggests that printing had a dramatic effect on personal celebrity: "The 'drive for fame' itself may have been affected by print-made immortality.... The wish to see one's work in print (fixed forever with one's name in card files and anthologies) is different from the desire to pen lines that could never be fixed in permanent form, might be lost forever, altered by copying, or-if truly memorable-be carried by oral transmission and assigned ultimately to 'anon'."

Preserving intellectual property rights-through both 'privileges' and patents-was a notion that grew out of the one-to-many power of the printing press. Eisenstein argues that this pride of authorship helped fuel the individualism that characterized the Renaissance. She also argues that the title page came to have promotional value for both author and printer, and that control of and the requirement for the publicity apparatus gave printers an important role in the rise of capitalism.

In recent years, copyright protection has been extended to computer software programs, highlighting the problems of copyrights and computers in general. The pirating of software was a problem before widespread networking of computers, but, again, the many-to-many aspect of networks dramatically exacerbates the situation. It enables (some would say it encourages) the unlimited reproduction and instantaneous distribution of digitized intellectual property of any kind worldwide virtually without cost. A good joke travels even faster on the Internet than it does on the street.

The source of this conundrum is as simple as its solution is complex. Digital technology is detaching information from the physical plane, where property law of all sorts has always found definition....Throughout the history of copyrights and patents, the proprietary assertions of thinkers have been focused not on their ideas but on the expression of those ideas...Copyright worked well because, Gutenberg notwithstanding, it was hard to make a book. Furthermore, books froze their contents into a condition which was as challenging to alter as it was to reproduce. Counterfeiting or distributing counterfeit volumes were obvious and visible activities, easy enough to catch somebody in the act of doing.

### *Acquiring Knowledge*

One of the immediate and recognizable impacts of the printing press was on how one learned. In educating the elite in the scribal culture, manuscripts were scarce, learning primarily involved listening (to someone read a manuscript or give a lecture), and-as above-memorization was paramount. Apprenticeship training and memorization were the primary means of educating the underclasses. That the printing press wrought significant changes in this system of learning cannot be doubted. As Eisenstein says, "Possibly no social revolution in European history is as fundamental as that which saw book learning (previously assigned to old men and monks) gradually become the focus of daily life during childhood, adolescence and early manhood.... As a consumer of printed materials geared to a sequence of learning stages, the growing child was subjected to a different developmental process than was the medieval apprentice, ploughboy, novice or page."

The structural changes are clear. People shifted from being listeners to being readers. Learning no longer required the presence of a mentor; it could be done privately. People talk of celebrated auto-didacts such as Tycho Brahe and Isaac Newton who learned primarily by reading. Such dramatic structural changes should lead to significant societal and cultural changes, but pinning those secondary changes down is very difficult. "Print is credited with altering personal consciousness either by shifting communicative formats from image to word or by transferring perceptual emphasis from ear to eye. The ways in which restructured consciousnesses rearranged particular societies in particular circumstances are left maddeningly fuzzy in such theories, although this is just what we want to know in order to take printing seriously as a historical agent."

Eisenstein emphasizes the difficulties by finding, for example, that despite the supposed shift from image to word, there was a reinforcement of the use of images in both printed works and art books. Similarly, while a reading public was more dispersed (and communal solidarity thereby diminished), vicarious participation in more distant events was enhanced. When subjected to careful historical scrutiny, "grand" theories about the implications of a culture of readers have been difficult to defend. More restrictive theories fare better. For example, "printed books in an educational setting signaled the abandonment of the principle that the material of knowledge and texts are dead things if they are not imprinted on the memory, or to use the biblical phrase, 'bound to the heart'."

The transformation of learners from listeners to readers, then, was a complex social and cultural phenomenon. It was also incomplete. Not until the industrial era did the concept of universal literacy take root. Nonetheless, it is generally conceded that, despite the ambiguity of its effects and its incompleteness, this transformation to learning by reading was a fundamental change in a world that was going from medieval to modern. Despite the invention and widespread utilization of other potential education-affecting technologies such as film, radio, and television, formal learning is still largely reading based today.

Computers, too, have the potential to affect how people interact with knowledge. In the western world, computers have inched their way into the curricula from kindergarten to graduate school. Their successes have been modest and their failures have been legion. Yet, even though we have not seen the full promise of networked computers, there are indications that they will enable a fundamentally different kind of interaction with knowledge. The first people to deal with computers were "programmers." As libraries of programs became available and computers became more powerful, cheaper, and friendlier, the people who interacted with them came to be called "users."

Early educational computer programs had users doing "drill and practice" exercises. These were interactive, but crude and repetitive. More recent efforts have young users interacting with the computer to develop correspondence (via e-mail), keyboarding, writing, editing, and publishing skills. Current encyclopedias on CD-ROMs represent a further step in this evolution of computer interactions. Full-text search capabilities allow instantaneous access to any word in the encyclopedia. The words are hyper-linked, which gives the user easy access to greater details on a given topic, and there are thousands of pictures, and hours of multimedia maps, movies, sounds, and narrated animations available for perusal (all for under $100).

In combination, full-text search, hypertext, multimedia and similar technologies provide a capability to interact with knowledge in a way that was unattainable before computers. They provide a user access to knowledge that is multimedia oriented and less sequential than the printed book. Connecting with the network adds three capabilities: access to a much wider array of knowledge, the potential for access to constantly-updated knowledge, and on-line help (today in the form of news groups and individuals that are available to answer questions). Serious questions asked in today's newsgroups rarely go unanswered.

Consider the auto-didact in the world of networked computers. These capabilities open up the possibility of just-in-time learning-having the ability to access information on a topic of immediate concern (the best time for learning) in ways that are self-paced and matched to a variety of learning styles. It is not too far fetched to talk about the shift from a 'reader' of printed knowledge to a much more interactively involved 'user' of knowledge and of other users (many-to-many). Whether these capabilities will be available on the "ultimate" network of computers or will be widely utilized are separate questions. It is clear from today's technology and industry focus, however, that networked computers enable a much more interactive user of knowledge. Further, that ability to interact is unique to the many-to-many communications era.

Every successful technology has unintended consequences. Sometimes the consequences are an inconvenience-cellular phones have created a tremendous burden on Forest Rangers because of the number of hikers who call asking for directions or assistance. Sometimes the unintended consequences are more serious-microwave ovens can be fatal for people with heart pacemakers. And sometimes the unintended consequences come to dominate the intended ones-Edward Tenner, for example, writes of methods for preventing forest fires that have been so effective in preserving dry underbrush that wildfires are now enormous conflagrations, destroying forests that survived lesser fires for centuries.

In the printing press era, there were efforts in both religion and science to "clean up the manuscripts"; to take the now-available copies of a variety of manuscripts and to edit and correct them into a clean copy. Briefly, the effort in religion was a failure; that in science, a success. But the more significant outcome was that, in each case, the effort to clean up the manuscript helped send its respective discipline on an importantly new trajectory.

The work of Erasmus paved the way for the Protestant Reformation and the work of Copernicus upset the entirety of Medieval cosmology. One can argue a variety of other major and minor unintended consequences, but these two absolutely dominated their respective intended consequences and arguably helped bring the European nation-states to world power. Has anything similar happened in the network age? Chris Kedzie argues there are causative links between democracy and interconnectivity. He suggests that governments who try to squelch the new information technologies to protect their monopoly on power do so at the peril of economic growth. He cites the Soviet Union having introduced or allowed new information technologies for economic reasons and found they played a role in supporting the emergence of democracy.

Less arguable are some dominating unintended consequences associated with the networking technology itself. Two have already been alluded to. The original intent of ARPANET was to share computational resources at a distance. By its second year of operation, users had "warped the computer-sharing network into a dedicated, high-speed, federally subsidized electronic post-office." The physicists at CERN who developed HTML were not trying to develop a WorldWide Web. Even Paul Baran, although he recognized early on that packet switching could lead to a large domestic communications net, was originally intent on developing a network that could withstand a nuclear attack.

A fourth dominating unintended consequence may be in the making. The Java language, that some suggest will dominate applications on the WorldWide Web and could bring the downfall of Microsoft, was originally developed for programming consumer electronic gadgets. Particularly in light of similarities with the printing press era, it would be surprising indeed if there weren't more dominating unintended consequences to come. This is not to suggest that we shouldn't take action for fear of unintended consequences. Far from it. It is to suggest that we are beyond our cause-and-effect reasoning abilities when it comes to networked computers and that we should be prepared for-and actively seeking-unintended consequences of actions we do take.

# 8

# Universal Access Communication and Information Services

## Right to Information

Information is power for development. For this reason, the right to information is an important human right. However, as many other rights, there are many pre-conditions which are related to economical, social, cultural and political development for realising the right to information. While developed countries seem to have important opportunities for the right to information, least developed countries and developing countries are far away from this right.

### *Intellectual Freedom and Right to Information*

There is a strong relationship between intellectual freedom and the right to information. In other words, the concept of the right to information is based on the concept of the freedom of information. Freedom of information means intellectual freedom. Both intellectual freedom and the right to information are human rights which protect the human life and human development. However, human rights which protect our lives need to be protected by a full democracy in the country. If there is not a full democracy, all members of the society can participate in the decision making process and for this reason they need the right to information. Unless there is a true democracy in a country, the problem of the right to information can not be solved, fully.

There is full democracy in many developing countries despite they have become a bit more democratic since 1980. In the majority of developing countries, democracy is not working completely. It is seen that only OECD (or developed) countries have established real democratic regimes. If we accept that a full democracy is a pre-condition for the right to information, it can be also said that developing countries do not have the chance to use the right to information wholly yet.

Human poverty constitutes a denial of fundamental human rights. To promote social progress and raise the standard of living within the wider concept of freedom, international human rights law... recognizes economic and social rights with the aim of attacking poverty and its consequences. Among these rights are an adequate standard of living food, housing, education, health, work, social security and a share in the benefits of social progress. These rights are "sine-non-quo" for using the right to information both on the national level and on the individual level. A man who does not have enough food, shelter, health, work, education and security does not need to use the right to informtion.

Table 1 shows that there are many countries which have not ratified or acceded some major human rights conventions. It means that these countries face the problem of human rights, and consequently the right to information.

*Table 1. Ratification status of major human rihts conventions, 1 March 1997*

| Countries that ratified Convention | Countries that have ratified or acceded | Countries have not or acceded |
|---|---|---|
| Economic, social and cultural rights, 1966 | 135 | 57 |
| Civil and political rights, 1966 | 136 | 56 |
| Elimination of discrimination against women, 1979 | 153 | 39 |
| Rights of the child, 1989 | 190 | 2 |

Source: United Nations (1997)

*Table 2. Regional aggregates of human developmend indicators*

| | Least developed Countries | Developing countries | Industrial countries |
|---|---|---|---|
| Life expectancy (years) | 50.4 | 61.8 | 74.1 |
| Adult literacy rate | 48.1 | 69.7 | 98.5 |
| Combined 1st, 2nd and 3rd level gross enrolment ratio | 36 | 56 | 83 |
| Access to health services (%) | 49 | 80 | - |
| GNP per capita (US$) | 210 | 1053 | 17221 |
| Human development index | 0.336 | 0.576 | 0.911 |

Source: United Nations (1997)

Two notions of human development can be discerned. One is on the level of the individual, the other on the national level. Table 2 shows us the regional aggregates of human development with some basic indicators and draws a profile of human development. Only educated (literate) people can use the right to information. Illiterates cannot use this right even if they need it. Srikantaiah and Dong point out that there is a definite correlation among the number of users of Internet and the GNP and the literacy rate. It can be said that there is also a definite correlation between the use of information and the literacy rate. Simply because that information user must be literate.

Ratio of enrolement by level of education by regions is a good parameter for the aspect of national level of the right to information. According to the combined 1st, 2nd and 3rd level gross enrolment ratios in Table 2, 64 % of least developed countries' population and 44 % of developing countries' population are not educated. That means, these countries cannot use the right to information and do not have such a priority. Article 29 describes the aims of education. So one has to conclude that the right to information-or in better terms: the right to access to sources of information-is related to an education aim, and put in a perspective of general education and human development.

Another negative situation is the relation of expenditures on education with %GNP. Though, least developed countries spend 3.1% of their GNP to education, this ratio is 3.8 for developing countries and 5.8 % for industrial countries (5). Unless developing (and least developed) countries increase their expenditures on education as much as industrial countries, perhaps much more, it is dificult to realize the right to information in these countries.

There is a meaningful difference in literacy rate between least developed/developing countries and developed countries. While the ratio of literacy is 98.5% for developed countries, it falls down to 69.7% for developing countries and 50.4% for least developed countries. That means half of the population of least developed countries and one third of population of developing countries cannot reach to written information. And it also means that the priority should be given to create the literate society in least developed and developing countries. One of the basic rights for a person or nation in life is to live healthily. An ill person or a country which has serious health problems on the national level does not need the right to information, as a priority. From the viewpoint of health there is a definite difference between developing and developed countries.

*Table 3. Communicate profile.*

| | Least developed Countries | Developing countries | Industrial countries |
|---|---|---|---|
| Radios (per 1.000) | 96 | 178 | 1.018 |
| Televisions (per 100) | 2 | 14 | 50 |
| Book titles published (per 100.000) | - | 7 | 52 |
| Main telephone lines (per 100) | 0.3 | 3.3 | 40.1 |
| International telephone calls (minutes per person) | 0.5 | 2.5 | 35.1 |
| Fax machines (per 100) | - | 0.1 | 2.8 |
| Internet users (per 10.000) - | 1.5 | 223.2 | |
| Personel computers (per 100) | - | - | 14.2 |

Source: United Nations (1997)

While the ratio of population with no access to health services in least developed countries is 51%, it is 20% in developing countries and less than 5% in industrial countries. These ratios show us that least developed and developing countries still have serious health problems. It will not be realistic to expect from a country which has health problems has to solve gives the priority to the problem of the right to information.

When we look at the communications profile of the developing countries and developed countries, (Table 3) it is seen that least developed and developing countries won't have the traditional media in the coming two years to 2000. 822 of 1000 persons do not have television. Book titles published per 100.00 is 7 for developing countries and 52 for industrial countries. Main telephone line per 100 is 0.3 for least developed countries, 3.3 for developing countries, but 40,1 for industrial countries. As of 1994 no daily newspapers were published in the 37 least developed and developing countries and their territories. The right to communicate is a base for the right to information. In this case, we can say that the right to information is still far away in the least developed and developing countries.

### *Population and the Right to Information*

World population is about 5.629.635.000 68% of this population is in developing countries, 10 % in least developed countries and 21% in developed countries. These ratios show that only one fifth of the world's population generally have the positive conditions for the right to information, and four fifth have many important problems which effect the solution of the right to information. For instance; while number of deaths at ages of 1-4 per 100.000 is 3128 in South Africa, it is 30 in Finland. The fundamental right for least developed and developing countries seem to be the right to live. Besides, over population in a country means many problems for it. The largest part of the world's population still live with many problems in the developing countries.

### *Libraries and the Right to Information*

Libraries, especially public libraries, as information and cultural centers have important responsibilities in safeguarding the public's right to information. When we look at the distribution of the public libraries in the world, it can be seen that there is an unequality and unbalance.

Development is the foundation which increase the public library use and consequently the right to information. Library services, and of course the right to information can be thought as a part of the national information policy. However, most of the least developed and developing countries generally do not have national information policies. Lack of a national information policy in a country affects library services and the right to information negatively.

## International Instruments for Access to Information for Knowledge

Access to information for knowledge has become a major concern of libraries serving the general public including those who cannot read conventional print materials due to vision problems, physical handicaps, dyslexia, or other disabilities. Referring the Article 27 of the Universal Declaration of Human Rights, the right of access to information has been identified as one of key factors of fundamental human rights. As globalization in all aspects of the society make people increasingly rely on information, access to information for those people with print disabilities has become more and more crucial for full participation in the society.

After the United Nations Decade of Disabled Persons, in late 1993, the UN General Conference approved the United Nations Standard Rules on the Equalization for Opportunities of Persons with Disabilities which refers the role of libraries among other cultural and educational organizations. At the same time, IFLA was also working out the UNESCO Public Library Manifesto 1994 upon request of UNESCO with an intention to attract policy makers' attention to library developments. The Manifesto was approved by UNESCO in 1994. As early as in 1990, the Section of Libraries for the Blind/IFLA started the discussion on a statement Access to Information for All which was approved by the IFLA General Conference in Barcelona, 1993, as its professional resolution.

The resolution deals with the fundamental rights on access to information of the blind and other print handicapped people and claims that the right of access to information should be clearly stated in specifically copyright related legislation of all levels to the effect that copyright protection should not prevent the access to information of people who require alternative access systems such as braille, talking books, tactile graphics, or electronic formats.

In 1995, United Nations World Summit for Social Development approved its extensive Declaration and Programme of Action with participation of major international disability organizations.

### World Summit for Social Development

United Nations World Summit for Social Development reaffirmed the rights contained in international instruments and declarations, such as the Universal Declaration of Human Rights, the Covenant on Economic, Social and Cultural Rights and the Declaration on the Right to

Development, with the recognition of the fact that more than one in ten, are people with disabilities, who are too often forced into poverty, unemployment and social isolation. One of the commitments declared by all gathered at the Summit was to "promote access for all to education, information, technology and know-how as essential means to enhancing communication and participation in civil, political, economic, social and cultural life, and ensure respect for civil, political, economic, social and cultural rights".

The Summit also recognized that the new information technologies and new approaches to the access to and use of technologies by people with disabilities and/or living in poverty can help in fulfilling social development goals. And therefore the Summit recognized the need to facilitate access to such technologies to those people. In the Programme of Action of the Summit, governmental responses are identified to include "Promoting the United Nations Standard Rules on the Equalization of Opportunities for Persons with Disabilities and developing strategies for implementing the Rules; governments, in collaboration with organizations of people with disabilities and the private sector, should work towards the equalization of opportunities, so that people with disabilities can contribute to and benefit from full participation in society; policies concerning people with disabilities should focus on their abilities rather than their disabilities and should ensure their dignity as citizens".

In order to implement and monitor the Programme of Action, at the national level, appropriate measures and mechanisms for implementing and monitoring the outcome of the Summit are to be adopted. At the international level, it was decided that the United Nations General Assembly should hold a special session in the year 2000 for an overall review and appraisal of the implementation of the outcome of the Summit and consider further actions and initiatives. The World Blind Union delivered a joint statement on behalf of international disability organizations including World Federation of the Deaf, International League of Societies for Persons with Mental Handicap, Rehabilitation International, and Disabled Peoples' International as follows:

" All the themes of this Summit are highly relevant to us. We are the poorest of the poor in most societies. Disability increases poverty and poverty increases disability. It is women who bear a particular burden of poverty, both as carers and as disabled persons. Two thirds of disabled people are estimated to be without employment. Social exclusion and isolation are the day to day experiences of disabled persons. Too many must live in institutions. We cannot and we will not tolerate such conditions any longer. Disabled people must be included in the decisions, and above all, in the follow-up of the implementation of the plan of action of this Summit..."

### *UN Standard Rules*

Standard Rules on the Equalization of Opportunities for Persons with Disabilities is a United Nations resolution adopted on 20 December 1993. With good reasons, the UN Standard Rules stresses the crucial importance of access to information services and documentation. Definition of the equalization of opportunity emphasizes the concern on accessibility to information.

The term "equalization of opportunities" means the process through which the various systems of society and the environment, such as services, activities, information and documentation, are made available to all, particularly to persons with disabilities. In spite of its importance, so far UN Standard Rules is not yet well recognized among librarians. However, the UN Standard Rules give strong support for efforts to make library services accessible to people with disabilities. The following is the most important part of the Rules related to information provision.

— The Rule 5 is designated to Access to information and communication. The primary responsibility of the state government is confirmed in this rule. Availability of access to "computerized information and service system" is demanded in this rule.

— 6. States should develop strategies to make information services and documentation accessible for different groups of persons with disabilities. Braille, tape services, large print and other appropriate technologies should be used to provide access to written information and documentation for persons with visual impairments...

— 10. States should ensure that new computerized information and service systems offered to the general public are either made initially accessible or are adapted to be made accessible to persons with disabilities.

— 11. Organizations of persons with disabilities should be consulted when measures to make information services accessible are being developed.

Libraries are identified in the Rule 10 as follows:

States will ensure that persons with disabilities are integrated into and can participate in cultural activities on an equal basis.

— States should ensure that persons with disabilities have the opportunity to utilize their creative, artistic and intellectual potential, not only for their own benefit, but also for the enrichment of their community, be they in urban or rural areas. Examples of such activities are dance, music, literature, theatre, plastic arts, painting and sculpture. Particularly in developing countries, emphasis should be placed on traditional and contemporary art forms, such as puppetry, recitation and story-telling.

- States should promote the accessibility to and availability of places for cultural performances and services, such as theatres, museums, cinemas and libraries, to persons with disabilities.

- In Rule 14, in addition to ultimate responsibility of states, those who are in charge of information provision are encouraged to accept responsibility for policy-making and planning to make their programmes available to persons with disabilities.

## UNESCO Public Library Manifesto

> "Freedom, prosperity and the development of society and of individuals are fundamental human values. They will only be attained through the ability of well-informed citizens to exercise their democratic rights and to play an active role in society. Constructive participation and the development of democracy depend on satisfactory education as well as on free and unlimited access to knowledge, thought, culture and information."

Unesco Public Library Manifesto, which was prepared by the IFLA, clearly states one of key issues of current information society, in which availability of information may limit or expand the potential role of a person in the community. With the recognition of this key issue, the Manifesto identifies the roles of the public library as follows, quote from the Manifesto:

> "The Public library is the local centre of information, making all kinds of knowledge and information readily available to its users. The services of the public library are provided on the basis of equality of access for all, regardless of age, race, sex, religion, nationality, language or social status. Specific services and materials must be provided for those users who cannot, for whatever reason, use the regular services and materials, for example linguistic minorities, people with disabilities or people in hospital or prison."

The Manifesto is neither an international convention nor a treaty. As you have noticed, the implementation of the manifesto relies on efforts of those who support it. The Manifesto is an international measure to improve and secure access to information through libraries for all general public including people with disabilities. Although the Manifesto is titled "Public Library Manifesto", the basic concept of the Manifesto is shared by all libraries serving the general public including those with disabilities.

## UNESCO and an Information Society for All

The United Nations Educational, Scientific and Cultural Organization (UNESCO) is mandated by its 184 Member States inter alia to promote the free flow of ideas by word and image and to foster international co-operation in the fields of communication, information and informatics in order to narrow the existing gap between the developed and the developing countries in these areas. UNESCO's medium-term strategy for 1996-2001 foresees a special focus on the application of communication and information technologies for development, democracy and peace. The present document gives an overview of the opportunities and challenges related to these technologies and outlines a framework for UNESCO action.

## *Opportunities and Challenges*

The dramatic acceleration in the development and use of information and communication technologies during the last few years has set in motion a worldwide process of transition from the "Industrial" to the "Information Society". The depth and non-linearity of this process seem to have much greater social, economic and cultural implications for humanity than the industrial revolution of the past. Business, education, training, research, entertainment - indeed, all aspects of life - are increasingly affected by electronic networks and multimedia technologies, which are opening up new opportunities and challenges for all.

As we move towards the third millennium, it is of the utmost importance to understand and to influence the fundamental changes brought about by the "communication and information revolution". The complexity and interrelation of today's world problems defy traditional explanations and solutions and require a completely new approach which must be both comprehensive and interdisciplinary. Moreover, individuals, groups and communities will need to develop not only new tools of analysis but also very different mentalities and attitudes in order to adapt to the emerging "new" civilization based on information and knowledge.

At the heart of this transformation are technological advances which include the digitalization of various types of information - text, numbers, sound and images - and their integration into a single commodity, so-called "multimedia"; artificial intelligence and the incorporation of user-tailored, interactive interfaces into information products and services; digital compression and switching techniques which facilitate the communication of ever greater volumes of information; an exponential increase in computing power coupled with dramatic reductions in cost; communication satellites with vastly increased power and accessibility, inexpensive optic fibre cable and new wireless technologies; and, perhaps most impressively, the explosive growth of computer networks and, in particular, of the largest among them, the Internet, which links millions of individual computers and users all over the world.

This combination and interaction of technologies is resulting in new products and services based on video, advanced image and voice processing, powerful techniques for automating information retrieval and routine transactions of all sorts, which are increasingly becoming accessible worldwide through interoperable networks. These "new" technologies - or, to be more exact, the new uses of technologies - are stimulating the convergence of industries. In industrialized countries, the last few years have seen strategic moves towards partnerships and alliances among cable companies, telecommunication operators, broadcasting networks and computer, publishing and entertainment enterprises. Markets for new information and interactive services are being aggressively explored and developed, as information providers and carriers seek to expand their activities beyond their traditional borders.

Most important of all, there is now a political will in many countries to support and encourage these processes. New legal frameworks and standards are being set up to promote the development and interconnection of national information infrastructures. Well-conceived information highways would further stimulate the already burgeoning national and international markets for information services and products. Today the industrialized countries have an overwhelming lead in all these advances, while for a great number of developing nations even "old" technologies, like television, telephone or even electricity, are still only a dream. However, a closer look reveals that the new information and communication technologies offer immense opportunities to all societies and individuals for alternative, truly universal and often cheaper ways of accessing and disseminating information.

Examples already abound of developing countries' using information technology in education or health to help break the vicious circle of poverty and isolation, or leapfrogging heavy industrialization by the creation of new sectors of sustainable economic development like software production or data processing. The importance of the information revolution has been recognised at the highest political levels in many developing countries. One recent example is the resolution of the Conference of African Ministers responsible for Economic and Social Development and Planning to set up a High-Level Working Group of African experts to develop a regional plan of action on information technologies—called Africa's Information Society Initiative—and to mobilize the necessary financial resources for its implementation.

The concerns of developing countries regarding their participation in the Information Society thus bear less on whether it should be accorded high priority, than on how to effectively apply information technologies to development so as to reduce, rather than widen and deepen the gap between "haves" and "have-nots" and worsen inequality across the technological divide. The major problems are posed not by the technologies as such, which can in general be acquired and adapted if appropriate resources are mobilized, but rather by political, social, organizational and ethical issues involved.

Whether humanity as a whole is to benefit from these opportunities will depend not only on the transfer of technology, but first and foremost on enhancing human capability to make the best possible use of information technology. Only on that condition can the Information Society hope to attain its ultimate goal - empowerment of all its citizens through access to and use of knowledge.

### *Opportunities for Development*

The economic and commercial opportunities of information highways are certainly significant, but the impact of information technologies on sectors of public concern is perhaps of even greater significance. Of particular interest and relevance to UNESCO is the impact of information highways and multimedia technologies on "intellectual" areas which are at the core of the development process. In the field of education, information technologies are viewed as a means of complementing traditional educational techniques to enable education systems to adapt to the different learning and training needs of societies. Computer simulation, telematics, and teleconferencing, alongside educational TV or radio, have great potential to reach larger audiences than the traditional classroom process, and to make learning more effective, attractive and stimulating.

The increasing variety of interactive media (e.g. compact disks and interactive TV) enlarges the scope and possibilities of self-directed learning. These tools provide an unparalleled opportunity for "reaching the unreached", particularly the 900 million illiterates in the world and the 130 million children unable to attend primary school, and for making lifelong education for all feasible, particularly for learners for whom access is limited by time and space, age, socio-cultural environment, work schedules and physical or mental handicaps. Modern distance education systems, of which UNESCO's "Learning without Frontiers" initiative is a forerunner, can not only give learners access to knowledge available in different parts of the world, but also ensure dialogue - the main factor in effective learning - both among learners and between learners and sources of learning.

Scientific research, where computer networks and many telematics applications originally developed, remains one of their most active consumers. For scientists, the major advantage of information highways is the possibility to access, disseminate scientific information and share research facilities more quickly, on a larger scale and in a more interactive way. Research groups in the natural and social sciences will increasingly become "virtual" - composed of interconnected specialists working on the same problem in different parts of the world. Electronic publishing will provide faster and cheaper access to the scientific literature, and facilitate the maintenance of an international archive of scientific accomplishments. These trends will be particularly beneficial to scientists in developing nations who would otherwise not have easy access to laboratories, documentation and databases; they will provide new opportunities to collaborate with colleagues elsewhere in the world, and mitigate, if not solve, the problem of South-to-North brain-drain.

In the field of environment, information technology will help to expand humanity's capacities to understand and manage physical and ecological processes, and to forecast and respond to disasters and catastrophes. The Global Observing Systems for environmental monitoring, being set up through a UN system-wide initiative in which UNESCO has a major role, are possible only because of advances in data sensing, processing, communication and presentation. Information technologies will also enable the establishment of better disaster warning systems and systems to help plan and coordinate response and relief efforts; the function of these systems to limit mortality, injury and loss of property will be facilitated by seamless links with the communication media available in the home and workplace.

In the field of culture, multimedia technologies already offer tremendous possibilities for the promotion and sharing of physical and non-physical cultural heritage. The availability of multimedia cultural products and services on information highways will provide limitless possibilities for everyone to enjoy the world's culture in all its diversity. At any time, one will be able to listen to a concert or visit a museum in a virtual mode without the necessity of travelling or queuing. Moreover, three-dimensional imaging and interactive interfaces open up vast new horizons for experimental art. On the whole, these technologies have an immense potential for enhancing cultural identities, promoting intercultural dialogue and stimulating artistic creativity.

The mass media have already adopted major technological innovations such as electronic editing and generation of images in TV programme production, as well as computerized and communication-assisted publishing of the printed press. Interactive television and multimedia open up yet unexplored perspectives not only for entertainment, but also for educational and cultural programmes and for the popularization of science, and are likely to enhance the role of public service broadcasting. News agencies are obvious beneficiaries of computer-based technologies which allow more efficient news production and distribution. If the rapidly developing media technologies are made available over a truly universal broadband network, the media's capacity to provide information and entertainment will increase almost beyond imagination.

Libraries - whether school, university, public or specialized - are certainly destined to play an ever greater role in the dissemination of knowledge and experience. Computerized and interconnected, they will be able to pool their resources and provide to their clients access to immense stores of information. Moreover, they are ideally placed to serve as public gateways to information highways, providing as they do both access and guidance and training to users. Archives will adapt their storage and preservation function to the impermanence of digital information which in many cases will replace paper documents. They will also become increasingly involved in electronic information provision as their clientele in government, research and the general public develops ever more sophisticated needs.

Professional and institutional distinctions in the dissemination of information and education will blur as new services develop and gain ground, driven by a market of aware and active citizens. While the focus for these services in industrialized countries will be the home and the workplace, in many developing countries, especially in rural areas, community-level access will be particularly important. Community tele-centres offering library, information and media access, social services like education and telemedicine and fora for participatory democracy, as well as personal communication facilities, will become possible, based on the cooperative organization of services and on enabling "last-mile" communication technologies.

### *Challenges to Society*

At the centre of the challenge posed by the emerging Information Society is the concept of universal service and how a "right to communicate" will evolve in a digital world where the basic services required by all citizens are becoming more extensive and complex. Access in this context involves not only physical availability and cost, but also ensuring that the user can benefit from the services concerned, through a minimum level of "digital literacy" and through appropriately adapted interfaces. In the increasingly competitive and commercial world of information and communication, the risks of exclusion of disadvantaged populations are substantial - both within and among societies. These risks are of particular concern to the developing countries which need clear and resourceful policies if they are to benefit from the emerging communication revolution.

An important facet of the "right to communicate" concerns access to telematics facilities at affordable cost by the "intellectual" sectors - education, science, culture, media, libraries and archives - which have a crucial role to play in the development of national information infrastructures. A study jointly carried out by the International Telecommunication Union (ITU) and UNESCO,,, offered a promising three-fold strategy to be pursued collaboratively in this context: (i) cooperation among the users in order to consolidate their demand for telematics services, (ii) partnership between telecommunication operators and users to develop and expand services based on market principles, and (iii) enlightened public policies to promote the building and use of telematics infrastructure in development-related sectors.

Another important issue is the maintenance of linguistic and cultural diversity in the Information Society. Technology-induced globalization is seen by many as a threat to local customs, values and beliefs, as exemplified by that fact that, today, 90% of the databases on the Internet are in English. Technology also offers possibilities for the development of specialized services to cater for diverse cultural needs and there is every reason to suppose that these will flourish where legitimate cultural, educational or scientific demands exist. These advantages are, however, counterbalanced by a danger that these groups of media users may prefer cultural specificity to diversity and dialogue, and thus run the risk of shutting themselves into a cultural ghetto. At the same time, it must be kept in mind that many small or even medium-sized countries do not have the critical mass, in either economic or demographic terms, to guarantee adequate national content and may thus largely depend on imported programmes and services. The rapid development of broadcasting technology and its convergence with computing and telecommunication give this issue a new complexity.

Increased access to interconnected networks and databases raises major ethical and legal issues. These include: privacy of information and the right of individuals to check data pertaining to themselves, which is widely recognized as a fundamental human right; regulation of content of information circulating through information highways (e.g. information of an intolerant, racist, violent or pornographic nature, and particularly its access by children); computer piracy and other informatics crimes; and copyright where efforts are required to extend legitimate intellectual property protection to the rapidly changing multimedia digital environment while maintaining access to information needed to promote societal and economic development. In all of these cases, the risks and advantages of coercive measures should be carefully weighed, and other solutions, for example involving consumer action or voluntary codes of conduct of information professionals, may well prove to be more attractive. This issue is not fundamentally altered by the fact that information technologies themselves are providing partial solutions to these problems.

The effects of computer technology on individuals and their social behaviour are also controversial. Already today, one can do almost anything on a computer: study, work, shop, watch a film or chat with a friend, visit a library or a museum, read a newspaper or play games. This provides immense opportunities for access, but it can also unduly privilege the "man-machine" relationship to the detriment of reflection, self-reliance and personal capacity-building. At a wider level, the emerging information highways constitute an important factor in major social transformations, such as the internationalization of trade and the development of a world economic market, the globalization of news and personal communication, and changes in the labour force due to the increased use of telematics. The risks associated with many of these phenomena are poorly understood, and deeper scientific analysis will be needed before they can be adequately considered by policy-makers.

Under its Constitution, UNESCO is required to contribute to "advancing the mutual knowledge and understanding of peoples, through all means of mass communication", "to promote the free flow of ideas by word and image", to "maintain, increase and diffuse knowledge", and to "give fresh impulse to popular education and to the spread of culture". With the advent of the information age, these tasks have not only retained their relevance but, indeed, have taken on a new urgency, and concrete ways to fulfill them will need to be adapted to the new technological environment. In an era where the distinction between different forms of information is blurring, the principle of the "free flow of information" - which until recently had been considered only in terms of mass media - must inevitably be applied to all types of information needed for the advancement of education, science, culture, peace and democracy.

Once accessible to all - irrespective of race, nationality, gender, location, occupation or social status - information and communication technologies can be instrumental for achieving a truly human-centred development. It is true that economic and commercial interests now seem to be the main driving force for the building of information highways. But it is also obvious that culture, education and science, as distinct and integral parts of our civilization, cannot be left totally at the mercy of market forces. Information highways must not simply provide new and more powerful channels for electronic consumption. They must have large spaces for knowledge and value sharing, artistic creation and public debate. Just as the existing media do, new electronic networks must transmit the widest possible variety of opinions together with information which may not be commercially profitable or may interest only minority groups.

In this regard, it is of the utmost importance to reaffirm the mission of public service media to meet the very basic educational, scientific and cultural needs of people in the new technological environment. The above conceptual framework is reflected in UNESCO's current Medium-Term Strategy and biennial programme which foresee that the Organization, in collaboration with the United Nations system and the international community at large, will:

— as part of its international intellectual co-operation function,

— encourage and facilitate the analysis of the societal impacts of communication and information technologies;

— contribute to the conception and promotion of international policies for the development of information highways, destined to embrace the developing countries in the Information Society and to avoid new types of exclusion within nations due to economic or other barriers;

— facilitate international debate on the human rights issues of the coming information age, including the rights to information access and to information privacy;

— promote international reflection on major ethical and cultural issues concerning information highways, including those related to content, in particular its cognitive dimension and the social acceptability of information of intolerant, racist, violent or pornographic nature;

— participate in the process of reviewing copyright and intellectual property conventions to ensure that they remain relevant and effective in the emerging information society;

— catalyze reflection on the issue of artistic integrity and moral rights which are endangered by new technological possibilities for distortion and for distribution of distorted works;

— encourage the development and dissemination of methods for handling and accessing information in the fields of education, science, culture and communication;

— reaffirm the mission of the public service media to meet the very basic educational, scientific and cultural needs of people in the new technological environment; and, as part of its technical assistance function,

— assist Member States in elaborating national policies and regional strategies for optimum use of and access to information through modern technology, and in creating conditions conducive to the development of electronic cultural industries;

— promote, for example through pilot projects and training, the use of information networks and innovative multimedia technologies to foster development in the Organization's fields of competence, in particular as regards:

— free flow of information in the fields of education, science, culture and communication, and the new role of libraries, especially public libraries, as gateways to electronic information;

— distance education and innovative approaches to non-formal and lifelong education and learning,—virtual scientific laboratories, in which researchers from developing and developed countries can collaborate through telecommunications and telematics on common projects;

— production and dissemination of diverse cultural products as a contribution to intercultural understanding and dialogue.

This strategy is designed to enable UNESCO to play its moral and intellectual role vis-à-vis the emerging Information Society, taking account of the educational, scientific and cultural needs of all nations and individuals and promoting a genuine symbiosis of cultures based on mutual respect and enrichment.

## 9

# International Information Agencies

In journalism, news agencies are bodies established to supply news reports to newspapers, magazines, and radio and television broadcasters. They are also known as wire services. News agencies can be either corporations that sell news, cooperatives composed of newspapers that share their articles with each other, commercial newswire services which charge organisations to distribute their news or government agencies. News agencies generally prepare articles that can be used by other news organizations with little or no modification, and then sell them to other news organizations. They provide these articles in bulk electronically through wire services (originally they used telegraphy; today they frequently use the Internet). Corporations, individuals, analysts and intelligence agencies can also subscribe. News agencies are distinct from news syndicates that distribute comic strips and other editorial material, such as columns and features, and also from PR services that distribute press releases.

### International News Agencies

Prominent international news agencies include:

— Agence France-Presse
— Associated Press (founded in 1848)
— Reuters
— The Press Association (UK)
— Canadian Press
— Canadian University Press (founded in 1938)
— Kyodo
— ITAR-TASS, Russia
— China News Service,China
— United Press International
— ANP (The Netherlands)
— DPA (Germany)
— Xinhua News Agency, China
— Yonhap, Korea
— Australian Associated Press

### Agence France-Presse

*Agence France-Presse* (abbreviated *AFP*) is the oldest news agency in the world. It is also the largest French agency and the third largest news agency in the world.

It is based in Paris, with regional centres in Washington, Hong Kong, Nicosia and Montevideo and bureaux in 110 countries. It sends out news in French, English, Arabic, Spanish, German, Portuguese and Russian.

AFP was founded in 1835 by Charles-Louis Havas as *Agence Havas*.

AFP is a nonprofit corporation autonomous chartered under a specific 1957 law, operating commercially and independently of the French government. It is administered by a CEO and a board comprising of 15 members:

— 8 representatives of the French press;

— 2 representatives of the AFP personnel;

— 2 representatives of the public services of radio and television;

— 3 representatives from the public services subscribing to the agency (one named by the prime minister, another by the minister of finances, another by the Minister of foreign affairs).

The board elects the CEO for a renewable term of three years.

AFP also has a superior council charged with ensuring that the agency operates according to its statuses, which mandate absolute independence and neutrality.

The primary client of AFP is the French government, which purchases subscriptions for its various services. In practice, those subscriptions are somewhat a subsidy to AFP, which is insecure financially.

### *Associated Press*

Among them China, Colombia, Republic of Korea, and Botswana. During this period, China and Korea were the fastest growing economies with average per capita GNP growth rates of 7.6 and 8.5% respectively.

The Associated Press, or AP, is an American news agency that claims to be the world's oldest and largest. The AP is a cooperative owned by its contributing newspapers, who both contribute stories to it and use material written by its staffers.

As of 2004, AP's news is used by 1,700 newspapers, in addition to 5,000 television and radio outlets. Its photo library consists of over 10 million images.

The collapse of United Press International, AP's traditional competitor, has left it as the only national news service in the US. Only a few foreign challengers, such as Reuters, exist for English-language news coverage. It is so omnipresent that the Associated Press Stylebook has become the *de facto* standard for news-writing in the country.

AP was formed in May 1848 by representatives of six competitive New York newspapers, who wanted to pool resources to collect news from Europe. Until then, newspapers competed by sending reporters out in rowboats to meet the ships as they arrived in the harbor. The following year it opened the first overseas bureau, in Halifax, Nova Scotia, to meet ships from Europe before they docked in New York City.

In 1861, facing censorship in covering the American Civil War, reporters first filed under the anonymous byline "from the Associated Press agent."

In 1876, Mark Kellogg, a stringer, becomes the first AP correspondent to die in the line of duty, at the Battle of Little Bighorn. His final dispatch: "I go with Custer and will be at the death."

In 1899, AP uses Guglielmo Marconi's wireless telegraph to cover the America's Cup yacht race off Sandy Hook, New Jersey the first news test of the new telegraph.

In 1914, AP introduced the Teletype, which transmited directly to printers over telegraph wires. Eventually a worldwide network of 60-word-per-minute Teletypes was built up.

### Reuters

Reuters is a company supplying global financial markets and news media with a range of information products and transactional solutions, including real-time and historical market data, research and analytics, financial trading platforms, investment data and analytics plus news in text, video, graphics and photographs.

The company was founded by Paul Julius Reuter, a pioneer of telegraphy services. In 1940, there was a Hollywood film about Reuter: A Dispatch from Reuters. Edward G. Robinson played the German-Jewish immigrant to London who as early as 1851 began transmitting stock-market quotes between Paris and London via the new Calais-Dover telegraph cable.

Reuter's agency built a reputation in Europe for being the first to report scoops from abroad, like the news of Abraham Lincoln's assassination. Today, almost every major news outlet in the world subscribes to Reuters. It operates in 200 cities in 94 countries. Reuters supplies text in 19 languages.

Reuters was floated as a public company in 1984 on the London Stock Exchange and on NASDAQ in the US.

Reuters continued to grow rapidly, widening the range of its business products and expanding its global reporting network for media, financial and economic services. Recent key product launches include Equities 2000 (1987), Dealing 2000-2 (1992), Business Briefing (1994), Reuters Television for the financial markets (1994), 3000 Series (1996) and the Reuters 3000 Xtra service (1999).

In the mid-1990s the company had a brief foray into the radio sector with London Radio's two stations, London News 97.3 FM and London News Talk 1152 AM, which replaced LBC in 1994. A Reuters Radio News service was also set up to compete with Independent Radio News.

In 1995, Reuters established its 'Greenhouse Fund' to take minority investments in a range of start-up technology companies, initially in the United States.

In July 1999 TIBCO completed an IPO on NASDAQ; Reuters retains a substantial proportion of the shares. Reuters announced in early 2000 a range of major initiatives designed to accelerate its use of internet technologies, open new markets and migrate its core business to an internet-based model.

### *Canadian Press*

The Canadian Press is a Canadian news agency established in 1917 as a vehicle to distribute Associated Press material to Canadian news media, mainly because it was very difficult to spread news across such a huge country, covering many time zones. It was important around this time to tell the news from overseas during World War I. Today, it is owned by many of Canada's own multimedia content provider companies. A French service was established in 1951. The CP has over 600 offices around the world and employs over 300 journalists.

Broadcast News is an arm of the Canadian Press. BN is the primarily broadcast section of the company, while CP focuses on print articles for newspapers and the web.

In the past few years, CP has covered such events as the 2002 Winter Olympics, the 2004 Stanley Cup, and the power outage crisis on both sides of the border in 2003 to name a few. When covering major events, CP mostly relies on the Associated Press, but their own reporters get Canadian comment to the event.

### *Canadian University Press*

Canadian University Press is a non-profit co-operative and newswire service owned by about 65 student newspapers at post-secondary schools in Canada. Founded in 1938, CUP is the oldest student newswire service in the world and the oldest national student organization in North America. Many successful Canadian journalists got their starts in CUP and its member papers. Its head office is in Toronto.

A national conference, which doubles as an annual general meeting, is held once a year in a different city. Each region holds two conferences a year as well. Each member paper exercises one vote at conferences. The president and national bureau chief are elected at the national conference, or Nash, while the regional CUPboard members and bureau chiefs are elected at the regional conferences.

Member papers contribute articles to the CUP wire, which also runs stories authored by CUP staff. There are news, features, opinions, arts, sports, graphics and supplements wires. After stories are edited by the national bureau chief, they are made available on the wire for publication in CUP member papers.

CUP wholly owns a multi-market ad placement agency, Canadian University Press Media Services Limited, which operates as Campus Plus, offering advertisers one-stop access to student newspapers.

### *Kyodo*

Kyodo News is a nonprofit cooperative news agency based

in Minato-ku, Tokyo. It was established in 1945 and it distributes news to almost all newspapers, and radio and television networks in Japan. The newspapers using its news have about 50 million subscribers. The subdivision Kyodo News International founded in 1982 is located in Rockefeller Center, New York. Their online newspaper is multilingual in Japanese, Chinese (Simplified and Traditional), and English.

### *ITAR-TASS*

ITAR-TASS, Information Telegraph Agency of Russia, is the major news agency of the Russian Federation.Its origin is in a letter sent by Finance Minister V. N. Kokovtsev to foreign minister on March 26, 1904 writing that "our trade and industrial circles, as well as the Finance Ministry, are ever more in need of an independent exchange of information with foreign countries by telegraph and of a way to make internal business developments widely-known".

In July 1904 a meeting was held about the setting up of an official Telegraph Agency. St. Petersburg Telegraph Agency (SPTA). The new agency's purpose was "to distribute political, financial, economic, trade, and other information of public interest within the country and abroad...". The St. Petersburg Telegraph Agency began work on September 1, 1904. On August 19, 1914 Petrograd Telegraph Agency (PTA) was decreed by the government to become the central news agency of the state.

On September 7, 1918 PTA was renamed into Russian Telegraph Agency (ROSTA). And on 25 July 1925 it became the Telegraph Agency of the Soviet Union or Telegrafnoe agentstvo Sovetskogo Soiuza (TASS) by decree of the Presidium of the Central Executive Committee of the USSR.

During the Soviet era TASS was the only source of news for all Soviet newspapers, radio and television stations. During the mid 1980s when TASS was at its peak, there were 14 affiliates in the Union republics:

— Ratau (Ukraine)

— Belta (Byelorussia)

— Uztag(Uzbekistan)

— Kaztag (Kazakhstan)

— Gruzinform (Georgia)

— Azerinform (Azerbaijan)

— Elta (Lithuania)

— Atem (Moldavia)

— Latinform (Latvia)

— Kirtag (Kirghizia)

— Tajikta (Tajikistan)

— Armenpress (Armenia)

— Turkmeninform (Turkmenia)

— Eta (Estonia)

TASS had bureaus and correspondents in 110 countries, with a daily output equal of 750 newspaper pages, translated into eight languages. It had nearly 5000 workers, with about a fifth being journalists.

In 1992, following the collapse of the Soviet Union, the name was changed to the Information Telegraph Agency of Russia - ITAR-TASS. It is still state-funded, and according to its website now produces about 700 newspaper pages per day, just under its Soviet peak. It has 74 bureaus and offices in Russia and other CIS countries and 65 bureaus in 62 foreign countries.

### *China News Service (CNS)*

The China News Service is the second largest news agency in Mainland China. (The Xinhua News Agency is largest.) CNS serves mainly overseas Chinese and residents of Hong Kong, Macau, and Taiwan.

CNS was established in 1952. Today, China News Service has established news offices and stations in every province in mainland China and in HK and Macau. CNS also has news offices in foreign countries, such as the U.S.A, Japan, France, and Australia.

### *United Press International (UPI)*

United Press International (UPI) is a global news agency headquartered in the United States filing news in English, Spanish and Arabic. Once one of the three biggest news agencies in the world, with Associated Press and Reuters, it has dwindled in size and continues to redefine itself.

Newspaper publisher E.W. Scripps combined three regional news services into the United Press Associations, which began service on July 15, 1907. Scripps founded United Press on the principle that there should be no restrictions on who could buy news from a news service. This formula made UP a direct threat to the monopolistic and exclusionary alliances of the major U.S. and European wire services at the time.

UP's announcement on July 15 said: "It is announced that the United Press will not be run on narrow or monopolistic lines, but will seek to give fair and impartial service to all legitimate newspaper publishers in the field."

Scripps later said: "I regard my life's greatest service to the people of this country to be the creation of the United Press," because the competition provided by UP prevented the Associated Press from having a monopoly in determining what news was provided to the public.

On May 24, 1958, United Press merged with International News Service, which had been formed in 1909 by newspaper publisher William Randolph Hearst, to become United Press International. UPI, in later 1958, launches the UPI Audio Network, the first wire service radio network.

UPI was hurt by changes in the modern news business, including the closing of many of America's afternoon newspapers, and was unprofitable for years. It went through seven owners between 1992 and 2000, when it was acquired by News World Communications, owner of the Washington Times. UPI's chief correspondent and most famous reporter, Helen Thomas, promptly resigned in protest of the Times' links to the Unification Church.

News people who work for UPI are nicknamed "Unipressers." Famous Unipressers from UPI's include journalists Walter Cronkite, David Brinkley, Howard K. Smith, Eric Sevareid, and William L. Shirer, who is best remembered today for writing Rise and Fall of the Third Reich. Helen Thomas retired after 57 years as UPI's Chief White House Correspondent was known as the "Dean of the White House Press Corps". Merriman Smith reported first-hand the deaths of two presidents, being in Warm Springs, Georgia when Franklin Roosevelt suffered his fatal stroke, and in Dallas, Texas with John F. Kennedy's motorcade when he was shot. His coverage of the assassination won him the Pulitzer Prize.

Arnaud De Borchgrave, Newsweek's chief foreign correspondent for 25 years, covering more than 90 countries and 17 wars, is currently UPI Editor-at-Large.

In 1908 UP pioneered the transmission of feature stories and use of reporter bylines. In 1914 Edward Kleinschmidt invented the teletype, which replaced Morse code clickers in delivering news to newspapers. Press critic Oswald Garrison Villard credits United Press with first use of the teletype.

In 1935 UP was the first major news service to offer news to broadcasters. 1945 saw it launch the first all-sports wire. In 1951 United Press offered the first teletypesetter (TTS) service, enabling newspapers to automatically set and justify type from wire transmissions. In 1952 United Press launched the first international television news film service.

On April 19, 1979, UPI announced an agreement with Telecomputing Corp. of America to make the UPI world news report available to owners of home computers. Later UPI was the first news service to provide news to dial-up services such as Prodigy and world-wide web search pioneers Yahoo! and Excite!

In 1982 UPI pioneered an eight-level Custom Coding system that allows clients to choose stories based on topic, subtopic and location. Developing one of the first news taxonomies, UPI use of meta-data helped define how information was categorized and customized to the user.

### *American Nazi Party (ANP)*

The American Nazi Party was an American Neo-Nazi political party formed in February 1959 by George Lincoln Rockwell. The organization was based largely upon the ideals and policies of the NSDAP in Germany during the

Third Reich. Following the assassination of Rockwell in 1967 by a disgruntled party member the group was taken over by Matt Koehl who renamed it the National Socialist White People's Party. In 1970, NSWPP member Frank Collin broke away from the group and founded the National Socialist Party of America which became famous due to its attempt to march through the largely Jewish community of Skokie, Illinois. The original American Nazi party never had more than 200 members despite its relatively high profile.

More recently a new American Nazi Party has been launched and is largely regarded as extremist, even for a fascist organisation. The new group claims to be the inheritor of Rockwell's legacy and is led by Rocky Suhayda. It was formerly known as the European American Education Association and is based in Eastpointe, Michigan. They use the Fourteen Words as their motto.

### *Deutsche Presse Agentur (DPA)*

Deutsche Presse Agentur (DPA) was founded 1949 in Germany and has grown to be a major worldwide service to print media, radio, television, online, mobile phones and national news agencies. News is available in German, English, Spanish and Arabic.

### *Xinhua News Agency*

The Xinhua News Agency is the official press agency of the government of the People's Republic of China and the biggest center for collecting information and press conferences in the PRC with a rank of class A among the world wide news agencies. The National Propaganda Department appoints publishers, chief editors, and other key officials of the above-mentioned newspapers—plus a few others—while provincial and local party leaders make similar appointments for party papers in their jurisdictions. It is an institution of the State Council of China.

It is one of the two news agencies in mainland China; (the other one is the China News Service). In many ways, Xinhua is the fuel propelling China's print media. Perhaps unique in the world because of its role, size, and reach, Xinhua reports directly to the party's Propaganda Department; employs more than 10,000 people—as compared to about 1,300 for the UK's Reuters, for example; has 107 bureaus worldwide both collecting information on other countries and dispensing information about China; and maintains 31 bureaus in China—one for each province plus a military bureau. Inasmuch as most of the newspapers in China cannot afford to station correspondents abroad—or even in every Chinese province—they rely on Xinhua feeds to fill their pages. People's Daily, for example, uses Xinhua material for approximately 25 percent of its stories. Xinhua is a publisher as well as a news agency—it owns more than 20 newspapers and a dozen magazines, and it prints in Chinese, English, and four other languages.

Like other government entities, Xinhua is feeling the pinch of reduced State financial subsidies. Beijing has been cutting funding to the news agency by an average of seven percent per year over the past three years, and State funds currently cover only about 40 percent of Xinhua's costs. As a result, the agency is raising revenues through involvement in public relations, construction, and information service businesses.

In the past, Xinhua was able to attract the top young journalists emerging from the universities or otherwise newly entering the field, but it can no longer do so as easily because of the appeal and resources of other newspapers and periodicals and the greater glamour of television and radio jobs. For example, midlevel reporters for the Xinmin Evening News often are given an apartment, whereas at Xinhua and People's Daily this benefit is reserved for the most senior journalists.

The Xinhua press agency was started in November 1931 as the Red China News Agency and changed to its current name in 1937. It began broadcasting to foreign countries in English from 1944.

The headquarter of Xinhua is located in Beijing. Xinhua News Agency established its first filiale abroad in 1948. Now it distributes its news in Asia, Middle East, Latin America, Africa where run the superior offices; in Hong Kong, Macau and many foreign countries and districts. It has more that one hundred Xinhua's filiales.

Today, Xinhua News Agency delivers its news across the world in 7 languages including Chinese, English, French, Russia, Spanish, Arab, etc., as well as news pictures and other kinds of news. It has made contracts to exchange news and news pictures with more than eighty foreign news agency or political news department.

Unlike the People's Daily, which is an organization of the Communist Party of China rather than of the PRC government, Xinhua rarely offers editorials, but rather passes through speeches by government officials. Its position set as a platform of receiving and distributing the information all over the world and thus it covers the world news, live news and exclusive reports.

Like many other media organizations, Xinhua struggled to find the "right line" to use in covering the Tiananmen Square events of April-June 1989. Although more cautious than People's Daily in its treatment of sensitive topics during that period—such as how to commemorate reformist

Communist Party leader Hu Yaobang's April 1989 death, the then ongoing demonstrations in Beijing and elsewhere, and basic questions of press freedom and individual rights—Xinhua gave some favorable coverage to demonstrators and intellectuals who were questioning top party leaders. Even so, many Xinhua reporters were angry with top editors for not going far enough and for suppressing stories about the Tiananmen Square crackdown. For several days after the violence on 4 June, almost no one at Xinhua did any work, and journalists demonstrated inside the Agency's Beijing compound.

In 2001, Hong Kong-listed media company Global China Technology Group Ltd invested in joint ventures with Xinhua News Agency to set up a market information Web site and offer audio and visual services planning and consulting.

The Chinese media's internal publication system, in which certain journals are published exclusively for government and party officials, provides information and analysis not generally available to the public. The State values these internal reports because they contain much of China's most sensitive, controversial, and high-quality investigative journalism.

Xinhua and many other Chinese media organizations produce reports for the "internal" journals. Informed observers note that journalists generally like to write for the internal publications—typically, only the most senior or most capable print and broadcast reporters are given such opportunities—because they can write less polemical and more comprehensive stories without having to omit unwelcome details as is commonly done in the print media directed to the general public. A Chinese historian has noted, as an example of such self-censorship, that only a minority of China's population are aware 30 million people starved to death in the early 1960s, because the Party has never allowed the subject to be openly explored in the media.

The Chinese Government's internal media publication system follows a strict hierarchical pattern designed to facilitate party control. A publication called Reference Information (Cankao Ziliao)—which includes translated articles from abroad as well as news and commentary by senior Xinhua reporters—is delivered by Xinhua personnel, rather than by the national mail system, to officials at the working level and above. A three-to-ten-page report called Internal Reference (Neibu Cankao) is distributed to officials at the ministerial level and higher. The most highly classified Xinhua internal reports, known as "redhead reference" (Hong Tou Cankao) reports, are issued occasionally to the top dozen or so party and government officials.

There are signs the internal publication system is breaking down as more information becomes widely available in China. A Hong Kong-based political journal circulated on the Chinese mainland has questioned the need for such a system in light of China's modern telecommunications and expanding contacts with the outside world. Internal publications are becoming less exclusive; some are now being sold illegally on the street and are increasingly available to anyone with money.

Xinhua's branch in Hong Kong was not just a press office. It was named a news agency under the special historic conditions before China resumed the territory's sovereignty from Britain. Until 1997, it served as the de-facto embassy of the PRC in the territory. It was authorized by the Special Administration Region government to continue to represent the central government after 1997, and it was renamed The Liaison Office of the Central People's Government in the Hong Kong SAR on January 18, 2000. The State Council appointed Gao Siren as the director in August 2002.

As suggested by the name change, Xinhua's present role is mainly about liaison with the broad spectrum of groups and associations in Hong Kong, or what is known as "united front" work in the terminology of the Chinese Communist Party.

According to some press reports in Hong Kong, the Liaison Office was under pressure from Beijing after the July 1 mass protest in 2003. Beijing officials reportedly criticised the Liaison Office for its inaccurate assessment of the public sentiment in Hong Kong during that period.

The former Hong Kong headquarters of Xinhua in Wan Chai was vacated in 2001, when the office relocated to Sheung Wan, and sold in September 2002. The 23-storey building will be converted into a four-star hotel with 480 rooms. Located at 387 Queen's Road East, the 1970s building had been Xinhua's home for more than 20 years.

Xu Jiatun headed the Hong Kong branch of Xinhua until 1990, when he fled to the United States amid accusations that he sympathized with Beijing students during the 1989 Tiananmen Square Crackdown.

Xu angered Beijing when he comforted Hong Kong students who staged a hunger strike outside the Xinhua office in support of the pro-democracy movement in Beijing in 1989. Years after, he joined to appeal for a reversal of the official verdict that the demonstrations were a "counter-revolutionary rebellion".

Zhou Nan succeeded exiled Xu Jiatun as the director of Xinhua in Hong Kong after the 1989 Tiananmen Square Crackdown. Zhou henceforth played a key role in the 13-year Sino-British argument on the handover in 1997.

During the hostile years, Zhou named Hong Kong's last governor Chris Patten as a 'sinner of a thousand years'. He said Patten had committed 'three violations', referring to Patten's political reforms, branded by Beijing as a breach of the Joint Declaration, the Basic Law, and understandings between the two sovereign nations.

Zhang Junsheng, former Xinhua vice-director, was brought into the agency by its former Hong Kong director, Xu Jiatun, in 1985. He was one of the few pre-1989 staff to survive the post-Tiananmen purge.

For 13 years, he was one of the few Xinhua officers who enjoy publicity by building up contacts in the film and arts world as the agency's cultural attaché.

His most famous manoeuvre was to repeat criticism of the Bill of Rights made in confidence by then-chief justice Sir Ti Liang Yang. Zhang also openly called Hong Kong's last governor Chris Patten a liar. He accused Patten of trying to create chaos in the civil service by undermining its neutrality.

A Xinhua News Agency branch was set up in Macau in 2000. The News Department of the Xinhua News Agency Macau Branch, a working organ sent by the central people's government of the PRC, is responsible for gathering news. The latter was renamed the Liaison Office of the Central People's Government in the Macau SAR.

### *Yonhap*

Yonhap news agency is the sole news agency in South

Korea that supplies domestic and foreign news and information to newspaper and TV broadcast and other subscribers in South Korea. It was founded on December 19, 1980 after the merger of Hapdong News Agency and Orient Press.

As the sole news agency in the Republic of Korea, Yonhap maintains contracts, news exchange and cooperation agreements and other pacts with 47 foreign news agencies including Associated Press, AFP, Xinhua, Kyodo, Itar Tass, and DPA.

Yonhap was the host news agency of the 1988 Seoul Summer Olympics, and was elected twice to the board of OANA.

### *Australian Associated Press*

Australian Associated Press is Australia's national news agency and is Australia's largest independent originator and aggregator of news and information, serving the media, government, business and financial markets.

AAP is owned by four Australian news organisations - News Ltd, Fairfax, West Australian Newspapers and the Harris Group.

### *Asian News International (ANI)*

Founded over 25 years ago, ANI is today South Asia's leading multimedia news agency with over 50 Bureaus in India and across the globe.

ANI's growth has been fuelled by the desire to fulfill the basic human need for knowledge and information, and ANI have done so with truth, credibility, quality and speed as its guiding principles.To cater to the ever-increasing spectrum of demand for news and information, in an era of rapidly evolving technologies, the pursuit of excellence sees ANI ever innovating, improving and redesigning products and services.

ANI's range of products encompass loosely edited news feeds and customized programmes for television channels, audio bytes for radio stations, live web casting and streamed multimedia / text content for websites and mobile carriers and wire services for the print section. ANI also provide a range of facilities for foreign and domestic channels to package their reports in India and uplink by satellite. These include provision of professional crews, editing and post production facilities, access to its archives, which are the most comprehensive collection of South Asian news videos anywhere in the world, uplinking facilities and providing fixers, coordinators, producers and correspondents, if required.

ANI cover almost all areas of interest to viewers including news, entertainment and lifestyles, health and science, business, sports, human-interest features and social and developmental issues. At ANI the pioneering spirit continues in line with our vision - that of providing a comprehensive array of news services, facilities, programmes and talent.

ANI provides unmatched news coverage from South Asia including breaking news and features with regional perspectives. ANI covers politics, business, technology, travel and entertainment. The New Delhi head office is staffed by professionals 24 hours and 7 days a week where the news content is collected, packaged and delivered in various formats.

## INTERNATIONAL ORGANSIATIONS

### *United Nations Educational, Scientific and Cultural Organization (UNESCO)*

The United Nations Educational, Scientific and Cultural Organization (UNESCO) is a specialized agency of the United Nations system established in 1946. The Organization's main objective is to contribute to peace and security by promoting collaboration among the nations through education, science and culture in order to further universal respect for justice, for the rule of law and for the human rights and fundamental freedoms (Article 1 of UNESCO's Constitution).

190 nations belong to UNESCO. The Organization is headquartered in Paris, France, with over 50 field offices and several institutes and centres throughout the world. UNESCO pursues its action through five major programmes: education, natural sciences, social & human sciences, culture and communication & information. Projects sponsored by UNESCO include literacy, technical, and teacher-training programs; international science programs; regional and cultural history projects, the promotion of cultural diversity; and international cooperation agreements to secure the world's cultural and natural heritage and to preserve human rights.

UNESCO has at times been highly controversial. During the 1970s and 1980s, Western countries, especially the United States and the United Kingdom, believed it was being used as a forum for Communist and Third World countries to attack the West. UNESCO developed a plan called the "New World Information Order", to stop alleged lies and misinformation being spread about developing countries. The West rejected it as an attempt by Third World and Communist dictatorships to destroy freedom of the press; the United States withdrew from the organization in protest in 1984, and the United Kingdom withdrew in 1985. (The UK rejoined in 1997, and the US rejoined in 2003.) UNESCO has also been criticized by some for its large and ponderous bureaucracy.

One of UNESCO's missions is to maintain a list of world heritage sites. These sites are important natural or historical sites whose preservation and safe keeping are deemed important for the world community. However once a site is on this list UNESCO does not get involved in any way with the preservation of the site.

UNESCO was also responsible for the founding of OANA. It provides funding to the International Council of Science. UNESCO is represented by UNESCO Goodwill Ambassadors.

### *International Telecommunication Union (ITU)*

The International Telecommunication Union (ITU) is an international organization established to standardize and regulate international radio and telecommunications. It was founded as the International Telegraph Union in Paris in May 17, 1865, and is today the world's oldest international organization. Its main tasks include standardization, allocation of the radio spectrum, and organizing interconnection arrangements between different countries to allow international phone calls. (In which regard it performs for telecommunications a similar function to what the UPU performs for postal services.) It is one of the specialized agencies of the United Nations.

The ITU decides matters between states through an extensive series of working parties, study groups, regional meetings, and world meetings.

*Examples:*

— World Radiocommunications Conference (WRC)

— World Administrative Radio Conferences (WARC)

The ITU is serving as the secretariat of the World Summit on the Information Society (WSIS). The World Summit on the Information Society (WSIS) is a UN world conference about information and communication. The summit happens twice: its first part was termed for December 2003 in Geneva, its second part should happen in 2005 in Tunis. The summit process was started with the first "Prepcom" in July 2002.

The UN General Assembly endorsed the proposal for a global summit on ICT issues in January 2002. The International Telecommunications Union (ITU) took the lead in organizing the event in which more than 50 heads of state participate. WSIS is also related to the UNESCO.

### *Global Information Infrastructure Commission (GIIC)*

The GIIC is a confederation of chief executive officers of firms that develop and deploy, operate, rely upon, and finance information and communications technology infrastructure facilities. Together as GIIC commissioners, these executives are dedicated to speeding the spread of information infrastructure throughout the world. The GIIC was established during a 1995 meeting in Brussels at which the political heads of the world's leading national economies formally and for the first time acknowledged the transforming forces of computer and telecommunications technologies and the emergence of an "information society."

# Bibliography


Negrine, R. and Papathanassopoulos, S. (1991). The internationalization of television. *European Journal of Communication, 6*, 9-32.

Noam, E. (1993). Reconnecting communications studies with communications policy. In M. R. Levy and M. Gurevitch (Eds), *Defining Media Studies: Reflections on the Future of the Field* (pp. 207-214). Oxford/New York: Oxford University Press.

Peng, B. (1986). *International Communication and Technology.* Taipei: San Min Book Store.

Picard, R. G. (1989). *Media Economics: Concepts & Issues.* Newbury Park, CA: Sage Publications.

Ploman, E. W. (1979). Satellite broadcasting, national sovereignty, and free flow of information. In K. Nordenstreng and H. I. Schiller (Eds.), *National Sovereignty and International Communication* (pp.154-165). Norwood, NJ: Ablex.

Rajagopal, A. (1993). The rise of national programming: the case of Indian television. *Media, Culture and Society, 15*, 91-111.

Roach, C. (1997). Cultural imperialism and resistance in media theory and literary theory. *Media, Culture & Society, 19(1)*, 47-66.

Rogers, E. M. (1986). *Communication Technology: The New Media in Society.* New York: The Free Press.

Rubin, R. B., Rubin, A. M. and Piele, L. J. (1993). *Communication Research: Strategies and Sources (3rd edition).* Belmont, CA: Wadsworth Publishing Company.

Schiller, H. I. (1971). The international commercialization of broadcasting. In *Mass Communications and American Empire* (pp. 94-103). Boston, MA: Beacon Press.

______________, (1986). Strengths and weaknesses of the new international information empire. In P. Lee (Ed.). *Communication for All: New World Information and Communication Order* (pp.17- 32). Maryknoll, NY: Orbis Books.

Schramm, W. (1957). *Responsibility in Mass Communication*. New York: Harper.

______________. (1964). *Mass Media and National Development*. Stanford, CA: Stanford University Press.

Sepstrup, P. (1989). Research into international television flows: A methodological contribution. *European Journal of Communication, 4*, 393-407.

Siebert, F. S., Peterson, T. and Schramm, W. (1956). *Four Theories of the Press*. Urbana, IL: University of Illinois Press.

Siune, K. and Truetzschler, W. (1992). *Dynamics of Media Politics: Broadcast and Electronic Media in Western Europe*. London: Sage Publications.

So, Y. K. (1997). *Market-driven journalism: A case study of Apple Daily*. In J. M. Chan, L. L. Chu and Z. D. Pan (Eds.), *Mass Communication and Market Economy* (pp.215-233). Hong Kong: Lo Fung Learned Society.

Sreberny-Mohammadi, A. (1996). The global and the local in international communications. In J. Curran and M. Gurevitch (Eds.). *Mass Media and Society (2nd edition)* (pp.177-203). London: Arnold.

Stevenson, R. L. (1994). *Global Communication in the Twenty-first Century*. White Plains, NY: Longman.

______________. (1996). International communication. In M. B. Salwen and D. W. Stacks (Eds.). *An Integrated Approach to Communication Theory and Research* (pp.181-193). Mahwah, NJ: Lawrence Erlbaum Associates, Inc., Publishers.

# Index